The New Vegetarian Cookbook

The New

Vegetarian Cookbook

GARY NULL

MACMILLAN • USA

Other Books by Gary Null:

The New Vegetarian

Why Your Stomach Hurts

Alcohol and Nutrition

Handbook of Skin and Hair

Successful Pregnancy

Macmillan General Reference
A Simon & Schuster Macmillan Company
1633 Broadway
New York, NY 10019-6785

Library of Congress Cataloging in Publication Data

Null, Gary.
   The new vegetarian cookbook.

   Includes index.
   1. Vegetarian cookery. I. Title.
TX837.N84   1980b   641.5′636   80-14603
ISBN 0-02-010040-X (pbk.)

16   17   18   19   20

Printed in the United States of America

Contents

Acknowledgments   vii

Introduction   ix

Stocking the Larder   1

Dairy Products   3

The Egg and You   11

Fruits   15

Vegetables   24

Beans (Legumes)   48

Soybeans and Soybean Products   52

Whole Grains, Cereals, Pasta and Bread   61

Nuts, Seeds and Sprouts   76

Seaweed   83

The Basics   88

Outfitting the Kitchen and Cooking Techniques   100

Planning the Vegetarian Menu   107

Recipes   111

Appetizers and Sandwiches   113

Soups   124

Vegetables   146

Cheese   171

Beans and Whole Grains   182

Pasta   192

Tofu Dishes   199
Salads   209
Salad Dressings, Dips and Sauces   225
Breads and Breakfasts   234
Desserts   258
Beverages   295
List of Suppliers   304
Index   305

Acknowledgments

I WISH TO THANK the New York Diabetic Association, 101 Productions, and Jeanne Jones (author of *The Calculating Cook*) for their cooperation in providing us with suitable recipes for those individuals with diabetes. I would also like to thank the New Jersey Hypoglycemia Association for their recipes so that those readers suffering from hypoglycemia can also enjoy this cookbook. I wish also to acknowledge the special talents of Ron Gilbert, America's foremost vegan gourmet chef, as they were of great help in helping us to select the best recipes for you. Ron was also of great assistance in writing the section titled "Stocking the Larder." In addition, thanks to Rose Freedman, Paul Manginelli, Gioia Fumo, and Ali Bouchekouk for their creativity, as well as Sharon Nickles, Gloria Sondheim, Heather Muir, and Helen Groll for their assistance.

Introduction

Eating natural foods is eating for pleasure and for good health. Although this cookbook serves as a guide to a better way of life, natural foods don't require a stiff, philosophical or moral conviction to eat them. You eat natural foods because they are tasty, zesty and budding with every gourmet delight ever to grace a table. In *The New Vegetarian Cookbook* you will find a collection of epicurean recipes coupled with enough information on ingredients and cooking techniques to suit anyone from novice to expert. All the steps to a better diet are in these pages: how to equip your kitchen, what natural foods are and how to use them, how to shop for them, and how to cook them. Take *The New Vegetarian Cookbook* to the market with you; use it to plan menus; consult it for cooking techniques and nutritional guidance. Most of all, enjoy the recipes.

Our approach here is to show you that natural foods are as good to eat as they are good for you. We discuss what you should be eating and how to cook food for the most pleasurable flavor, so you can soon enjoy the vast array of natural, pure vegetables, grains, dairy products, nuts, seeds, and fruits that are widely available at your local market. If you've never cooked before, we tell you what you need to know to cook well. If you're single or an older American on a limited budget, this book will demonstrate how to economically prepare natural foods at home. By trimming down the recipes to one serving or using the recipes to plan ahead and cook several meals at once you provide that extra incentive to eat better by eating in. You will save time and money, and—especially for those who work all day and don't want to come home and start cooking from scratch—these meals prepared earlier will be very satisfying. We also show you how to stretch your food dollar by getting the best buys in fresh produce and grains, seeds and beans. Each and every recipe in this book has been devised to get you the utmost in taste and nutrition for your money.

Even if you're on a special diet—whether diabetic, hypertensive or hypoglycemic—you'll find recipes for you, as well as for everyone else.

Don't worry about how the rest of the family might react to natural foods after years of eating additives and other chemicals. If you involve them, encourage them to participate and plan meals, even difficult children will be amenable to a change in diet. They should be able to help in the kitchen, sample the fruits of their efforts and take pride in being part of an important change in their family activities.

A word or two about the recipes: All of them are original and have been tested and retested, some of them by upwards of ten thousand people. We offered sample releases on our radio show "Natural Living," and listeners offered their suggestions and comments after trying them at home. From their comments, we were able to adjust the recipes until they burst with flavor, were most nutritious and most economical to produce. They range from appetizers to desserts, including seasonal favorites. We gave special attention to those who must give specific consideration to their diet. Many recipes, therefore, are prepared without salt for people on low-sodium diets; there are also recipes for mouth-watering desserts made without sugar or artificial sweeteners for those with an active sweet tooth. Natural ingredients are used to make all the recipes—no artificial flavors, colors or synthetic additives!

The suggestions in the following chapters will help you to get the most out of your food dollar in terms of economy, nutrition and taste as you do your shopping. The various tips we offer on selecting the foods you buy will guide you in making the most knowledgeable choices. We've devoted more space to describing some foods than others to give you a hint that these foods will play a more important role in your diet.

As a companion to *The New Vegetarian, The New Vegetarian Cookbook* translates theory into practice so that you can join the swelling ranks of people who eat well without fuss or bother. Remember, the word "vegetarian" finds its root and home in the Latin verb *vegetare*, "to enliven." That is what we're trying to do: invigorate your health through the pleasure of eating the best food.

Stocking the Larder

Dairy Products

The highly versatile dairy products contain the proper amount of amino acids, in correct proportions, to promote protein synthesis in the body. They are thus complete proteins. Whether it be a banana yogurt pie or a cheese soufflé, many of the recipes in this cookbook call for one or more types of dairy products. Here's what's available.

MILK

Four glasses of milk a day supply you with all the fat, calcium and phosphorus you need each day; one-half of your daily protein requirement; one-third of your vitamin A requirement; and one-fourth of the calories you need. As a complete protein, milk is a very important part of the vegetarian diet, and anyone who isn't allergic to it should consume 3 glasses every day. Note well we said *consume*, not *drink*. There are many alternate ways of adding milk to your diet. For example, powdered milk can be added to bread doughs and casseroles for an extra nutritional boost, or you may consume your milk quota in the form of thick, creamy, delicious yogurt. Additionally, natural cheeses are a tasty way to "eat" your milk, while at the same time expanding your menu with a wide variety of different tastes and textures.

Whole milk should be as fresh as possible, so keep it in the fridge and use it within a day or so of purchase. Powdered milk, on the other hand, can be kept for a longer period of time if it hasn't been mixed with liquid. Store it in an airtight container to preserve its freshness. Powdered milk, by the way, is a good buy. If you want to save money and calories, mix the powdered half and half with whole milk. You'll find there's hardly any difference in the taste. If your family won't drink powdered milk, you can still save money and calories, as well as get the benefits of whole milk, by substituting powdered milk in recipes requiring milk. Spray-dried powdered milk is best, because it is processed at lower temperatures to preserve more of its nutritional quality. To determine if milk is spray-dried, write the manufacturer for information on processing. When shopping, look for the U.S. Extra Grade shield on the label to insure you of sweet, pleasing flavor and natural color.

You can easily make yogurt from dry milk, too. Use 1 cup of plain commercial yogurt to 1 quart of prepared powdered milk. Place the yogurt in the top of a double boiler and let stand covered at room temperature for 2 hours. Then add the quart of milk, which should also be at room temperature. Heat the milk and yogurt over the hot water until the mixture comes to a boil. Stir constantly to make a very smooth yogurt. Turn off the heat and let the mixture cool until it's about 120 degrees (F). Keep the pot covered until the mixture "sets," which will take about 4 to 8 hours. Once the yogurt is set, chill it until ready for use. This recipe makes about 5 cups of yogurt.

Powdered milk will also whip up frosty drinks with a real nutritional "pow." To make 1 serving, use 3/4 cup of milk and 1 teaspoon honey, 1 tablespoon of dry milk and chunks of your favorite frozen fruits in a blender. Blend at high speed until smooth. Serve over ice. It's good!

BUTTER

Real butter enhances the flavor and texture of everything you cook. For peak flavor, sweet butter is best, because salt is only added to butter as a preservative. Any sign of rancidity will, therefore, be much more apparent in unsalted butter. Unfortunately, dairies are not required by law to state if they have added chemicals to color or preserve the butter they produce. If you really want to find out what's in the butter you buy, write the company and ask.

We save money by making something we call "butter spread." It has the flavor of butter but goes a lot further and lasts longer. Here's how to make it: Soak 1/4 cup agar-agar in 1 pint of milk. Heat the milk in the top of a double boiler until the agar-agar is dissolved. Melt 1 pound of butter over hot water, then whip the agar mixture into it, a little at a time. If bubbles appear, keep whipping until they subside, then pour the mixture into molds. Chill before using. Keep this spread refrigerated and use within 3–5 days.

Another way to make butter go further is to make flavored butter spreads, although the taste is better than the savings, since the butter isn't stretched much. Combine softened butter with any of the following: honey, applesauce, peanut butter, soft cheese, or your favorite blend of fresh or dried herbs. (Add no more than 1/4 teaspoon of herbs to a pound of butter.) These seasoned butters are a real treat on homemade bread!

CHEESE

Natural cheeses can substitute for or supplement milk or eggs in the vegetarian diet. For people who won't drink their milk, the multiple uses of cheese are a perfect way to round out your daily menu. Half the fun of cheeses is learning the differences between them and the variety of tastes and uses for them. You can even make your own cheese at home. Soft cheeses such as cottage and other unripened cheeses are not difficult to produce. For instructions on making your own cheese, write for government bulletin #129, available free from the Government Printing Office, Washington, D.C. 20402.

Natural cheeses are a nutritional bargain, and in most cases don't cost more than processed kinds. Be sure, however, to check labels carefully because even some "natural" cheeses may contain chemical colorings or preservatives. A natural cheese is allowed to ripen and age, whereas processed cheeses are made by mixing different types of hard cheeses and then emulsifying them with inorganic salts. Often the processed cheese contains chemical stabilizers and artificial flavoring. "Cheese foods" can legally contain up to 44 percent water, hardly a bargain at cheese prices. In any event, something that has to be labeled "food" to be identified as such has to be a little suspect. There are so many different types of natural cheeses that it is impossible to list them all. So, for the sake of simplicity, here is an outline of the 3 major types, some subtypes, and a few tips on storing and using them.

SOFT CHEESES

These unripened cheeses are all highly perishable and must be kept refrigerated and used within 3 to 4 days of purchase.

Cottage cheese: This is an all-time favorite among the soft, unripened cheeses. Its creamy texture, fine flavor and low price make it one of the best cheese bargains. Although you could hardly ask for more, it's also low in calories, high in nutrition and easy to digest. It has a protein content of 15.8 percent versus the 3.2 percent of whole milk, thus making cottage cheese the protein equivalent of concentrated milk. And its high protein content makes it a perfect companion for incomplete protein foods such as grains, nuts, seeds and vegetables. One cup of uncreamed, skimmed milk cottage cheese will provide you with 38 grams of protein, 6 grams of carbohydrate, 202 mg. calcium, 0.9 mg. iron, 20 I.U. vitamin A, 0.07 mg. thiamine, 0.63 mg. riboflavin, 0.2 mg. niacin, and only 195 calories.

The different types of cottage cheese are simply varying combinations of 3 different factors. First, the type of milk used to make the cheese can be either whole or skim. If skim milk has been used, then the cheese is labeled "low fat." Secondly, the size of the curd can be fine, medium or large. And third, the cheese can be cream-style or plain. Cream with 18 percent fat is added to the curd to produce cream-style. Pot and farmer's cheeses are variations of cottage cheese. Pot cheese has large, dry curds and is somewhat crumbly, while farmer's cheese has very tiny curds and generally comes in a bar, as cream cheese does. It's very creamy and makes a tasty spread for bread or toast.

Look for high quality fresh cottage cheese and check the container to see what the ingredients are before purchasing. Ideally, the cheese should contain nothing but milk, cream, cultures or enzymes and salt. Unsalted varieties are also available in most stores. Open the container and look at the curds; they should be uniform in size, and the cream dressing should appear to be well integrated with the curds. The surface of the cheese should be shiny and set, with the aroma sweet and milky. Check the date on the container to make sure you're getting the freshest one you can. Store the cheese in the refrigerator and use it within 5 days of purchase.

Better yet, make your own cottage cheese at home. Heat 1 gallon of nonfat milk in the top of a double boiler (or a stainless steel soup pot) until it reaches a temperature of 72 degrees (F). While the milk is heating, crush 1 vegetable enzyme tablet in 1/4 cup cold water. Add the enzyme solution along with 1/4 cup cultured buttermilk to the warm milk and stir well. Remove the milk from the heat and let stand, covered, in a warm place for 12 to 18 hours. A firm curd should now have formed. In the pot, cut the curd into 1/2-inch cubes, then return the pot to the top of the double boiler and heat until the curd reaches 110 degrees (F). Maintain this temperature for 15 to 20 minutes, stirring at 5-minute intervals. Line a colander with several layers of cheesecloth and pour the curds into it. Lift the cheesecloth with the curds from the colander, then immerse it in a pan of ice water. Work the curds gently through the cheesecloth with your fingers for about 5 minutes, and then lift the cheesecloth out of the ice water. Let the liquid drain off and squeeze the bag gently to get rid of more liquid. Let the bag drain in the colander for another hour or so. Now add salt if you wish and 1/4 cup milk or cream. Chill the cheese before eating it with fruit or using it in your favorite recipe. This will make about 3 cups of sweet, fresh cheese.

A versatile food, cottage cheese appears on the menu as anything from an appetizer to dessert. Serve it in creamy salad dressings or combine it with other cheeses to make dips and spreads. Cottage cheese–noodle casseroles make tasty main dishes, and a creamy cottage cheese sauce is a fine foil for any cooked vegetable. Whip 1 cup of cottage cheese in the blender with 1 tablespoon each of oregano, basil and cumin, 1/2 cup yogurt, and 2 tablespoons safflower oil to make almost 2 cups of a superlative, low-calorie dressing. Or for dessert, use it instead of part of the shortening in baked goods, or try a cottage cheese and fruit pudding. With or without fruit, cottage cheese makes a fine first food for baby. Just whip it in the blender till it's smooth.

Ricotta: This Italian cousin of cottage cheese is fine grained and bland. Use it in lasagna or ravioli, of course. But also try it in desserts or served with fruit.

Feta: This Greek goat cheese has a longer shelf life than the other unripened types because it is preserved in brine. However, this soaking sometimes makes feta too salty; so taste it before using. If it's overpowering, try using it in a bland, unsalted cooked dish.

Camembert and Brie: These soft French cheeses are mold-ripened, and both come with rind that's edible if soft. The taste of these two cheeses changes as the cheese ages. For instance, new Camembert will be firm and bland, but after it's allowed to ripen for a while, it becomes soft and buttery within its rind with a much more robust flavor. Camembert and Brie are best served with crackers, bread and fruit for dessert.

SEMIHARD CHEESES

Once the package is opened, the cheeses that are either mold- or bacteria-ripened should be kept chilled. They will keep longer than soft, unripened cheeses.

Gorgonzola, blue and Stilton: These crumbly cheeses are characterized by blue mold formations (veining) throughout. They will last a long time if closely wrapped, and will even gain flavor by aging in the refrigerator. Use them as dessert cheeses, spark up your salad dressings with them, or combine them with yogurt or sour cream for a tasty dip.

Muenster, brick, Port Salut, Bel Paese, Jack and mozzarella: Similar in texture, all of these cheeses are bacteria-ripened and have a wide variety of flavors, which tend to be less sharp than the mold-ripened cheeses. They all melt well and make delicious grilled sandwiches and casserole toppings.

HARD CHEESES

After it has been aged, cheese gives more concentrated protein in every bite; hard cheeses retain only about 30 percent of their moisture, as compared to the 45 to 85 percent retained by soft, unripened cheeses.

Cheddar: For macaroni and cheese lovers, cheddar is the choice. It comes in varying degrees of sharpness, from mild to extra sharp, and melts well for use in sauces and casseroles where its tangy flavor accents the taste of the dish.

Swiss: Natural Swiss has a sweet, nutty flavor and is popular in sandwiches and casseroles. Swiss, and its close relative Gruyère, is a favorite choice for fondue, where the cheese is melted into a "bath" for chunks of bread or vegetables. Incidentally, natural and nourishing Swiss is the only type of cheese that can be used in a fondue; processed Swiss does not melt properly and makes a sticky mess.

Parmesan and Romano: Often these popular cheeses are grated as a topping for spaghetti and au gratin dishes. Both of them also make a nice addition to after-dinner cheese platters or as finger foods with fruit and crackers. For grated cheese, try to buy Parmesan and Romano in bulk and grate them yourself to keep them fresher and more flavorful.

FERMENTED MILK PRODUCTS

When milk is fermented, it changes in taste, texture and nutrition. The chemical process is accomplished through the addition of bacteria. Far from being a threat to good health, these bacteria are a healthful aid to digestion, making fermented milk products the perfect answer for people who have trouble digesting milk. The fermentation process is easily stopped by chilling after it is completed; so, keep all of these fermented products in the refrigerator. Enjoy them as a wholesome part of your daily dairy requirement.

YOGURT

In the past few years this creamy concoction has steadily been gaining popularity in the average American household. For a delicious, convenient way to "eat" your milk, yogurt can't be beat for its refreshing pick-up. Good commercial brands of natural yogurt are available, flavored or plain. However, even these sometimes contain sugar. Therefore, read the labels carefully and be sure to pick a brand without additives or sugar and with live bacilli. For fun and to save money, try making your own. The following recipe uses whole milk (for one that uses powdered milk, see page 4):

Use 1 tablespoon of plain, natural yogurt for every 2 1/2 cups of milk. In the top of a double boiler, heat the milk to the boiling point and then allow it to simmer for a minute or so. While the milk is cooling, stir the "starter" yogurt in a bowl until it's smooth and liquid. When the milk has cooled down to 106 degrees (F), stir the starter yogurt into it. Cover the bowl with plastic wrap and place it in a warm, draft-free spot for 8 hours or overnight. When done, it should be thick, creamy and custardlike. Chill your homemade yogurt before you serve it with fruit or use it in cooking. Remember to save some to start the next batch, and you'll never have to buy yogurt again. If you feel this method is too haphazard, there are yogurt-making machines on the market that guarantee perfect results every time.

Yogurt is an ideal snack, but have you used it for cooking? It makes a fine substitute for sour cream in any recipe, and yogurt dressings are creamy and low calorie. For a summertime treat, top cold soups with a spoonful of plain yogurt, or mix yogurt and honey to make a salad dressing for chilled fruits. For the ultimate yogurt exhilaration, take a tip from Middle Eastern cuisines and make yogurt drinks by thinning yogurt with ice water, then adding crushed dried or fresh mint. Simply euphoric!

BUTTERMILK

This creamy, low-calorie (only 43 per glass) milk product not only makes a tart, thirst-quenching drink during the summer, but it's ideal as a tasty addition to salad dressings and some types of baked goods. Buttermilk can take the place of baking soda to act as a natural rising agent in breads and biscuits. True buttermilk is the whey left after the cream has been churned; however, what we buy at the market is cultured buttermilk, made by injecting a buttermilk culture into either skimmed or whole milk. The result is a product of uniform taste and creaminess and a source of easily digestible and delicious protein.

SOUR CREAM

You should check the label on the carton to make sure that the sour cream you're buying doesn't contain stabilizers or gelatin. Sour cream is properly made by adding a culture of acid-producing bacteria to fresh cream. In addition to being easily digestible, sour cream has all the nutrients of cream and may be used in a variety of ways. Float sour cream on cold soups or use it in salad dressings or baked goods. You may wish to make crème fraîche, the French version of heavy cream, by adding 1 tablespoon of sour cream to a pint of heavy cream. Shake this mixture in a jar until well blended, then allow it to sit overnight at room temperature. You will then have the heaviest and most luxurious cream you've ever tasted. A spoon or so of this thick, rich goodness enhances any dessert. Use as much as you like and refrigerate the rest for up to a week.

The Egg and You

Eggs are not only one of the most versatile of the complete protein foods, they are also easy to digest, and cooking with gentle heat won't destroy their protein. In protein content, the egg scores a remarkable 94 on a scale of 100 and has the additional benefit of being low in calories (81.5 for a large one).

Choosing the right egg for any purpose requires an understanding of the government standards for grading eggs. Three grades are used: AA, A and B. The letters label appearance more than anything else. Grade AA eggs have thick whites and small, firm yolks. Grade A eggs are about the same; however, AA eggs have yolks that are more well centered. If you want to choose an egg for its appearance, decide how centered you want the yolk. Grade B eggs are used for general purposes. All three grades have the same nutritional value.

The size egg you choose is simply a matter of personal preference. Jumbo eggs weigh 30 ounces a dozen, extra large eggs tip the scales at 27 ounces, while medium eggs weigh 21 ounces, and the small are 18 ounces a dozen. We find that individual servings are better served by the larger sizes; we use smaller eggs for general cooking purposes. The color of the egg shell has no bearing on what's inside. Also, don't be fooled into thinking that eggs with deep orange yolks are better for you. The color is the result of the hen's having been fed a harmless substance, xanthophyll, that has no nutritional value. "Organic" eggs have no more food value than regular eggs; however, they are free of the chemical residue found in eggs laid by chemically fed and treated chickens.

Finding the freshest egg is not simple. In some states, cold-storage eggs may still be legally labelled "fresh." A truly fresh egg should have no off-odor, nor should the yolk break easily when the egg is opened. The yolk should be shiny and round and the white fairly thick. The overall flavor of a fresh egg is much better than that of a cold-storage one. While still at the egg counter, be sure to check the carton by opening it and surveying each egg to make sure no egg is cracked. Never, never, use a cracked egg. Because even the pores in an eggshell are large enough to admit salmonella bacteria, a cracked egg can harbor hordes of harmful organisms. If you're doubtful about the freshness of an egg, test the egg by placing it in a bowl of cold water. If the egg floats, discard it.

Most people think that cooking an egg is the simplest thing in the world after boiling water. That isn't so. An egg's tender protein demands precise and careful cooking to preserve its nourishing power. A few tips, then, are in order.

HARD-BOILED EGGS

Start with the egg at room temperature. If the egg has been sitting in the refrigerator, warm the egg by running warm water over it for a minute or so. Then pierce the end of the shell with a pin to prevent it from cracking while boiling and to make it easier to peel after cooking. Lower the egg into enough boiling water to cover it by about an inch. When the water returns to boiling, begin timing. Let the water simmer gently, not rapidly or furiously. Boil for 4 1/2 minutes; then pour off the hot water and run cold water over the egg until cool enough to handle. Peeling can be made easier by chilling the egg for 30 minutes. In any event, the best way to peel an egg is to roll it back and forth on a hard surface until it is cracked all around; then, starting at the top, remove the shell in large pieces, taking with it the white membrane.

SOFT-BOILED EGGS

Timing, not technique, makes an egg hard or soft-boiled. Again, start the egg at room temperature, warming the egg by running warm water over it for a minute or so if the egg has been refrigerated. It's not necessary to pierce the end first, but the boiling water should cover it one inch when lowered into the pot. When the water returns to boiling again, lower the heat so that the water just barely bubbles and start timing. Allow 3 minutes for a very soft egg and 4 minutes for a medium egg. If the egg is cold when you start, add 2 minutes to each of the times. After simmering is completed, pour off the hot water and rinse the egg under cold water. Serve it at once or else it will continue to cook in its own heat.

POACHED EGGS

While special pans or forms can be used to get uniform-looking poached eggs, the true gourmet would assert that a free-form egg is the only "real" poached egg. The question is how to achieve this perfection with the minimum of ragged edges. Into a skillet, put enough water to cover the egg. Heat until it comes to a boil, then add 1/2 teaspoon salt and 1 teaspoon of vinegar. Break the egg into a small saucer or dish. Remove the skillet from the heat and slip the egg into the hot water. Let the egg sit in the water until the desired degree of doneness is achieved. Remove the finished egg from the pan with a slotted spoon and drain it on a paper towel before serving.

FRIED EGGS

Frying eggs with overly intense heat will result in tough and rubbery eggs. Be gentle. The best method is to melt butter in a skillet until the butter just begins to bubble, then add the egg and lower the heat. Fry until done to your liking. Another good method is to heat the butter until quite hot but not smoking, then break the egg onto the heated surface, covering the pan and removing it from the heat. Leave the egg in the pan until done (about 3 or 4 minutes). This is an appetizing method if you like the white of an egg to be set but the yolk runny.

THE OMELET

The mystique of the perfect omelet has led too many people to believe creating one is an arduous task. It isn't; although attention to detail and precise timing are required. Begin with the eggs at room temperature. If the eggs are cold, run them under warm water for a minute or so. The pan used must be smooth so that the eggs can slide easily. We find a 7-inch cast-iron-on-stainless-steel pan perfect for making a 2- or 3-egg omelet. To make a puffy omelet, separate the yolks from the white, and beat the whites until they are fluffy but not stiff. Fold the beaten yolks into the white while you heat a tablespoon of butter in the pan until it just starts to sizzle. Now pour the eggs into the pan, and lower the heat. As the eggs start to set, rotate the pan to allow the uncooked portions to flow underneath and come in contact with the cooking surface. When the mixture is no longer runny, use a pancake turner to fold one side of the omelet on top of the other. Allow the folded omelet to cook for another 20 seconds or so, then turn it out onto a plate. Season to taste with salt and pepper. To make a French-style omelet, use the same procedure, except instead of beating the whites and yolks separately, whisk the whole eggs together until they're frothy. Omelets make a fine main dish, and can be filled while cooking or after they're done. Fill them with cheese, mushrooms or vegetables before you fold them over. They can also be served with your favorite sauce.

SCRAMBLED EGGS

Concentration is the key to making a truly luscious batch of scrambled eggs, because of the three equally important factors involved: temperature, the proper cooking surface and the regulation of heat during the cooking process. Use the same type of smooth pan you would use for an omelet. Melt butter in it until the butter starts to sizzle. Meanwhile, whip the eggs gently with a fork, seasoning to taste with salt and pepper. If you want, add a spoonful or two of milk. Lower the heat, and add the eggs to the pan. You have two choices at this point: If you like dry eggs with small curds, start stirring the eggs immediately. Or if you prefer creamier, larger curds, let the eggs set for 10 seconds before you start to gently scoop them up and turn them, allowing the uncooked portions to come in contact with the cooking surface. As soon as the eggs are done to your liking, scoop them out onto a plate and serve immediately.

Fruits

From the complete protein foods, we move to the sections of the market that display fruits and vegetables, incomplete proteins but the suppliers of the bulk of nutrients you need in your diet. The great variety of succulent tastes provided by fruit will make your new eating habits a delight to live with.

Ideally, fresh fruits should be bought when they're in season; however, and unfortunately, this isn't always possible, and sometimes a package of frozen fruit is a better bargain than expensive, out-of-season fruits. Canned fruits are the worst buy of all because of the way they're processed. Most of them are packed in sugar-laden syrups that add empty calories to your diet. And yet, if you're lucky enough to have an abundance of fresh fruit, you may can your own, secure in the knowledge that your canning will contain only natural products. So if you can't buy in season or can your own, buy frozen or dried fruits, always reading the labels to make sure you aren't getting a lot of sugar and chemicals along with the fruit.

APPLES

From the middle of autumn to the start of spring, apples are reaching their peak season, and a wide variety of types is available almost everywhere to suit every purpose. Generally speaking, apples fall into two categories: cooking and eating apples. While cooking apples may be eaten out-of-hand, eating apples are not suited for cooking. The best eating apples include such paradisial delights as red Delicious, Pippins, Northern Spys, Wealthys and McIntoshes. For cooking and eating, try yellow Transparents, Baldwins, Jonathans, Staymans and Winesaps. Rhode Island Greenings, if you can find them at your market, may be the best cooking apples of all. Depending on where you live, you will also find additional varieties of apples well worth trying. If you're not sure whether they'll hold up in cooking, ask the locals.

Most apples are marketed according to a set of standards rating color, uniformity of size and shape and freedom from superficial defects. They will be labelled with either a U.S. Extra Fancy or a U.S. Fancy stamp. Select carefully by avoiding soft spots and bruises, and keep an eye out for the ones with the best color. As apples ripen, they show decreasing degrees of firmness and a change in color. To tell if apples are ripe, press against them with your fingertip. They should yield very slightly and emit a slight but noticeable aroma. If the apples bought are very firm, store them in a cool, dry place until they ripen. Ripe apples should be stored in the crisper bin of the refrigerator and used within a few weeks.

APRICOTS

Like apples, apricots appear in the market in October and last up to March. Look for firm, yellow apricots with no bruises or discoloration, and look out for soft spots. Don't bother buying green apricots; they won't ripen. Ripe apricots can be stored in the fridge and used within a few days of purchase. Dried apricots tend to be more expensive, but they are very high in nutrients and make chewy, sweet snacking. When you use dried fruit, the package should be rewrapped after opening and stored in a cool place.

AVOCADOS

These delectable fruits brighten up a green salad or sandwich, as well as many dishes. The avocado is a rich mine of vitamin A, thiamine, potassium, riboflavin and niacin. If you wish to use an avocado right away, choose one with a dark purple skin. Another test for ripeness requires nothing more than applying slight pressure to the avocado; if an indentation appears, the avocado is ready for use. If you buy an unripened avocado (it will be emerald green in color), store it in the refrigerator because it spoils quickly. Ripened avocados last 6 or 7 days and are available all year long.

BANANAS

The banana is available year-round; some markets carry not only the green and yellow ones, but red bananas as well. Choose firm, slightly green or solid yellow bunches and allow them to ripen at 70 degrees (F) until flecks of brown freckle the skin. Never chill bananas. It's best to buy whole bunches, and avoid tearing the stem end of the bunch when removing a banana, as this will hasten spoilage of the entire bunch. Dried bananas can be found in some stores, and they make a delicious candylike treat. They should be kept in a plastic bag in a cool place once the package is opened.

BERRIES

There are over two hundred kinds of berries and berrylike fruit, with many varieties available depending on what part of the country you live in. All berries are an excellent source of vitamin C as well as other nutrients. Some of the most popular include strawberries, mulberries, juiceberries, raspberries, blackberries, blueberries, huckleberries, elderberries, gooseberries and dewberries. Frozen strawberries, raspberries and blueberries are available year-round. Although not the real thing, they'll do in a pinch. Look for berries that are frozen without syrups and additives. If you have a garden patch, you might also want to freeze some of your own berries, as most stand up well to this treatment.

Blueberries are in season from May through September and are a good source of iron and magnesium. They also contain some vitamin A and C. Plump, brightly colored berries with no soft spots are the most flavorful. Store them in the refrigerator and use within a day or two. Rinse the berries well before serving with yogurt or cream. Blueberries are excellent eating with cereals, in muffins, and in bread—and don't forget to make a blueberry pie with natural sweeteners and a whole wheat crust.

Strawberries are brightest in the spring and are an excellent source of vitamin C. They also contain good amounts of vitamin A, calcium, phosphorus, iron and potassium. Buy bright, undamaged, plump berries with green caps. Green strawberries don't ripen, so avoid them. If they're in a covered basket, check the bottom for staining, indicating crushed berries on the bottom. When you get your purchase home, remove the berries from the carton, pick them over and discard any spoiled ones. Store them, unwashed, in the refrigerator and use within 2 days. For a healthful and delicious treat for any member of the family, blend 1 cup of very ripe strawberries with 1/2 cup yogurt, and freeze the mixture. The children will want more and more. An excellent dessert sauce can be made by simply crushing a cup of berries with 1–2 tablespoons of honey.

A good source of vitamin A and potassium, blackberries are in season from July to September. They also contain calcium, phosphorus and vitamin C. Choose ripe, plump undamaged berries, and avoid those with caps because they were probably picked when green. If the berries come in a wrapped container, check the bottom of the basket to make sure it's not stained with juice. If it is, then the berries are overripe and will soon get moldy. When you get them home, take them out of the carton and pick through them before storing in the refrigerator. Don't rinse them until ready for eating, which should be within a day or two. Boysenberries, loganberries and dewberries are all close relatives of the blackberry and should be treated in the same way.

June and July is too short a season, but that's the only time for fresh red and black raspberries. They are a good source of vitamins B and C and are best when plump, ripe and with no signs of mold or decay. Sort out the ripe ones from any damaged ones, and store in the fridge. However, ripe raspberries should be eaten as soon as possible.

CHERRIES

The great variety of cherries are in season from June to August and should be plump, glossy, and unbruised when you buy them. Cooking cherries are tarter and firmer than eating cherries. Kentish, Montmorency and May Dukes are the most popular for cooking and preserving, while Bings, Lamberts and Royal Annes are the favorites for out-of-hand eating. Rinse and dry the cherries before storing in the refrigerator.

Frozen cherries are a good buy if they have been processed without sugar or additives. Some cherries taste even better after being frozen, and if you have your own cherry tree, consider freezing the excess crop for later eating. To freeze cherries, either pit them or leave them whole after carefully washing and drying them. Pack the fruit in plastic bags and seal well. No liquid is necessary, and, if you maintain a zero-degree temperature, they will keep well for several months in your freezer.

CRANBERRIES

Legend has it that Peg Leg John, an early Maine settler, used to sort his cranberries by throwing them down the steps from the attic. The firm fruit would bounce to the bottom and the unsound cranberries would remain on the steps. Perhaps this may have led to the cranberry separator, which works on the same principle. This is all good to keep in mind when choosing and sorting cranberries: they should be firm enough to bounce, so discard any that don't. Peak season is September to December. Don't wash the berries until you're ready to use them; until you are, keep them in a plastic bag in the refrigerator. Cranberries also freeze well: just put them in a plastic bag and store in the freezer until ready to use. You need not defrost them first.

COCONUTS

They may be hard to break, but they're worth all the trouble. To choose a coconut, look for one that's heavy for its size and sloshes when you shake it. Pierce the "eyes" on the top of the nut with an ice pick, and then drain out the milk for drinking. Crack the nut with a hammer and remove the meat. If the nut seems impervious to the blows of the hammer, a short stay in a 250-degree oven should make things easier. If you have an excess of meat, grate and dry it in a warm oven for future use.

GRAPEFRUIT

Both pink and white grapefruit are available all year round (although they're juicier September to October), and their vitamin C is an invaluable addition to your diet. The fruit should be heavy for their size, with no spots or mold. Thinner rinds generally indicate juicier fruit. Grapefruit should be kept chilled; never buy green fruit because it won't ripen. Top some grapefruit halves with a little honey and butter, then broil them for a minute or so to make a different, tantalizing dessert.

GRAPES

Available year-round, grapes are well worth their often high price for both nutrition and flavor. Grapes should be plump and undamaged, with glossy color and a nice "bloom." Stems shouldn't be brittle, and any bad grapes should be removed before storage in a plastic bag in the refrigerator. In addition to the black Concord grape, so popular for juice and jelly, grapes come in a wide variety of types, both for the table and other uses. Thompson seedless, white Malagas, red Tokays and the firm but juicy Emperors are very popular. But the spicy Muscat is perhaps the most distinctively flavored table grape and must be very ripe to be fully appreciated. Ripe grapes make an excellent topping for yogurt. Don't forget or ignore raisins; they have all the nutrients of grapes in a more concentrated form. Kids, backpackers, and brown baggers all enjoy them.

LEMONS AND LIMES

These citrus fruits are indispensable in the preparation of a myriad of foods and are the main ingredient for many a cool, thirst-quenching drink. Sprinkling lemon or lime juice on other, cut fruits will prevent them from darkening. The lemon and lime should have thin rinds, look bright and be unblemished. Keep them well chilled until ready for use.

MANGOES

This tropical fruit is an excellent source of vitamin A and also contains vitamin C, iodine, niacin, potassium, calcium, phosphorus and sodium. Available from May to September, mangoes are colored from green to gold to red, and they are about the size of an avacado. The juicy flesh of the mango is orange-yellow, and its abundant sweetness is reminiscent of apricots and pineapple. The mango should have a smooth skin with the beginnings of a rosy blush. Ripeness is easily tested by applying pressure with the fingertip against the fruit; if ripe, the flesh will yield slightly to the touch. You may buy them unripened and bring them to their full succulence by keeping them at room temperature and out of direct sunlight. Once ripened, mangoes should be stored in a plastic bag in the fridge. Eat as soon as possible, especially after chilling them. Remember to remove the long, flat pit you'll encounter when cutting the fruit. Mangoes make any combination fruit salad more exciting, and mango juice is one of the most divine nectars imaginable.

MELONS

So many different varieties! From May to November, the market will have melons like cantaloupe and muskmelon, distinguished by orange flesh and slightly craggy skin; honeydews with smooth yellowish skin and bright, spring green flesh; Persian melons, which look like large cantaloupes; and Cranshaws, whose skin is dappled and flesh is slightly pink. And no list of melons would be complete without mention of that perennial American favorite, the watermelon. Melons are sweetest if vine ripened. You can tell if the fruit was vine ripened by looking at its stem end: It should have a scar that's slightly shriveled, and it should smell faintly sweet if you sniff it. To locate a ripe watermelon, scratch the skin with your fingernail. If it's ripe, you'll come away with a thin green paring. Choose firm, unblemished melons with no soft spots or mold, and store them in the refrigerator until ready to eat.

NECTARINES

Nectarines have a taste all their own, despite their peachlike appearance. Select firm, orange-yellow fruits, free from bruises or soft spots. When they develop a rosy blush, they're ready to eat. To test for ripeness, press lightly with your fingertip. If the flesh yields slightly, it's ready to eat. Nectarines are available from July to August and can be stored in the refrigerator—but eat them as soon as possible.

ORANGES

On the vitamin C scale, oranges (available year-round from Florida and California) rate high, as they do for other vitamins. Florida Temples or Tangelos, which are actually a cross between a tangerine and a grapefruit, make excellent choices, while the year-round availability of the California Navel has the added attraction of providing a fruit that is easily peeled and sectioned without making a mess. Valencias, Kings and Blood oranges are very reliable juice oranges. When choosing oranges, don't go by color alone, because russet or greenish oranges are as good, if not better, than the brighter orange types—which may have gained their intense color from being dipped in a vat of dye or given a whiff of gas. The fruit should be heavy for its size, with no soft or moldy spots. The thinner the rind, the juicier the orange. Both oranges and orange juice should be chilled before using. If you can find oranges that haven't been dyed, try making some candied peel or marmalade. Dried orange peel can also be tossed into the fireplace for a sweet, citrusy smell, or stud a whole orange with cloves, roll it in powdered orris root, and hang it in the closet for a long-lasting fragrance.

PAPAYAS

An outstandingly rich source of vitamins A and C, papaya also contains potassium, calcium and phosphorus. Papaya has the added bonus of providing the enzyme papain, which aids in digestion. Additionally, the small black seeds of the fruit contain another aid to digestion, pepsin. The seeds make an attractive and healthful garnish for salads. Papayas reach their peak in May and June; very ripe papayas are bright yellow. If you don't intend to use the fruit right away, choose one that's speckled with yellow over about one-third of its surface. Look for medium-sized fruits with no spots or bruises. At room temperature, the papaya will ripen within 2 or 3 days, and should be chilled before serving.

PEACHES

The fuzzy fruit should be firm and yellow with a rosy blush when bought. A ripe peach will yield slightly when pressed with a fingertip. Don't bother buying green peaches—they don't ripen. Ripe peaches may be stored in the refrigerator; however, eat them as soon as possible. Besides using them in desserts, broiled peach halves make an excellent side dish with casseroles or baked beans.

PEARS

From October to May pears grace the shelves with their variety. This is one fruit that should be bought when quite firm and allowed to ripen at home. Place the pears in a brown paper bag and leave them at room temperature until the flesh yields slightly when pressed with a fingertip. Eat as soon as possible when they become ripe, or store them in the refrigerator. Avoid pears that are bruised, soft or mushy. If you're wondering why some pears that look fine on the outside are brown and mushy within, it's because they've been stored too long at low temperatures. From July to September, juicy Bartletts make their appearance. Boscs come later in the season, with their russet skins and sweet flesh. After that, look for Comice pears and sweet Anjous. In some areas, the tiny Seckel pears are available, and they're delicious for out-of-hand eating or for turning into spiced preserves.

PINEAPPLES

Hawaiian and Caribbean pineapples are available year-round; the difficult part is finding a truly ripe one. Only fruit ripened before picking is very sweet. Avoid pineapples with dried-out leaves or those that are discolored or green. To serve pineapple, slice off the crown, peel the fruit, and discard the hard, inner core. The fruit may be diced, sliced or chunked, but chill it well before serving. Save the sliced-off top to make an attractive houseplant by placing the crown in a shallow dish of water in a sunny spot until tiny rootlets appear. Then pot the plant in light, sandy soil and watch it grow!

PLUMS

Four or five standard varieties of plums are to be found throughout the year in most markets, although peak season is July to August. Fruits should not be very hard, wrinkled or shriveled. Choose firm, glossy fruits with a nice bloom on them, chill and eat. Red and greenish plums are somewhat soft when ripe, while the Italian or Damson types retain their firmness even when ripe.

TANGERINES

Tangerines reach their peak just in time for stuffing into the Christmas stocking. These brightly colored fruits should be deep orange, heavy for their size, and sweetly fragrant. Tangerines should be chilled before serving.

Vegetables

Vegetables are the ubiquitous building blocks of the vegetarian diet, for nutrition and for variety. Fortunately, it's possible to vary the types of vegetables you serve since a wide range is available at any time. Special attention, however, should be given to their selection, storage and preparation to take advantage of their benefits. Selecting different vegetables is important because each vegetable has its own special character. Each has a different nutrient makeup. To enable you to make your selections in a balanced way, in this chapter we mention the important nutrients of each vegetable. You should also be aware of how to combine the incomplete protein in vegetables with other foods for complete nourishment, and that information is provided in the chapter on menu planning. Vegetables should be selected in their proper season, and with a view to serving a diverse number of tastes, textures and colors.

Vegetables are a bargain in every sense of the word. Besides being relatively low in cost, vegetables provide every important vitamin and mineral your body needs, except vitamin D, which is supplied by the sun. Vegetables are low in calories, so that dieters can get vital nutrients without consuming a lot of empty calories. Most cooked vegetables will net you only 50 calories for a 1/2-cup serving, while the same portion of starchier vegetables—such as beans, potatoes, peas, and corn—will have between 50 and 100 calories.

One convenient and robust way to enjoy your vegetable requirements is to consume them in the form of juice. Tomatoes, celery and beets, for example, can be juiced solo or in combination. Just remember, however, not to juice and drink more than you would normally consume of the whole vegetable, for juice is highly concentrated. Juice can also be extracted from different types of sprouts and combined with other juices for a nourishing drink. If you plan to make a lot of juice or if you want to juice some of the harder vegetables, an electric extractor is a must. Carrots and turnips, for example, make wonderful juices but require good technology to grind them up.

Vegetables can be loosely classed into 3 main groups: stems, roots and leaves. The dark green, leafy vegetables such as kale, collard greens, mustard greens and spinach are valuable sources of vitamin A and calcium. Stem and flower vegetables like broccoli, asparagus, celery and cauliflower are important sources of fiber necessary to promote good digestion, as well as being simply good sources for nutrients. Turnips, potatoes, beets and other root vegetables add bulk to the diet. The deep orange types, like carrots and sweet potatoes, are an important source of carotene, which your body uses to convert into vitamin A. The most nutritious way to eat root vegetables is to eat them without peeling. Turnips, however, are an exception; they are usually waxed to protect them from shipping damage. Watch out for waxed vegetables in general. Cucumbers, tomatoes, peppers and eggplants are frequently waxed, and leave you no choice but to peel them.

If you live in the country or can drive there in the spring, you might enjoy foraging for vegetables that grow in the wild. Make sure to gather wild greens, such as dandelion or watercress, only in areas that have not been sprayed with insecticides. Among the wild greens, try fiddlehead ferns in spring: their tender young shoots can be steamed and eaten like asparagus. Pungent wild onions, which look like scallions, only smaller, are used in much the same way as their domestic cousins. Wild spearmint will make a tasty drink and is also very high in carotene. Be careful before you forage, and consult a reliable field guide to make sure the plants you gather are edible, not poisonous. This is especially true for those who wish to gather mushrooms; avoiding poisonous species takes a keen eye and a lot of knowledge and experience.

When bought in season, fresh vegetables are the best buy nutritionally and economically. If your market carries vegetables wrapped in plastic or packed in plastic-topped cartons, check your purchases carefully and don't hesitate to return any produce that doesn't measure up. Look for the freshest, brightest produce you can find, and then store it carefully. Unwrap the produce when you get home, check it for damage and then rewrap it before storing. This is particularly important for leafy greens such as lettuce. If the greens remain in a tightly sealed store wrapping, they will deteriorate rapidly if the produce has any rotted spots. For more tips on choosing and storing produce, check each of the following sections under the heading of the appropriate vegetable.

While it is most desirable to get fresh produce from the farm, this is not always possible. Thus, if you long for some broccoli, but it's not in season, you'll have to resort to frozen. Unlike canned vegetables, which often contain chemical additives, some frozen vegetables are good buys. Check the package to make sure no chemicals have been added. If the vegetables you buy are of high quality and flash frozen, you will have produce almost as good as fresh. Buying frozen those vegetables that are out of season will save you money over buying them fresh. We especially like the large "economy size" bags that allow you to pour out just the amount you need and put the rest back in the freezer for future use. Make sure any frozen produce you buy is frozen solid and stays that way until you're ready to use it. Never refreeze partially thawed produce, but use it right away. Refrozen food of any kind is a possible source of bacterial contamination.

The chapter on cooking techniques will outline how to boil, steam or bake vegetables; nevertheless, two important points must be remembered in vegetable eating. First, whenever possible, eat them raw. Many people have never savored the pleasures of snow-white raw mushrooms or tiny raw artichokes, or even tiny, very tender, raw sweet corn. Secondly, when you cook, cook as briefly as possible, with as little peeling, scraping or soaking as possible. The more water and heat used, the more nutrients are lost.

ARTICHOKES

The peak season for these globe-shaped "flowers" is from March through May, but it's sometimes possible to get "frost-kissed" artichokes in November, and their flavor is especially fine. Artichokes are a rich source of potassium, sodium and calcium, and also provide vitamin A and riboflavin. Frozen artichoke hearts are available all year-round and since there is little waste to them, they're economical to use in many of your favorite dishes. Occasionally, and all too seldomly, "baby chokes" can be found in Italian produce markets. These delectable "flowers" can be eaten whole, either raw, lightly boiled, or pickled. When choosing artichokes, look for a bright green color (except for the frost-kissed kind, which may be striped with bronze), tightly closed leaves and no bruises or discoloration. Size does not affect flavor, but uniform-sized artichokes insure even cooking results when cooked together. Artichokes should be stored in the crisper bin of the refrigerator and used within 3 to 4 days of purchase. To prepare boiled artichokes, pull off some of the tough outer leaves and cut off the stem, then rinse the choke under running water, spreading the leaves out. Peel the stem and add it to the pot along with the chokes. The pot should have 2 to 3 inches of water in it, and lemon juice can be added to prevent discoloration. Bring the water to a boil, cover the pot and simmer until tender. To test for doneness, pull out one of the leaves at the base of the choke. If it comes out easily, they're ready for draining and eating. Artichokes are eaten leaf by leaf by dipping the tender base of the leaf in a sauce and scraping off the base with the teeth. The hard upper tip is discarded. As leaf after leaf is eaten, the center cone finally emerges, where tiny, pinkish leaves protect the "fuzzy" choke. Remove the cone and scrape out the choke, then cut up the bottom, dunk it in the sauce and eat it. The heart of the artichoke has an excellent flavor. If you wish to prepare stuffed artichokes, remove the choke before cooking. You may also pull all the leaves off a raw artichoke, clean the bottom and then boil gently to serve as a little "platter" for cheese dip or sautéed mushrooms. Boil the leaves and serve them at another meal or use them to make soup. For that matter, the cooking water from boiled artichokes can be added to broth or stocks for a rich, unusual flavor. Boiled artichokes are well served with melted butter, mayonnaise or French dressing to dunk the leaves in. Tiny chokes are an elegant appetizer, while stuffed artichokes make a good main dish for any festive occasion. After the artichoke has been prepared for stuffing, fill each with a mixture of brown rice, pine nuts and raisins or use your favorite grain or bread stuffing. Artichokes can also be baked in a low oven (about 325 degrees) with a little bit of water, wine or tomato juice in the bottom of the pan. Or if you tie them securely with string, you can boil them gently in 2 or 3 inches of water.

ASPARAGUS

Asparagus heralds spring, with the spears at their best from March through May. Frozen spears are found all year. Asparagus may be either green or white (the green spears more fortified with vitamin A). Asparagus is a good source of fiber, its roughage content long considered a "spring tonic" for cleaning out the body's system. Vitamins B_1, A, and C, and some riboflavin are found in the vegetable.

Asparagus's low sodium content makes it an ideal choice for people on a low-salt diet. The asparagus spears come both pencil thin and fat and hefty, but the thin stalks are more tender and can be eaten raw in a salad or used as a dipper for a cheese spread. Choose uniformly sized stalks with tightly closed buds. Remember when buying by the pound that the white ends will be discarded; therefore, look for bunches that have only small amounts of white at the bottom. If you don't have a special asparagus cooker, you can get both the stems and tips of the vegetable uniformly tender by standing the stalks upright in a coffee percolator with the ends submerged in 2 inches of water. Simmer until just barely tender, then serve with a cheese sauce or melted butter. The cooking water may be used in soups, and any leftover spears may be cut up and added to tossed salads. Try stir frying asparagus tips with a bit of oil and soy sauce, then toss in some tofu cubes for a satisfying main course. Wilted asparagus can be revived by standing the spears in a jar of water for an hour or so. A cross cut in the butt end of each spear will help the spear absorb water more efficiently. Store uncooked asparagus in the refrigerator and use within 3 days.

BEANS: GREEN SNAP AND YELLOW SNAP

From the first tiny tender "snappers" of the season to the larger green and yellow beans available later, these vegetables not only burst with flavor but with vitamins A, B and C and potassium. Although in season from May to October, they are available year-round because they freeze well. Beans should be bright, uniformly sized, with blemish-free pods and no signs of wilt or bruises. One pound of beans serves three people. The modern greenbean is a far cry from what Grandma called a "stringbean." Fortunately, new hybrids have developed that don't need "stringing." Just rinse well, snap off the ends and simmer in just a few inches of water. Beans can also be steamed, or sliced and stir fried in hot oil. Store snap beans in a plastic bag in the fridge and use within 3 to 5 days.

BEET GREENS

Although available all year, beet greens reach their peak from June to October. They can be bought in bunches, or they may come as a bonus with a bunch of beets. Beet greens are a source of potassium, magnesium, iron, thiamine and riboflavin, and also contain vitamins A and C. They should not be overcooked! Simmer the greens, uncovered, very briefly, and then serve them with a sprinkling of lemon juice. Very tender young greens may be added to salads. When choosing beet greens look for bright green, unwilted leaves with no spots or discoloration. Store them in the fridge in a plastic bag with a bit of damp paper toweling to keep them fresh. Beet greens should be used within 2 or 3 days of purchase, and should be rinsed very carefully because they often harbor a lot of grit and sand.

BEETS

From June to August, fresh beets are at their best: use in soups, juices, salads and main dishes. Tiny beets can be well scrubbed, sliced and eaten raw. Larger beets, after baking or boiling, may be added to salads or pickled. Don't peel beets or trim the tops too closely before cooking or their rich color will bleed out. The exception comes when making soups. Otherwise, just scrub them well, trim the top a bit, and then boil in a large amount of water or bake in a 325-degree oven for an hour. Beets should look and feel firm, be well rounded and bright red with fresh, springy tops. Store in the crisper bin of the refrigerator and use within 2 weeks. Beets are a good source of vitamins A and B_1 and also contain riboflavin, potassium and magnesium.

BROCCOLI

In season from October through May, broccoli is a good source of vitamins A, B_1 and C, and contains potassium, calcium, sulphur and iron. The trick to getting tender, nonmushy tops during cooking is to cut the stems into smaller pieces and start them off first in a covered pot with a few inches of boiling water. When the stems are just beginning to get tender, add the tops and simmer for a few more minutes. If you lift the cover off the pot every now and then to let steam escape, the broccoli will stay greener. You may also use the stems, cut into julienne strips, for stir-fry dishes and save the tender buds to be steamed until just tender, all served with a drizzle of melted butter. Cold broccoli also makes a good addition to tossed salads, or it can be marinated in French dressing to serve as an appetizer. Broccoli should be bright green, with tightly closed heads and no signs of yellow. Count on 1/2 pound of broccoli for each serving. Store the head in a plastic bag in the fridge and use within 2 days.

BRUSSELS SPROUTS

These tiny "cabbages" are available from September to February, although frozen sprouts can be had year-round. If properly prepared, the frozen sprouts can taste as good as the fresh. However, overcooked sprouts are a disaster. They're smelly, tasteless, colorless and bound to turn anyone off. Brussels sprouts, like other sulphur-high vegetables, smell unpleasant when overcooked because heat releases the sulphur. In addition to having sulphur, Brussels sprouts are a source of vitamins C, B_1 and A, and also contain calcium and potassium. They should be bright green with compact heads and no traces of yellow when bought at the market. Remove some of the outer leaves for cooking, but don't carry this process too far or you'll end up with the tiniest sprouts ever! Rinse well before boiling them in enough water to just cover them, and don't cover the pan. They should be ready in 5 to 10 minutes, depending on their size. Brussels sprouts store easily in a plastic bag in the fridge and should be used within 2 days of purchase.

BURDOCK

Burdock can be found in the wild and is often sold in Oriental food markets, where it's known as *gobo*. Burdock is the root of a prickly plant that's covered with burrs. The wild variety has small roots, while those cultivated, mainly in Japan and Hawaii, have large, bulbous greyish-brown roots. Peel burdock and boil it before using in tempura or stir-fry dishes. Keep the roots in a cool, dry place, and use within a week or 2.

CABBAGE: RED AND GREEN

If familiarity breeds contempt, then perhaps cabbage is suffering from overexposure. Cabbage is abundant throughout the year and is one of the least expensive vegetables. However, it has suffered from poor preparation. Overcooked cabbage is about as dull and lifeless as a food can be! But if stir fried or briefly steamed, the flavor is sweetly fragrant and tasty. Cabbage contains vitamins C, B_2 and some amounts of phosphorus, magnesium and potassium. Raw red or green cabbage makes a colorful addition to tossed salads, besides being the basis for the familiar standby, cole slaw. If you want a different flavor in your slaw, make it with yogurt instead of mayonnaise in the dressing and toss in some celery seeds. When cooking red cabbage, add some lemon juice to preserve its bright color. A lovely vegetable dish is made by simply steaming some shredded green cabbage until just tender, then dressing it with melted butter and caraway seeds. And don't forget to save those outer leaves—which, by the way, contain the most nutrients—to make stuffed cabbage. Cabbage should have firm, blemish-free heads with tightly packed leaves and no sign of wilt or discoloration. Wrap cabbage snugly in plastic wrap and store in the refrigerator. Use within 2 weeks of purchase.

CARROTS

Available all year, carrots are a favorite with children and grown-ups alike. Raw carrots are often loved by children, and they should be encouraged to continue to eat them that way. For carrots provide them with large amounts of vitamins A and B₁, riboflavin, potassium and sodium. We like fresh carrot juice more than any other vegetable juice, and even if you don't share our fanatical enthusiasm for it, you'll like it if you try it. Don't be deceived by canned carrot juice if you've ever tried it. The fresh juice is very different and infinitely more wholesome. When choosing carrots, find smooth, uniformly sized roots with no bumps or blemishes. Try to get carrots with the green tops, so that you can chop a handful of carrot greens into your next salad. The smaller the carrot, the sweeter the flavor, and the finger-length ones are a special treat. Unless the carrots on hand are very large or old, it is better not to peel them. A good scrub with a stiff vegetable brush under running water is all you need to do. Boil, steam or fry carrots until just barely tender. Store carrots in a plastic bag in the refrigerator, using them within 2 weeks.

CAULIFLOWER

Fresh cauliflower is available at the market from September to November, while frozen cauliflower is available throughout the year. If not overcooked, the frozen cauliflower tastes just fine. Cauliflower supplies vitamin C and B₁, as well as riboflavin, phosphorus, magnesium, potassium, calcium and sulphur. The heads should be firm and creamy white, with no green or speckling. The small "flowerettes" can be served raw as an appetizer or marinated in French dressing. When cooking cauliflower, be sure to stop at the point when it's just tender. Don't overcook. It's best to follow the cooking directions given for broccoli, above. Allow 1 medium-sized head for 4 servings, and store wrapped in plastic in the fridge until ready for use.

CELERY

For the compulsive nibbler who is trying to bring his weight down, celery is the savior because it's available year-round and has only 9 calories per cup. It's also one of the least expensive vegetables, and all parts of it may be eaten. Use the leaves in salads or soups or dry and store them for those times when you want just a hint of celery flavor in a dish. Celery is a good source of roughage, and its high water content makes it the perfect balance for foods that are high in protein or starch. To take advantage of celery's vitamins A and B_1, and its riboflavin, calcium, phosphorus and sodium, eat the vegetable raw or cooked until tender-crisp. Celery juice—the old "celery tonic"—is very refreshing and nourishing. We like to combine celery juice with tomato or carrot juice for a thirst-quenching drink. The two most widely available types of celery are the green Pascal and the Golden type, which is really a creamy white. Choose stalks with bright coloring, absence of spots or blemishes, and with fresh, springy leaves. Celery that has wilted a bit can easily be restored by cutting some notches in the root ends of the stalks and standing them upright in a glass of water for an hour or so. Store celery in a plastic bag in the fridge and eat within a week of purchase.

CHARD, SWISS

Chard is actually a member of the beet family, but never develops the bulbous roots typical of that vegetable. It's available during the summer months and provides vitamins A, B_1 and C, and riboflavin, iron and sulphur. Chard's flavor is similar to that of spinach, and the leafy sections of the plant can be treated as you would spinach. Stems should be cooked separately or started first so that the tops won't be overcooked. Simmer the stems in boiling water for 5 minutes before adding the leaves. Or stir fry the stems and save the leaves for another meal. Refrigerate chard in a plastic bag; use within 2 days.

CHICORY OR CURLY ENDIVE

This curly salad green should not be confused with its relative the Belgian endive, which, while a variety of the same plant, has quite a different taste and appearance. The slightly tart greens are found in bunches in the market all year-round and are a source of vitamins A, C and B₁, and additionally of riboflavin, calcium, phosphorus and iron. No wilt or discoloration should mar the bright green leaves when you buy them, and chicory should be used within 2 days. Store in the refrigerator in a plastic bag. In addition to adding the chicory to a salad, it can also be steamed briefly and treated like any cooked green.

COLLARD GREENS

Vitamin A, vitamin C, riboflavin, thiamine, niacin, magnesium, calcium, phosphorus, sodium, potassium and iron make collard greens one of the most nutritious vegetables. Collards are freshest from June to September and, as with kale, may actually taste better after a light frost. Collards should be bright green with no sign of discoloration or wilt; 1 pound will serve 4 people. Wash the greens well before cooking to remove any traces of grit, then boil uncovered for 5 to 10 minutes. The cooking water can be saved for use in soups. The greens should be used within 3 days of purchase and kept refrigerated in a plastic bag.

CORN

This great American favorite is found every month of the year but is at its peak of flavor when it comes to market in May through September. The prices are lowest during this period of the year. From December to April, the corn comes from Florida and is not as sweet or as economical as locally grown ears. Flash-frozen corn can be had all year, and though the flavor is more starchy than sweet, it is still a good vegetable entree. Corn can be prepared in so many ways that it's likely each area that grows corn has its own local dish. Popular types of corn include the yellow Golden Bantam or the white Country Gentleman, while Florida types include such names as Iobelle, a common variety during mid-season, and Florigold, whose peak is in the spring. Another variety, Sugar 'n' Cream, features mixed golden and white kernels and has been gaining popularity in recent

years for its sweetness and ease in preservation. In addition to pro-
ducing sweet corn, the United States annually grows large quantities
of field corn for use as animal fodder and dried corn (for information
on dried corn, see the chapter on grains). Corn provides vitamin A,
thiamine, riboflavin, niacin, phosphorus, magnesium, iron, and copper.
The natural sugars in corn begin to turn to starch as soon as it's
picked—so that the fresher picked the better. Chilling does retard this
conversion to starch, so it's wise to keep fresh corn unhusked in the
refrigerator. Pick ears with fresh, green husks and light golden silk.
Peel back the husk on one of the ears to make sure the kernels are
plump and even, with no signs of insect damage. Boil corn, uncovered,
in unsalted water until just tender, about 3 to 8 minutes. Or corn can
be husked, buttered, and wrapped in tin foil and then roasted over
coals or in the oven. If you don't like your corn on the cob, cut the
kernels off with a sharp knife, pressing down well to make sure that
you get all the germ and juice. Then simmer them in their own juice
until just tender, adding butter or a little cream. If you like, use this
method and then add some lima beans to make a tasty dish of
succotash that will provide the complete protein of the grain-bean
combination. Leftover corn can be used in soups, casseroles or
whipped up into a batch of corn fritters. Try serving corn fritters with
a dish of applesauce.

CUCUMBERS

Cucumbers are available all year; however, look for them during the
summer months when local, unwaxed types find their way to the
market. The unwaxed cucumber can be recognized by its dull-looking
skin. If the cucumbers are waxed, as is the case during most months,
peel the skin off before using. Because of their high water content,
cucumbers help to wash out the system and aid in digestion. They are
an excellent balance food if served with high-protein food and starch.
These crunchy vegetables are also a good source of vitamin B_1 and
riboflavin. "Cukes" come in a range of sizes, from tiny gherkins to
the fleshy 12- to 15-inch-long Europeans. Sometimes Oriental vegetable markets have small, chubby cucumbers that are extremely crisp
and almost seedless. These Kirby cucumbers add a bracing accent to
any salad and are a good buy because they are unwaxed and never
bitter. Buy cucumbers with bright green skins and no soft spots or
yellowing. The slender, medium-sized cuke usually contains fewer

seeds. To make a cucumber truly crisp, salt after slicing and let stand an hour or so, then rinse. This salting process draws out a lot of the excess moisture. For the same reason, if you want to braise or stir fry cucumbers, don't salt them until after cooking or the dish will turn out to be too liquid. Slices of dewatered cucumber and bread can be fried in the same way you would an eggplant or zucchini. Keep cucumbers unwrapped in the crisper bin of the refrigerator. Eat them within a week of purchase.

DANDELION GREENS

Cultivated dandelion greens are in the market in early spring and summer. Lighter in color than the wild ones, they have a milder taste. Dandelion greens are an excellent source of vitamin A as well as a good source of iron and other minerals. Choose bunches with tender, crisp leaves, preferably with the roots still attached. Trim away the roots, and rinse the greens carefully before storing them in the fridge in a plastic bag with some paper toweling wrapped around them to absorb excess moisture. Use them raw in salads or steam them for 5 minutes and serve as you would spinach.

EGGPLANT

While eggplants are available all year, the peak season runs from August through September. Eggplant can be sliced, mashed, stewed, chopped, baked or fried. Dress it up with yogurt for a relish or make pickles from tiny, baby eggplants. For the dieter, the eggplant's 19 calories per cup are a godsend. It will fortify you with vitamins A, C and B complex, not to mention its high-fiber content for roughage. Variations of eggplant include the Morden with tiny fruits; white eggplants that look like eggs; and a variety that has fruits the size and shape of cucumbers. Most of the eggplant grown in the United States, though, is deep purple, globular and includes such types as Black Beauty, Florida Market and Black Magic. It's sometimes possible to buy finger-sized eggplant in Italian or Oriental food markets; these are especially tasty. Eggplant contains a lot of water: "dewater" by salting eggplant slices, letting them stand for an hour and then rinsing and draining them. Dewatered eggplant won't absorb as much oil when fried. Some eggplants are waxed, unfortunately; if there is any doubt in your mind as to whether it's waxed, peel the eggplant. Its meaty texture makes eggplant ideal for a main dish in a vegetarian meal. It can be used in casseroles, as French-fried chips or for crispy fritters. Team it up with cheese, as in eggplant parmigian, and eggplant becomes the basis of a complete protein meal. It can be fried with peppers and onions to make "poor man's caviar." Eggplant stuffed with rice, bread dressing or grains provides for a complete protein meal that can be served on a regular basis throughout the year. Eggplant is best stored in a plastic bag at 60 degrees (F) and should be used within 2 days of purchase.

ENDIVE, BELGIAN

These creamy white, cylindrical sprouts of the chicory family are available during the winter months and are at their best from November to April. They should be crisp, creamy white, with tightly closed tips and no stains or blemishes when you buy them. Refrigerate them in a plastic bag, and use within 2 days, either raw in salads, steamed or sauced.

ESCAROLE

A close relative of curly endive (and often confused with it), escarole is found in the market year-round, although its peak season is from June to October. It is a good source of vitamins A and B₁, and has riboflavin, calcium, phosphorus and iron to round out its nutrients. Escarole should be bought fresh, with no wilting or yellowish leaves. It may be eaten raw in salads or steamed as well as sauced. Store escarole in a plastic bag in the fridge with a bit of damp paper towel to keep it crisp. Use within 3 days.

GARLIC

Garlic enhances so many different dishes that some people find it impossible to cook without this pungent bulb seasoning some part of the meal. Garlic is available fresh all year. Of course, one of the great interests of garlic is its use in folk medicine, where it has the reputation for remarkable curative powers. Even if you're not using garlic for medicine, make sure to keep enough around for cooking. Choose firm white bulbs with fat cloves and no signs of discoloration or shriveling. Don't buy too much at once. Store in a cool, well-ventilated place, and it will often keep for up to a month.

KALE

This dark green, curly vegetable is sold in bunches during the winter months. The flavor of kale is improved if it's picked after a light frost. Its peak season, however, is from December through April. Kale is a good source of vitamin A, while also containing vitamins B_1 and C and riboflavin, calcium and other trace minerals. Look for dark green, crisp leaves with no discoloration or signs of wilt. Remove and discard the tough outer leaves and cut out any tough ribs. Rinse the kale well to remove all traces of grit, then boil in a covered pot in an inch or so of water. Again, don't overcook; it only takes about 5 minutes for kale to become properly tender. Refrigerate kale in a plastic bag and use within 5 days.

LETTUCE

Your market undoubtedly carries many different kinds of lettuce all year-round, and it is worthwhile trying them all or combining several to add interest to your salads. Lettuce is a good source of thiamine, riboflavin and potassium, and also contains vitamins A and C. The darker the green of the lettuce, the more vitamins A and C are present. Make sure to buy lettuce that is fresh, with bright green leaves free of insect damage or wilt. The round, pale Iceberg lettuce is perhaps the most common type on the market. Smaller heads tend to be more flavorful. Bibb lettuce has small, bright green leaves that are very tender, but be sure to wash the leaves carefully because it does tend to be sandy. Boston lettuce is pale green and loosely packed as well as very tender. Romaine or cos has long, crisp, bright green leaves and good flavor. Use it right down to the inner core, which should be thinly sliced before you add it to the salad bowl. Loose leaf lettuce comes in several different types: curly, red-tipped and flat leaf like Ivy Leaf and Salad Bowl. Loose leaf lettuces are fragile and care should be taken not to bruise their delicate leaves when rinsing them.

All types of lettuces should be stored unwashed in a plastic bag with a bit of damp toweling to keep them fresh. Keep lettuce well chilled and also chill washed lettuce before serving it in a salad. Use the loose leaf types within 3 days and head lettuce within 5,

Some important words on salad making: Besides dressing, the most important secret to good salads is proper preparation of the greens. Wash the greens carefully in cool water, then dry them in a clean dish towel or with paper toweling. Wet lettuce will not hold salad dressing, thus losing important flavor. Tear the greens into bite-sized pieces, then chill until dinnertime. Don't add the dressing until the last minute or the greens will get soggy. For the simplest and perhaps best salad of all, just toss the greens with oil first, then gradually sprinkle on either some apple cider vinegar or lemon juice. As you continue to toss, taste, and add more vinegar, salt and pepper and perhaps a pinch of your favorite herb. The basic proportions for salad dressings are 2 parts oil to 1 part vinegar; however you may use lemon juice instead of vinegar, or use mayonnaise to replace part or all of the oil. Add your own flavor touches such as garlic, chives, Worcestershire sauce or cheese. Try creamy yogurt dressings, or add homemade ketchup to homemade mayo for a creamy French dressing. Capers, olives and pickles all add spicy accents to dressings. There are a host of greens other than lettuce to enliven any salad: chicory, endive, escarole, dandelion greens, raw spinach, watercress, raw shredded cabbage or sorrel. The key word to making good salads is experiment! Creativity and combinations reap the rewards of healthful and delicious eating!

LIMA BEANS

Fresh and frozen lima beans are around all year and are a good source of protein, carbohydrates and vitamins C and A. Dried lima beans are a good staple item for the vegetarian kitchen; we include information about them in our chapter on beans. Choose fresh limas with pods that are bright green and well fleshed out. Allow 1 pound of unshelled beans per serving. The two main varieties of limas found at the market are the large, meaty Fordhooks and the smaller, more tender Baby limas. Shell the beans just before cooking, and save the pods to add to soup stock for flavor. Boil the fresh lima beans in a covered pot, using a small amount of water. Don't salt them until they've been cooked. Again, don't overcook! They take only 5 to 15 minutes, depending on the size of the beans. Lima beans combine well with other vegetables such as corn, peas, tomatoes and peppers. Store the unshelled beans in a moisture-proof container in the fridge and use within 3 days.

MUSHROOMS

Snowy white or creamy beige mushrooms are commercially grown and are found throughout the year. They are a good source of thiamine, riboflavin, potassium, phosphorus, copper and iron. Look for unblemished caps with tightly closed gills. Cartoned mushrooms should be removed from the plastic as soon as you get them, and then stored in a single layer in a flat pan. Mushrooms must be kept well chilled until ready for use, and make sure they don't get damp, because they decay quickly. Rinse them just before cooking, and dry mushrooms carefully. Mushrooms soak up moisture like a sponge; therefore, don't immerse them in water. A handful of snow-white, raw mushrooms gives a great, earthy flavor to salads as well as to many other dishes. Mushrooms give out a lot of liquid during cooking, thus adjust the cooking liquids accordingly. Mushrooms tend to be quickly perishable and should be used within a day or 2 of purchase.

MUSTARD GREENS

Fresh or frozen, the pungent flavor of mustard greens is a welcome change from other greens anytime during the year. They are stores of niacin, calcium, phosphorus, iron, sodium, potassium and iron. One pound should be enough to serve 3 people; choose dark green, unwilted leaves with no signs of yellow. Small, tender, mustard greens can be used raw in salads. Cook larger leaves as you would spinach. Refrigerate them in a plastic bag and use within 3 days.

OKRA

Although available frozen all year-round, fresh okra is available from June to September. Its slender, bright green pods are a source of vitamins A and C, and provide calcium, phosphorus, potassium and magnesium. The slender, unblemished pods with bright color should be no more than 4 inches long when bought at the market. Because of its slightly gelatinous quality, cooked okra is often used to thicken soups and stews; it's also good when coated with cornmeal and deep fried or stewed with corn and tomatoes. To cook okra, trim off the ends and then either leave it whole or slice before boiling, uncovered, in a small amount of water. Never overcook or it will be mushy and disagreeable. Store okra uncovered in the fridge and use it within 3 days.

ONIONS

Many types of onions are available throughout the year, and they can be used in a multitude of dishes and eaten in a variety of ways. They are a source of vitamins A and C, of calcium, phosphorus, potassium and sulphur. Look for firm onions that are not blemished and have thin, brittle skins and firm ends. Small white onions are generally served as a cooked vegetable or, when pickled, as a cocktail tidbit. The mild, red Italian onions are delicious when sliced thin and added to sandwiches. The brownish-yellow, all-purpose onions can be used both raw and cooked. Large ones are also good when stuffed and baked. When buying onions to cook as an entree, count on 1 pound to serve 4 people. Before boiling the peeled onions, cut a cross in the root end of each one to prevent them from bursting. Store onions in a cool, well-ventilated place and they will keep up to several months.

PARSNIPS

Parsnips, in season from March through June, are a good source of vitamin C, phosphorus, calcium and potassium. Pick small, well-rounded bulbs with no bruises or discoloration. Parsnips provide soup stock with a good flavor and are tasty boiled, mashed and served with lots of butter. Small parsnips can also be peeled, sliced thinly and added to salads. To conserve the nutrients, peel parsnips after, not before, boiling. Store them uncovered in the refrigerator, and they will keep for 2 weeks.

PEA PODS, EDIBLE OR SNOW

These small, crisp pods are occasionally found fresh in local and Oriental markets or frozen at any time of the year. The pod, as the name implies, is edible. The smallest specimens are best. Wash them and dry well before stir frying them in a small amount of oil or butter. It's essential not to overcook them; if you do, the wonderful, crisp texture will be destroyed. They add an Oriental accent to any meal. Store snow peas in a plastic bag in the refrigerator and use within 2 days.

PEAS, GREEN

Fresh green peas are around from March to June. They are a source of vitamins A and C and also provide a small amount of protein, thiamine, calcium, phosphorus, riboflavin, iron and potassium. Frozen peas, when properly prepared, are usually satisfactory enough pea-eating for the rest of the year. Peas should be bright green, with unblemished pods that are well filled out. Small, fresh peas can be eaten raw in salads or as a cocktail snack. Add a few empty pods to intensify the flavor when boiling peas. Pods also are good for flavoring soup stocks. To be at their best, peas should not be overcooked. Therefore, boil them in unsalted water, without a cover, for 8 to 12 minutes. One particularly good pea recipe calls for placing the shelled peas in a heavy-bottomed saucepan with 1 or 2 tablespoons of water. Top them with a handful of shredded cabbage, cover the pan with a tight lid, simmering gently until just tender. Store fresh peas in their pods in a plastic bag in the refrigerator. Use within 2 days of purchase.

PEPPERS, SWEET, GREEN AND RED

Unlike their fiery cousins the chilis, sweet green and red peppers are used as a vegetable, not as a seasoning. At their best in the summer months, they are a good source of vitamins A and C, as well as a source of calcium, phosphorus, sodium and potassium. Peppers should be bought large, firm and unwrinkled, with no soft spots or bruises. They come both in bell and long tapered shapes, and may be green or red depending on their ripeness. If you have to cut down on calories, peppers are a delight, having only 25 calories per 1/2 cup. If the peppers are waxed (something to avoid), then you will have to peel them. If you must peel, try this method: Char the skin over an open gas flame or under the broiler. When the peppers are black all over, put them in a paper bag for 10 minutes. Then simply rub off the charred skin with your fingers and rinse the peppers under cold water. The flesh will taste smokey and delicious. Large bell peppers make an unusual entree when filled with your favorite grain or bread stuffing and topped with some cheese. We like to keep a bag of chopped peppers in the freezer and add a handful to different dishes for both color and flavor. Store peppers in a plastic bag in the refrigerator, and use them within 1 week of purchase.

POTATOES

Any time of the year, 4 types of potatoes can be found at the market. They are a source of vitamin C, niacin, iron, potassium and phosphorus. It is important to remember that new potatoes retain more vitamin C than mature ones, and that all potatoes should be eaten with their skins for maximum nutrition. Different types of potatoes are suited for different cooking methods. The Burbank or Idaho potato is russet, with a fairly thick skin and numerous eyes. Because of its high starch content, it's especially good for boiling and baking, where its texture will be fluffy and mealy. Katadins are creamy buff potatoes that are low in starch, making them good candidates for pan frying, scalloping and cold salads, where they will keep their shape. The California Long White is, as its name implies, a long, somewhat flattened spud with a thick skin and few eyes. Red Pontiacs are large round tubers with thin red skin, which is sometimes dyed. New potatoes are the immature specimens of any variety, about the size of Ping-Pong balls. Quite often they are also subjected to dye to appear in the russet shade people expect. Tubers should be bought when firm, well shaped, with as few rough spots or eyes as possible. Avoid buying withered or damaged potatoes or those with any green tinge. This hue is caused by solanin, a mildly toxic substance that develops in potatoes overexposed to light.

Potatoes are America's most popular vegetable in great part because they can be prepared in so many ways and still be delicious and nutritious. To bake potatoes, choose high-starch types, scrub them well and pierce the skin in several places to allow for the escape of steam. Bake them in a preheated oven at 450 degrees (F) for about 1 hour. When they test done—are tender when pricked with a fork—remove them from the oven, cut a slit in the top and squeeze to fluff the flesh out. Serve with yogurt, butter or sour cream. You may wish to pan roast potatoes in butter or oil. Peel or not, as you choose, then quarter and place in a baking dish with butter or oil, turning them so they are well coated on all sides. Bake them in a preheated 350-degree (F) oven for about an hour and a half. Keep checking them, and turn them every now and then to make sure they get brown and crisp on all sides. To boil potatoes, either peel them or scrub them well, cut into quarters, and boil in salted water for about 35 minutes. When the spuds are done, drain off the water and return the pan to the burner. Shake it over medium heat until the potatoes are dry and fluffy. Once potatoes are peeled, they tend to darken. So once peeled, keep them submerged in cold water. We don't recommend this, however, as it tends to leach out some of the nutrients. When making fried potatoes, slice them thinly before drying them well with paper towels. Fry them in a small amount of oil or butter, turning them often to get an even brown color. Leftover boiled or baked potatoes are also good when fried in butter or oil with a bit of chopped onion. Don't discard the water in which potatoes have been boiled because you can add it to soups or use it as the liquid in any bread dough recipe. Store potatoes in a cool, well-ventilated place with a minimum of light. Don't expose them to moisture or they will either sprout or rot. Properly stored potatoes will last 2 to 3 months.

RADISHES

The peak season for radishes is between April and mid-July; however, different types of radishes are available throughout the year. They are a good source of vitamin C, calcium, iron, sodium, phosphorus, sulphur and potassium. In addition to the common, round red ones, there are white and black radishes, as well as red-and-white-striped types. They all taste much the same. Try to buy firm and uncracked tubers, with bright smooth skin and with the green tops still on. When you get them home, remove the tops and as you would with any vegetable green, place them in a plastic bag with a bit of damp paper towel. Use the tops as a salad green or steam them briefly and serve with a sauce. Use the tops within a day or two. The roots should be stored in a plastic bag in the fridge and used within 2 weeks. In addition to eating them raw, try steaming them and serving with melted butter some time. Radishes are also a good tempura item when thinly sliced, and may be used as a substitute for water chestnuts in Chinese dishes.

SCALLIONS

Scallions can be obtained all year-round and are a source of vitamins A, C and B₁, with the added benefits of calcium, phosphorus, potassium, sulphur and riboflavin. Scallions should be bright green with a firm white bulb at the end. If they come wrapped with a rubber band, remove it and store them in the refrigerator in a plastic bag with a bit of damp paper toweling. Salads are enhanced by scallions; try them in Chinese dishes as well. They are particularly delicious if they are served lightly steamed with melted butter atop. Scallions should be used within 5 days of purchase.

SPINACH

Serve spinach often because of its nutritional value and its year-round availability, both frozen and fresh. Fresh spinach comes either in loose bunches or "precleaned" in plastic bags. The bagged product is somewhat cleaner, yet it should still be carefully rinsed to rid it of any traces of sand. Spinach is a good source of vitamins A and C and also provides riboflavin, potassium, calcium and iron. The leaves should be crisp, deep and dark green, with no signs of wilt or decay. Once spinach starts to decay, it does so very quickly, and therefore it is wise to pick over the spinach as soon as you get it home. Remove any damaged leaves and then loosely repack it in a plastic bag and keep it refrigerated. Use the spinach within 2 days of purchase. Count on 1 pound serving 2 or 3 people.

To cook spinach, first rinse it in several changes of warm water and remove any tough stems. Place the greens in a pot that has a tight lid. It isn't necessary to add more water because the water clinging to the leaves should provide enough moisture. Cover the pot and simmer over very low heat until the spinach is tender. This will take 3 to 5 minutes. Check once or twice to make sure it isn't too dry. If it is, add a teaspoonful or so of water. Steamed spinach, done in a basket over boiling water, is especially delicious. Add leftover cooked spinach to soups and omelets, or make it into a puree and season it with cream sauce. Don't neglect to add raw spinach to your favorite tossed salad, and mince very finely to add to sandwich spreads.

SQUASH, SUMMER

All the different types of squash are a good source of vitamin A, potassium, phosphorus, calcium and vitamin C. Summer squash differs from the winter type by being more tender and having a thinner rind. This skin should not be discarded because it contains many valuable nutrients. You will find summer squash in all shades of yellow and green, in shapes that vary from the bulbous-ended crook-neck to the slender straight zucchini. Choose smooth, unblemished squash with no soft spots. Gently scrub the squash with a vegetable brush under cold running water, and you are ready to cook it or slice it thinly to add to salad. Summer squash is best when either steamed or simmered in a small amount of water until just barely tender. Because it has a high water content, it's best not to salt squash until after cooking or too much water will cook out. Try some deep-fried zucchini sticks as an alternative to the ever-popular French fry. Dry the julienne sticks well with paper towels before deep frying them in hot oil. Keep all summer squashes unwrapped in the fridge, and use them within 3 days of purchase.

SQUASH, WINTER

Winter squash adds variety to the vegetable menu from fall to early spring. They're a good source of vitamin A, calcium, phosphorus and potassium. Some of the most familiar varieties include the dull green acorn squash, shaped just as its name implies, or butternut squash, cylindrical with a bulbous end and a creamy tan rind. Hubbard squash, noted for its sweet, tender flesh, is globular with a tapered neck and a hard, warty rind. Select winter squash that has a hard, blemish-free rind and store in a cool dry place. It will keep for several months. Winter squash is low in sodium, which makes it good for the salt-free diet. The meaty and satisfying flavor makes it a good main course choice for the vegetarian menu. Try an acorn squash cut in half and filled with your favorite grain or bread stuffing, or make squash patties by combining cooked, mashed squash with beaten egg and bread crumbs until it holds together. Shape into patties and fry in butter until browned on both sides, then serve with a zesty tomato sauce. To make plain baked squash, cut the squash in half lengthwise, remove the seeds and put a lump of butter in the cavity. Bake in a 375-degree (F) oven until tender, about an hour. Save and wash the squash seeds. When they're dry, toast them in the oven and eat them as a snack.

SWEET POTATOES AND YAMS

While in the market all year-round, their peak season is from March to June. Sweet potatoes and yams are full of vitamins A and C, and their natural sugar makes them a good candidate for the healthful dessert department. The bright orange ones are the yams, and the lighter-colored tubers are the sweet potatoes. Select smooth, un-withered, well-shaped roots, with no blemishes or spots. You may boil them, but they taste better baked in a 350-degree (F) oven till tender (about an hour). Don't forget to eat the skins because they contain many of the nutrients. Store the tubers in a cool, dry, dark and well-ventilated place and never allow them to become chilled. Properly stored, they will keep for a month or so.

TOMATOES

For nutrition and taste, a vine-ripened tomato, perfumed with the aromas of summer, is without comparison. Unfortunately, it's not always possible to get good tomatoes. The best bet is to find locally grown produce from July to September. Tomatoes are a good source of vitamins A and C and also contain calcium, phosphorus, potassium and sodium. Enjoy them raw or cooked; savor their ruby juice. There are hundreds of different types of tomatoes: they range in size from the tiny "cherry" to the 1-pound beefsteaks; they come round and plum-shaped; and their color will vary from the usual red to the yellow of low-acid types. Good news for the dieter: tomatoes have only 30 to 35 calories per medium-sized fruit.

Pick firm, unblemished fruit with no bruises or discoloration. They should be deeply colored, unless you plan to ripen them at home by storing them at room temperature, out of direct sunlight, until ready to eat. Ripe tomatoes should be stored unwrapped in the refrigerator and used within 2 days. Gardeners should beware the first frost. Once green tomatoes have been chilled by frost, they will not ripen. However, they may be used to make green tomato relish or breaded and fried like eggplant. You'll save a lot of money if you buy when tomatoes are overflowing from a local bumper crop, and they'll taste best at that time. You can make tomato sauce or stewed tomatoes and freeze batches for later use. You can also freeze whole tomatoes by first dropping them into boiling water, then slipping the skins off and draining them. Pack them in plastic containers and store in the freezer. If you have a juicer or blender, make up batches of juice to freeze. Just remember to shake well after defrosting and before drinking. Make tomato soup with the juice, or mix tomato juice with other juices for nutrition-packed drinks. Use the sauce to enliven pastas, cooked vegetables, and casseroles. Hollow out large tomatoes and serve them stuffed with kasha, rice or cottage cheese. Tomatoes may be easily peeled by dipping them briefly in boiling water then in cold water. The skins should slip right off.

TURNIPS

Both white and yellow turnips can be found from October to March, and they provide vitamin C, calcium, sodium, phosphorus and potassium. Frozen turnip greens are available in some areas, and properly cooked make a nourishing addition to any meal. Look for smooth, unblemished, even-shaped roots with no soft spots. If you can get them with the tops on, so much the better. Thinly sliced, raw turnips are good in salads, or stir fry matchstick-sized pieces of turnip in hot oil and then season with tamari. Yellow turnips are especially good when mashed and served with melted butter. You might decide to combine them with an equal amount of mashed potatoes for those who don't favor the turnip's distinctive taste. Store turnips in a cool, dark well-ventilated place and use them within 3 months.

Beans (Legumes)

The bean is truly a winner in economy and nutrition, providing an important source of incomplete protein, minerals and vitamins. Combined with complete proteins such as dairy products, they can form the mainstay of the vegetarian diet. Since beans combine so well with so many other foods, they add a lot of variety to the menu as well as providing bulk. Fortunately, beans are one of the least expensive foods you can buy, and only a handful or so goes a long way to stretch any dish. Not only can beans be cooked, but dried legumes can also be used in the form of flours or flakes. Beans can also be sprouted to add crisp, fresh vegetables to the salad bowl. For directions on sprouting, see the chapter on nuts, seeds and sprouts. The soybean is perhaps the most important of all the beans. Its forms and uses are so many that we have devoted a complete chapter to the soybean.

Some people develop gastric disturbances when they eat beans, and the unfortunate bean has been the subject of unflattering doggerel regarding its gas-producing abilities. If this is a problem for you, it's probably because your diet has been too low in roughage. Introduce beans into your diet gradually, coupling them with other high-roughage foods such as whole grains and fresh raw fruits and vegetables.

All dried legumes should be carefully washed and sorted before cooking to remove any small stones, bits of earth or other foreign matter. Plan on 1 cup of dried beans to serve 4 people, and wash them in several changes of lukewarm water. Either soak the beans overnight or precook them (see instructions for each variety) by bringing them to a boil in a generous amount of unsalted water (salt tends to toughen them), removing the pot from the heat and letting it stand, covered, for 1 hour before the final cooking. You may also cook beans in a pressure cooker. Do be careful, however, for some types, like soybeans, tend to splatter off their skins and clog the vent. Following is a rundown on the most commonly available beans and how to choose and use them.

ADZUKI BEANS

Never pressure cook these small red beans or they'll be bitter. Soak or precook them first, then simmer until just tender (about 1 1/2 hours). Mix some of the cooked beans with water, soup vegetables and seasonings for a tasty soup. Mixed with brown rice, pickles and seaweed, they make a filling and nourishing main dish. Adzukis may be purchased at your local health food store.

BLACK OR TURTLE BEANS

These are small oval beans with back skins and white interiors. Again, don't try to pressure cook them or their skins will clog the vent. Soak or precook them, then simmer until tender in a kettle with a tight lid. Black and turtle beans are a good source of vitamin C, riboflavin, B vitamins, phosphorus and potassium. They combine well with tomatoes, onions and green peppers, making them good for soups and casseroles.

GREAT NORTHERN AND NAVY BEANS

The familiar beans of Boston fame, these two are used interchangeably. Both provide potassium, thiamine, riboflavin, niacin, other B vitamins, iron, calcium, phosphorus and sodium, and rate well in the protein department. Northern and navy beans should be presoaked or precooked before final cooking. Make your baked beans with natural sweeteners like honey and slowly cook them with fresh tomatoes and spices. And don't forget, they make a hearty soup.

KIDNEY BEANS

One of the most versatile of beans, the kidney bean is a source of protein, vitamin A, thiamine, riboflavin, niacin, iron, vitamin B_6, calcium, phosphorus, sodium and potassium. Use them in chili, or dress cooked beans and serve them in a salad. For a different vegetable dish, combine them with stewed tomatoes, onions and green peppers. Pureed kidney beans can also be combined with tomato paste, spices and cheese for a tasty dip or sandwich spread.

LENTILS

Lentils are among the tastiest of beans, need no soaking or pre-cooking and take only 30 minutes to cook. Wash them carefully and discard any lentils that float in the rinse water. Lentils are a good source of protein, vitamin A, thiamine, riboflavin, niacin, iron, calcium, phosphorus and potassium. Simmer them until just "al dente," then drain and pour on some French dressing, toss, chill and serve as an appetizer instead of the usual salad. Besides making a good soup, lentils also combine with other vegetables and grains for complete protein.

LIMA BEANS

Dried limas provide protein, thiamine, riboflavin, niacin, phosphorus and potassium. Soak or precook them first, then simmer until tender. They combine well with corn and peas to make succotash, or use them in soups and casseroles.

MUNG BEANS

They are best known for their sprouts (see chapter on sprouting), but they may also be used as a cooked bean. Mung beans are full of protein, vitamin A, thiamine, riboflavin, niacin, iron, phosphorus and potassium. Cooked mung beans are rather bland and are best combined with more flavorful vegetables or served with a piquant dressing.

PEAS

The dried pea family has a number of different relatives that vary in color, taste and method of preparation. They all provide protein, vitamin A, thiamine, riboflavin, niacin, iron, calcium, phosphorus and sodium. Black-eyed peas, sometimes called cow peas, cook quickly and are a southern favorite when combined with rice. Chick-peas are also called garbanzo beans, or ceci, in Italian. They have an irregular texture and a nutlike flavor. They can be toasted and eaten as a healthful snack or milled into flour used to make delicious flat breads. Try chick-peas in minestrone or serve them with a vinegar and oil dressing as an appetizer. Hummus, the paste made from mashed cooked chick-peas, is a favorite Middle Eastern dip you'll enjoy with crackers or pita bread. Whole dried green peas can be used to make hearty soups or added to combination vegetable dishes. Soak or precook them before the final cooking and when selecting remember the ones with the wrinkled skins are sweeter. Pigeon peas must also be presoaked or precooked. They combine well with rice and are used extensively in Indian cooking. Split peas come in both green and yellow types and cook rapidly with no presoaking necessary. Add them to a generous amount of water and simmer for 45 minutes, adding seasonings and perhaps some soup vegetables. When the split peas are tender, you can serve the soup right away or store it in the fridge for another meal. Pea soup thickens on standing, so dilute with water before reheating.

PINTO BEANS

These mottled pink and brown beans are a good source of protein, thiamine, riboflavin, niacin, iron, phosphorus, sodium and potassium. A great favorite in the Southwest and Mexico, pinto beans are used extensively in chili dishes and casseroles. Pinto beans make the best refried beans. To make refried beans, heat oil in a skillet and sauté some garlic until golden. Add well-drained cooked pinto beans, sauté and mash until crusty and brown. Refried beans can be eaten as a side dish or added to a taco along with sauce and chopped lettuce. If you use pinto beans to make chili, you can delight even the nonvegetarian by adding soy flakes to the pot. They lend a wonderful meaty flavor and texture.

Soybeans and Soybean Products

The soybean plays such an important role in vegetarian diets that it merits a whole chapter. Soybeans come from a plant that's a bushy member of the legume family, and may very well be one of the world's most important food sources. Surprisingly enough, 67 percent of the world's supply of soybeans is grown in the United States; a surprise considering we take so little advantage of this nutritious legume. As a high-quality, low-cost source of protein, soybeans may very well be the answer to the world's food crisis. They are high in B vitamins, minerals and lecithin.

Aside from its amazing benefits, the bland quality of soybeans makes them a perfect partner for many other foods, and they come in a remarkable array of forms. Beyond the raw and dried bean, they are used to make diverse products including tofu, soy sauce, soy flour and soy milk. Each is so different that we have outlined them separately and devoted some space to let you know exactly what they are and how to use them.

Textured soy protein can be found in many new-wave supermarkets and is worth looking into. For those new initiates to a vegetarian diet, it can provide a satisfying substitute for meat. Try, as well, roasted soybeans. They come in jars, salted or not, and make perfect nibbling. The soybean's nutritional richness and its versatility can certainly stand up to and outrank that all-American favorite, the peanut!

WHOLE, RAW SOYBEANS

Fresh soybeans come in fuzzy green pods, which should be bright green and well filled out without bruises. Cooked soybeans provide protein, vitamin A, thiamine, riboflavin, niacin, iron, calcium and phosphorus. Raw soybeans don't contain any sodium, perfect for people on salt-free diets. Refrigerate soybeans unshelled until you're ready to cook them. Shell and pop them into a kettle of water and boil for 10 to 15 minutes. Cooked fresh soybeans can be used in any way you would use fresh peas or lima beans.

DRIED SOYBEANS

Dried soybeans come whole or split; the flavor is the same, but the split beans cook faster. Carefully rinse and pick over the beans before cooking them. You can prepare them in a pressure cooker by using 2 1/2–3 cups water for every cup of soybeans. When pressure is established, cook for 90 minutes. To cook soybeans in a kettle, soak them overnight, then simmer for 3 hours in the same water in which they were soaked. To tell when they're done, press one against the roof of your mouth with your tongue. It should yield to the pressure and burst open. Never throw out the cooking fluid, which can be used to enrich soups, stews and sauces. Don't salt the beans before they're done or they'll get tough. Cooked soybeans are a nutritious addition to soups, stews and casseroles, and can even be added to bread dough (they won't give the somewhat bitter flavor that soy flour does). Try combining soybeans with finely chopped onion, celery and green pepper. Mash everything well, then blend in a beaten egg. Form this mixture into patties, roll the patties in crumbs and fry them in butter until well browned. They are delicious served with tomato sauce.

SOYBEAN MILK

Soybean juice can be used cup for cup in any recipe calling for cow's milk. How does it compare for nourishment? It has the same amount of protein, but only one-third the fat. Soybean milk does lack carbohydrates and vitamin B_{12}, as well as having little calcium, but these deficiencies are easily made up for. One cup of fortified soybean milk will net you: 7.6 grams of protein, 90 I.U. vitamin A, 0.18 mg. thiamine, 0.07 mg. riboflavin, 0.5 mg. niacin, 1.9 mg. iron, 4.0 mg. vitamin B_{12}, 350 mg. calcium and 110 mg. phosphorus. Soy milk, plain or fortified, can be bought ready made. Unfortunately, however, commercial soy milk is expensive and sometimes contains additives.

So make your soy milk at home. It's easy and a lot cheaper! We have chosen to outline the Cornell method for making soy milk, which eliminates a lot of the slightly bitter flavor of soy milk. First, pick over 1 cup of dried soybeans and discard any broken ones. Rinse carefully and soak them in 3 cups of water overnight. Drain the soybeans and rinse them well under cold water, then divide them into thirds. Preheat your blender by blending 2 cups of boiling water in it for about 1 minute. Grind each portion of beans with 2 cups of boiling water for 2 to 3 minutes. Keep your kettle boiling, as it's essential that the water be very hot because the hot water is what inactivates the lipoxidase—the substance that has the bitter flavor. Use caution when doing all this to prevent splattering of hot liquid, and use a blender with a nonmeltable top. Strain the resulting mixture through a colander lined with cheesecloth and placed over a 1-quart bowl. Squeeze the cloth to extract as much juice as possible. The resulting milk must then be heated in a double boiler for at least 30 minutes. Stir it every now and then to keep it from scorching and to prevent the formation of a skin on the surface of the milk. Add a little water to make up for what's been lost through evaporation (you should have 2 1/2 cups) and then allow the milk to cool. Once cool, it should be refrigerated. You may use this unfortified milk to substitute for the cow's milk in a recipe, or you can fortify it for use as a beverage by adding 1 teaspoon safflower oil, 1 teaspoon honey and 1/2 teaspoon calcium carbonate per cup of milk. You can get calcium carbonate at many health food or drug stores. You may also wish to add 1 well-crushed vitamin B_{12} tablet to each batch you make. This enriched milk, which tastes fine plain, can also be flavored with natural fruit syrups or made into fruit shakes with whole fruit in a blender. Fortified soy milk will give you the same fat, carbohydrate and calcium content as cow's milk. Remember to shake it before pouring, because the calcium carbonate doesn't dissolve completely.

SOY FLOUR

Full-fat soy flour is less bitter than defatted, making it good for adding to breads, cakes and pastries, while defatted soy flour contains more protein (50 percent as compared to 40 percent in the full-fat). Full-fat soy flour is 20 percent oil. One cup of full-fat soy flour will supply 26 grams of protein, 80 I.U. vitamin A, 60 mg. thiamine, 0.22 mg. riboflavin, 1.5 mg. niacin, 0.40 mg. vitamin B_6, 5.9 mg. iron, 140 mg. calcium, 390 mg. phosphorus, 1 mg. sodium and 1,200 mg. potassium. Don't use soy flour unless it's been exposed to heat to destroy the protein-inhibiting enzymes present in the raw product. Soy powder is available already heat-treated for use in beverages so you can use it without further preparation. Add it to shakes and use in cooking. Soy flour is good to add to bread doughs; the amino acids it contains complement the ones in grains. When using it to bake, maintain a ratio of 1 part soy flour to 8 parts wheat flour. In yeast baking, you may have to add a bit more leavening, since soy flour is somewhat heavy. You can also use this versatile flour to enrich soups, casseroles and cereal dishes.

SOY GRITS, SOY FLAKES

Soy grits are toasted soybeans with a nutty crunchiness that makes them a tasty addition to grain dishes, cereals and breads. One cup of grits provides 52 grams of protein, 120 I.U. vitamin A, 1.5 mg. thiamine, 0.4 mg. riboflavin, 3.4 mg. niacin, 1.2 mg. vitamin B_6, 14 mg. iron, 350 mg. calcium, 850 mg. phosphorus, 8 mg. sodium and 2,600 mg. potassium. Soy flakes are an air-puffed light cereal. Both soy grits and flakes are a good source of many nutrients, and adding them often to soups, stews and casseroles provides a meaty flavor and nutritional boost.

TEMPEH

Until recently, this soy product was not well known in the United States. It's a cheap and tasty source of protein made from split, cooked soybeans and rhizophus mold. The beans are fermented overnight and the white mycellium that forms partially digests them. This fermentation process deactivates the trypsin enzyme (a digestive inhibitor) and results in sweet, fragrant cakes that are now totally digestible. Tempeh can be baked or fried, tasting a bit like veal or chicken. It is also a good source for nonmeat vitamin B_{12}. It's now possible to buy rhizophus mold to make tempeh at home. Tempeh-making kits, complete with starter, beans, instructions and recipes, are available from Farm Foods. A full price list is available by writing to Farm Foods, 156 Drakes Lane, Summertown, Tennessee 38483.

TAMARI

Commercially produced soy sauce is often called tamari. It is naturally fermented soy sauce, having a bouquet and flavor all its own—and it's good for you! Tamari is 9–18 percent complete protein and easily digestible because the fermentation process it undergoes destroys the protein-inhibiting enzymes. Tamari contains B vitamins, riboflavin and niacin, and is one of the best nonmeat sources of vitamin B_{12}. This flavorful sauce is made by soaking and steaming barley, rice or wheat and then adding koji spores (mold spores) and cooked soybeans to the warm mash. After the mix is salted, it's allowed to ferment anywhere from 6 months to 2 years. The liquid at the top of the vat is soy sauce, while the pressings at the bottom become nutrient-rich tamari. Use it as a seasoning in soups, salads or any dish, but use it sparingly. Tamari has a high salt content (11–18 percent), so a little goes a long way.

MISO

Miso is a paste made from fermented grains that has long been a staple seasoning and food in the Oriental kitchen. Its highly concentrated flavor makes miso seem to be a seasoning, while in fact its high protein concentration actually makes it a food that combines especially well with grains. Only 1 teaspoon of miso added to cereal will supply you with 1.8 grams of protein, 10 I.U. vitamin A, 19 mg. thiamine, 0.01 mg. riboflavin, 0.1 mg. vitamin B_6, 0.3 mg. iron, 0.12 mg. calcium, 53 mg. phosphorus, 500 mg. sodium and 57 mg. potassium. Miso's high salt content, like that of tamari, makes modest use imperative. The fermentation process used to make it predigests the protein in miso; therefore, miso is especially easy for the body to assimilate. Because miso is made by combining grains and soybeans— which complement each other nutritionally—miso is a complete protein and contains the eight essential amino acids in addition to nine nonessential ones. It's also an aid to digestion because it contains natural digestive enzymes and lactic acid bacteria. Like all fermented soybean products, miso is also an important nonanimal source of vitamin B_{12}, an important plus for the vegetarian. And miso is very low in calories (11 per gram of protein).

Miso may be found on some supermarket shelves, but for the most part, look for it in Oriental food markets and at local health food stores. Miso is relatively inexpensive and is sold in both natural and "quick" forms. The natural product is recommended because it contains no chemical additives and has been aged slowly to fully develop its nutrient value. The three major kinds of miso are made from soybeans and rice, soybeans and barley and mame miso, which is made from soybeans alone. Rice miso is the most popular, and if a recipe just calls for miso it usually means rice miso. Similarly, though there are sweet and salty misos, when a package or recipe doesn't specify, it's salty miso that's meant. Although there are many kinds of rice miso, the most popular are red miso, light yellow, mellow red, mellow biege, mellow white, sweet red and sweet white. The red and light yellow types are salty, with a tart pleasing flavor and textured from chunky to smooth. The mellow misos have a flavor somewhere between sweet and salty, while the sweet types are suitable for spreads, dips and desserts. Barley miso is darker and saltier than the rice type and has a chunky texture. Its rich, mellow flavor adds a distinctive taste to soups and vegetable dishes. There are numerous "special" misos that are a combination of miso and other ingredients such as vegetables, nuts or seaweed. They are mainly intended to be used as a seasoning or topping for other foods.

Three types of "modern" miso have been developed; since 1945 they have been available in the United States. Akadashi miso is sweet and dark brown, consisting of a mixture of different types of miso that have been blended, pasteurized and packaged. This type of miso sometimes contains other ingredients such as sugar, MSG and preservatives; check before buying. Dehydrated or freeze-dried miso is made by freeze-drying regular miso, and the resulting product contains 32.2 percent protein, 18.5 percent salt and 35.8 percent carbohydrate. It's most often found in instant soup mixes that come in foil packets. The powder in the packets is mixed with boiling water for a quick soup. Lower-salt/high-protein miso is also available in a freeze-dried form that comes in a jar. It contains 14 percent salt, 26.4 percent protein, and 53 percent moisture.

Try different kinds of miso until you find the flavors you enjoy most. All types of miso should be stored in a cool, dark place; the sweet varieties should be kept in the refrigerator. Miso packed in plastic bags should always be kept tightly wrapped, and miso in kegs should be wrapped in plastic or kept in a tightly closed container.

Use miso as a seasoning in much the same way tamari is used. It adds body and flavor to soups, sauces and grain dishes. Sweet miso can be used in desserts, dips and sandwiches. Remember that miso is a "live" food; too much heat will kill all those valuable micro-organisms! Add miso to hot dishes just before you remove them from the heat, or use miso without heating at all.

TOFU

As a high-quality source of complete protein, tofu (soybean curd, usually called bean curd) is hard to beat, not to mention inexpensive, low in calories and versatile. Tofu's bland, meaty quality makes it a perfect candidate for the backbone of the vegetarian diet. Dried, frozen tofu has one of the highest percentages of protein found in any food. One small piece of tofu provides 9.4 grams of protein, 0.07 mg. thiamine, 0.04 mg. riboflavin, 0.1 mg. niacin, 2.3 mg. iron, 150 mg. calcium, 150 mg. phosphorus, 8 mg. sodium and 50 mg. potassium. A meal featuring tofu in combination with grains will supply complete and complementary proteins. The preparation of tofu makes it one of the most digestible forms of soybeans, and it's an ideal food for dieters—1 gram of usable protein will contain only 12 calories!

Tofu in many forms is available at Oriental and regular markets, or make your own at home. Enjoy its many uses in soups, dips, main dishes and desserts. Since tofu is gaining popularity in the United States, you should be able to purchase it locally. The most popular type is the plastic-packed medium or firm Japanese style; Chinese doofoo or bean cake runs a close second. Kinugoshi, the soft-style tofu, comes in tubs or cartons and has a smooth, silken texture. Deep-fried tofu comes in cubes or pouches. Tofu also comes in cubes, pudding, patties, with vegetables and dried yuba, which are bean curd sheets. Dark brown, pressed tofu can also come either plain or seasoned with soy sauce and spices.

Look for the freshest tofu you can find. Packaged brands are usually dated, so choose the package with the latest date on it and check the label to be sure a nigari-type solidifier, rather than a chemical, has been used. The label should say that the product contains either nigari, calcium chloride or magnesium chloride nigari. Fresh tofu is highly perishable and must be kept under constant refrigeration. If packed in water, drain the water off and replace it with fresh. Do this daily until you're ready to use the tofu, but for best flavor and nutritional value this should be within no more than a few days. The dried types of tofu that come in cellophane or plastic packages should also be kept in the fridge once the bag is opened.

For do-it-yourselfers, instant homemade tofu mix may be found in some markets and will provide beginners with foolproof results. Or try the following recipe: Prepare enriched soy milk according to the recipe on page 53. Dissolve 1 teaspoon of magnesium sulphate (available at health food or drug stores) in 1/4 cup hot water, and gently stir the mixture into 2 quarts soy milk that you have heated at 180 degrees (F). Leave the pot undisturbed for about 10 minutes. By then, a curd should have formed. Dip off the whey as much as possible, and gently place the curd in a cheesecloth-lined mold. An empty tuna can with both ends cut off works well. Weight the top of the mold with a 1-pound weight. When the curd becomes firm, increase the weight to 2 pounds. Let the weighted mold stand in the refrigerator overnight on a plate. If you aren't going to use the tofu immediately, cover it with water and store in the refrigerator until ready for use. If you like your tofu firmer, drain it after weighting it, place it on a folded towel and let it stand overnight. You can also squeeze it in a clean cloth and then knead it for a few minutes to expel as much moisture as possible. To press tofu, slice the cakes and lay the slices on a towel. Cover the slices with another towel and put a large cutting board or anything heavy on top of the covered tofu. Let sit for about 20 minutes and the tofu is ready to use. Some recipes call for scrambled tofu, which you can prepare by cooking the curd over medium heat for 4 to 5 minutes while breaking it into small particles with a whisk.

With tofu in hand, here are a few suggestions on how to use it: Fresh bean curd can be added to all sorts of vegetable dishes. Dice or cube it, then gently stir it into the vegetables at the last minute, allowing it to just heat through. Try it with bean sprouts, snow peas and soy gravy, or combine the cubes with fried rice or kasha. Remember, it need not be cooked, just heated. Slices of fresh bean curd make a nice addition to clear soups, or you can deep fry pieces of curd that have been dipped in a batter of whole wheat flour for a crunchy treat. Try stuffing bean curd cakes. Make a slit in the side of the cake, open it up carefully and fill it with chopped vegetables, kasha or rice, then gently fry the "pockets" until golden brown. Scrambled or pressed bean curd should be used in dishes that require longer simmering, as their firmer texture will keep them from falling apart. Mashed bean curd can be used in many of the ways you normally use cottage cheese. Serve it with pickles, relishes or make a sandwich spread out of it. You can also combine the mashed bean curd with chopped vegetables and beaten egg, making patties out of the mixture and frying them in oil or butter. Serve thin slices of bean curd with whole wheat bread, lettuce and mayonnaise for a tasty "cheese" sandwich. Bean curd sheets must be soaked in hot water for 10 minutes before using. They are then ready to be added to soups or can be deep fried for a crunchy snack. Packaged, deep-fried pouches can be stuffed before heating or served as is. Soft bean curd makes an interesting dessert when combined with fruit.

As you become more familiar with tofu, you'll come up with many of your own innovations. But no matter how you choose to serve this natural, high-protein food, serve it often and savor its benefits!

Whole Grains, Cereals, Pasta and Bread

Whole grains are indeed the staff of life, and have played a major role in the development of man's diet through the centuries. As early as 9,000 B.C., man was gathering wild grains and using them for food. Probably the first way that grains were consumed, before the advent of cooking vessels, was a sort of aspic-like porridge made by soaking grain in water and then keeping it warm near the fire. Later on, toasted grain was mixed with water and then eaten as a paste. Then someone thought of baking the paste and the first bread was made.

Every culture in the world has one or more types of grain that form the mainstay of the diet for the majority of the population. It may be rice, millet, corn or wheat consumed in the form of porridge, flour, bread, noodles, sprouts, or just plain cooked as a cereal dish.

Grains give the vegetarian diet bulk, variety and nutrition. Whole grains are vital to your diet. Milling and refining rob whole grains of much of their nutritional value; refined grains lack the trace vitamins and minerals found in the outer layer of the grain. They're also harder to digest than whole grains. Substantial amounts of the vitamin B complex, vitamin E and unsaturated fatty acids, not to mention quality protein, are part of whole, natural, unrefined grain.

The flour you use should also be from whole grain. To get the best nutrition and taste, grind your own. While refined flours will keep for a long time because they're essentially "dead," whole grain flours must be stored more carefully to prevent spoilage. Once ground, the oil in the whole grains will cause them to eventually become rancid. A nutritious alternative to whole grain cereals and flours are grain flakes cooked for 15 to 20 seconds under radiant heat and then dropped onto rollers and flattened. Since no moisture is used in this process, flaked grains have not been leached of their nutrients. They're convenient, too, as they cook in half the time it takes to cook whole grains.

In the following section, we have presented the individual types of whole grains with suggestions for storage and use. For information on sprouting, see the chapter on nuts, seeds and sprouts.

BARLEY

Barley is one of the most ancient of grains used by man, along with wheat and millet. Barley was used as a staple in the form of porridge and added to soups and stews or mixed with vegetables to make a sort of pilaff. Barley is low in sodium, which makes it good for low-salt diets. It's high in other nutrients, and 1 cup of whole grain, hulled barley will provide 19 grams of protein, 0.42 mg. thiamine, 0.14 mg. riboflavin, 7.4 mg. niacin, 5.4 mg. iron, 68 mg. calcium, 580 mg. phosphorus and 590 mg. potassium. The tough hull on barley has to be removed by a process known as "pearling" before it can be cooked. Some pearling processes go way overboard and rub off too much of the outer layer of the grain. So choose darker kinds of barley—subjected to less milling. When cooking barley, allow a little more than twice as much liquid as grain. Simmer in a covered kettle for 30 to 35 minutes, or pressure cook the grain for 20 minutes. Cooked barley is excellent in soups, casseroles and stuffing combined with other grains and vegetables. One particularly tasty combination is cooked barley mixed with chopped cooked kale and seasoned with tamari. Barley flour can be used in breads in a ratio of 1/2 cup barley flour for every cup of whole wheat flour.

BUCKWHEAT

Not really a grain, buckwheat is actually a type of grass related to burdock and rhubarb; however, its nutritional value and taste put it in a class with the whole grains. Buckwheat is available both in whole and unhulled forms and can be roasted or cut. Often, it is called kasha or groats. The best buy in buckwheat is the whole unroasted kind. You can roast your own and grind your own flour, if you like. Toasting improves the naturally bland taste of buckwheat. To toast, combine 2 parts water with 1 part buckwheat, then simmer for 15 to 20 minutes. If you like a more cereal-like consistency, use more water. A good main dish can be made by combining millet and buckwheat with stir-fried vegetables. Or serve the buckwheat with sauce or gravy. We like to stir yogurt into hot buckwheat for a special flavor. Buckwheat also makes a tasty stuffing for cabbage leaves, grape leaves or knishes. The flour can be used in breads and is a favorite for pancake batter. Because light buckwheat flour is made from sifted flour rather than whole unroasted groats, either look for darker kinds of flour or grind your own. You can make a creamy cereal by browning buckwheat flour in a little oil or butter, gradually stirring in hot water. Bring to a boil, simmer for 10 minutes, then serve the cereal with milk or fruit. Buckwheat contains very little sodium, so people on a low-salt diet may enjoy it. One cup of cooked buckwheat will provide 7.6 grams of protein, 0.39 mg. thiamine, 0.1 mg. riboflavin, 2 mg. iron, 74 mg. calcium, 180 mg. phosphorus and 290 mg. potassium.

CORN

Dried corn is an important source of flour and meal. When corn is allowed to dry out, its simple sugars turn to starch and it keeps indefinitely. You can buy cornmeal or corn flour—or grind your own. Because the "germ" of the corn starts to deteriorate in food value as soon as the corn is ground, the freshest is undoubtedly homeground just before you're ready to use it. The only difference between meal and flour is the fineness of the particles. One cup of cooked cornmeal will provide 11 grams of protein; 620 I.U. vitamin A; 0.46 mg. thiamine, 0.13 mg. riboflavin, 2.4 mg. niacin, 3 mg. vitamin B_6; 2.9 mg. iron, 24 mg. calcium, 310 mg. phosphorus, 1 mg. sodium and 350 mg. potassium. Dried corn can also be sprouted (see the chapter on nuts, seeds and sprouts). To use dried corn as a vegetable, soak it overnight and simmer it in a generous quantity of boiling water until tender. Serve it in soups, combined with other vegetables or cream-style. When serving dried corn or cornmeal dishes, be sure to include high-protein foods, as cornmeal ranks lowest in protein of all the grains. Cornmeal makes a good hot cereal, and with cheese added is a nourishing side dish. If you grind your own meal, you won't have to add white flour to make cornbread. Processed cornmeal, however, makes bread that's too crumbly without the addition of white flour. Make hush puppies, cornmeal muffins, spoon bread and tortillas to add different accents to your meals. Cornmeal dumplings and pancakes are unusual ways to serve this versatile grain, and corn flour can be used to thicken sauces and gravies as well as to bake fine-textured breads and cakes.

MILLET

It's too bad that millet is somewhat overlooked by the American household, because it is a good source of low-gluten protein and is easily digested. In some parts of Africa where the climate is too dry to raise rice and too hot to grow wheat, millet is the staple. It's usually served as a porridge or combined with vegetables. Of all the grains, millet comes closest to being nutritionally perfect. One cup of cooked millet will supply 5.7 grams of protein, 0.42 mg. thiamine, 0.22 mg. riboflavin, 1.3 mg. niacin, 3.9 mg. iron, 12 mg. calcium, 180 mg. phosphorus and 250 mg. potassium. To cook millet as a cereal, simmer it in 2 parts water to 1 part grain. Millet is good when combined with kasha or vegetables and has a better flavor when toasted first. Millet sprouts are also a good source of nutrients (see chapter on nuts, seeds and sprouts). The meal ground from millet can be used in all the same ways as cornmeal; its flour can be mixed with whole wheat flour to make breads, muffins and rolls.

OATS

There are many uses for this nutritious grain besides as a breakfast cereal. Oats may be bought as whole oat groats, sometimes known as Irish oats, Scottish oats or steel-cut oats. Most of the time, they are most widely available as rolled oats. Rolled oats are shot with steam and then pressed, a process that causes some loss in nutrients but allows a shorter cooking time. One cup of rolled oats will provide 4.8 grams of protein, 0.19 mg. thiamine, 0.05 mg. riboflavin, 0.2 mg. niacin, 1.4 mg. iron, 22 mg. calcium, 140 mg. phosphorus, 520 mg. sodium and 150 mg. potassium. Whole oat groats must be soaked overnight before cooking. Try using them in soups. Rolled oats are a fine addition to breads, cookies, pancakes and desserts. You can grind rolled oats into a flour that can be used in equal measure with wheat flour when baking. Oat flour can also be used as a thickener in sauces and gravies and makes a crispy coating for fried foods.

RICE

What wheat is to the West, rice is to the East—the staple of life. When we refer to rice we mean brown rice, not the white kind, which has had the bran removed and much of the nutritional value of the grain with it. Brown rice comes in short-, medium- and long-grain varieties. The shorter-grained kinds have more gluten and will cook up somewhat thicker. There is also a type of glutinous rice which is very sticky and is used for desserts. Rice bran or polishings can be bought and used in the same ways as wheat germ. Rice cream and rice powder are used as a cereal and for coating foods that are to be fried. Rice flour is a finer form of rice powder and can be used in breads, cakes and pastries. Rice flakes are processed in such a way that there is very little loss of nutrients, and they make an interesting addition to casseroles and breads. A rice-based grain milk called kohkoh can be found in some stores. It's a mixture of roasted ground rice, sweet rice, soybeans, sesame seeds and oatmeal. Used in cereal or tea, kohkoh is a nutritious addition to breakfast.

When buying rice, check the package label for the source of the grain, because rice is one of the most chemically treated food crops. The box should say the rice is unsprayed or organically grown. To cook rice, combine it with water in a heavy-bottomed pot in the following proportions: short-grain rice, 2 1/2 cups rice to 1 cup water; medium-grain rice, 2 cups rice to 1 cup water; long-grain rice, 1 1/2 cups rice to 2 cups water. Pour the rice into the water, bring to a boil, stir once, and lower the heat to medium while covering with a lid. Simmer slowly, without stirring, until most of the water has been absorbed by the rice. At this point, the surface of the rice should be covered with what the Chinese call "fish eyes," small craters or holes in the surface indicating the rice is done. Fluff the grains with a fork before serving. If some of the rice sticks to the bottom or inside of the pot, replace the lid and cook over very, very low heat for 30 minutes or so. Keep an eye on it to make sure it doesn't burn. At the end of that time, the rice should have formed a crust that's pulling away from the sides of the pot. Allow it to cool, and remove in large pieces. This crust is delicious when deep fried and makes a tasty snack, or use as a base for a stir-fry dish. To pressure cook rice, use the following proportions: short-grain rice, 2 cups water to 1 cup rice; medium-grain rice, 1 1/2 cups water to 2 cups rice; long-grain rice, 1 1/4 cups water to 4 cups rice. When the rice is cooked, allow the pressure to drop slowly so the cooking steam will be absorbed by the grain.

Rice has so many uses: we like it with milk and cinnamon for breakfast. Rice casseroles are a favorite for lunch or dinner, and rice balls with small pieces of pickles or seaweed inside them are a favorite snack food. Don't neglect rice at dessert time, either. Make a creamy pudding or a rice-flour cake. Leftover rice can be added to soups or stir fried with tamari and vegetables to make a tasty side dish or a light luncheon choice. Take advantage of the versatility of rice and serve it often.

RYE

Rye comes as whole "berries," cream of rye, and rye flour. Flour is sold both dark and light; the dark version has more nutrients. One cup of dark rye flour provides 21 grams of protein, 0.78 mg. thiamine, 3.5 mg. riboflavin, 3.5 mg. niacin, 0.38 mg. vitamin B_6, 5.8 mg. iron, 69 mg. calcium, 690 mg. phosphorus, 1 mg sodium and 1,100 mg. potassium. Use cream of rye as a breakfast cereal by combining it with water in a ratio of 4 cups water to 1 cup meal. Simmer this mixture for about 15 minutes and serve the porridge with milk or fruit. Combine whole, cooked rye berries with rice and other grains. Their sweet, nutty flavor adds a pleasant note to casseroles or vegetable dishes. Rye berries also make nutritious sprouts (see chapter on nuts, seeds and sprouts). Rye flakes make an interesting addition to soups or stews and can be eaten as a cereal if you soak them overnight. And, of course, not to ignore the obvious, rye flour makes that fragrant, caraway-speckled loaf that everyone likes.

TRITICALE

Although a nourishing whole grain, triticale is little known. It comes in berries, flakes, and flours. The berries have a sweet, nutty flavor that blends well in casseroles and soups. To make a main dish, combine it with rice and stir-fried vegetables. One cup of triticale contains 25 grams of protein, 0.8 mg. vitamin B_{12}, 51 mg. calcium, 76 mg. phosphorus, 7 mg. sodium and 680 mg. potassium. Triticale flour and flakes are high in protein and can be used in many ways to enrich your diet. Try the flakes in casseroles and stews. Because it is low in gluten, triticale flour needs to be combined with an equal amount of wheat flour when using it to make bread, cakes and pastries.

WHOLE WHEAT

High protein and adaptability, its quantity of vitamin **E** and the properties that make it rise make whole wheat an invaluable addition to man's diet. The first grains that were gathered were rendered edible by either toasting or soaking in hot water to make a sort of porridge. Later, man discovered that toasted grain could be pounded and mixed into a paste that was digestible and most nourishing. Either by accident or by design, this paste was left near the fire and bread was created. Herein is the point: Risen bread can only be made light and palatable with the addition of whole wheat flour. The secret that the golden grains hold within them is gluten, the elastic substance that supports the yeast culture and gives bread its light, digestible texture. Though other flours may be added to the bread dough, for the characteristic taste and texture of risen bread, wheat flour is essential.

The wheat kernel or berry consists of three layers. The outer layer, which is high in fiber, is the bran; the central portion is the white starch mass that contains 70 percent of the kernel's protein and starch; and the small germ found at the central base of the kernel contains the vitamin E and fatty acids. To reap the complete nutrition of wheat, we must consume the entire kernel. Ay, there's the rub. For wheat flour has had the bran and germ removed—rubbed away! Yes, the bran may be bought separately and used in your food; however, that's rather silly when you can have the whole kernel in the first place. Wheat germ and bran, as well as other wheat products such as meal, cereal, flakes, bulghur and couscous, make good additions to the diet, but the mainstay should be the whole wheat berry. One cup of raw, hard red winter wheat will provide 22 grams of protein, 0.91 mg. thiamine, 0.21 mg. riboflavin, 7.5 mg. niacin, 6 mg. iron, 80 mg. calcium, 620 mg. phosphorus, 0.8 mg. vitamin B_6, 5 mg. sodium and 650 mg. potassium. Add whole wheat berries to rice or other grains to make tasty pilaffs or serve them in soups, breads and stews. For a different texture, crack the berries or buy cracked wheat, and serve it as a cereal by simmering it in water in a ratio of 3 parts water to 1 part grain.

To get the best nourishment, it is important to know the different kinds of wheat. Hard winter wheat is high in protein and gluten, making it the best choice for all-around cooking and baking. Soft winter wheat is most suitable for cakes and pastries, because it can be ground into a very fine flour. Durum wheat has the highest protein and gluten content and, while excellent for use in pastas, it makes rubbery baked goods.

For freshness, flavor and to avoid preservatives, grind your own flour from whole wheat berries or buy a stone-ground product. Graham flour is simply unsifted flour; make your own or buy it for use in baking. By grinding wheat berries coarsely, you make wheat meal, which can be used to make a tasty, nutlike cereal. Commercial brands of wheat cereals are available such as Wheatena, Cream of Wheat and farina, although they don't use wheat meal. Wheat berries also make nutritious and sweet-tasting sprouts that can be used in salads and desserts (for directions on sprouting, see chapter on nuts, seeds and sprouts). The wheat berry can be added whole to almost any main dish, soup or bread for a nutty crunch.

Bulghur is parboiled, cracked wheat and only requires soaking in hot water to prepare, since it has already been partially cooked. Presoaked bulghur can be used in salads or appetizers. Couscous, that North African favorite, is made of soft, refined durum wheat that has been steamed, then cracked and dried. Steam some as a foil for a vegetable curry. Use wheat flakes as a cereal or add them to soups, stews and casseroles.

Wheat germ is the richest known source of vitamin E and is a good supplier of the B complex vitamins so sadly lacking in processed foods. Buy wheat germ at the market in cereal form and use it to enrich your foods. Sprinkling wheat germ as the final touch to any dish is like adding edible, nutritious gold dust. The beauty of wheat germ is that it adds flavor to any dish. It can also be eaten alone and unadorned as a cereal with milk. It perks up cottage cheese, yogurt or fruit. Toasted wheat germ tastes better, so if you buy it raw, toast it yourself. Add it to breads, casseroles, breadings for foods, soups, salads and sweets. Wheat germ has a high unsaturated oil content. Store it in a tightly closed jar in the refrigerator.

Try making wheat gluten by mixing whole wheat with water in a ratio of 1 1/2 cups water to 2 1/2 cups flour. Knead this mixture as you would bread dough, then let it sit for an hour or so to let the gluten develop. Then knead it under cold water to remove the starch from the mixture. Keep kneading and changing the water until it runs off clear, not cloudy—perhaps three times. Form the results into a loaf, then slice and steam it or boil it for about 30 minutes. Kofu, as it is called, can also be fried after initial cooking.

GRANOLA

Granola is a mixture of grains and nuts, seeds and fruits, and no matter how you mix it, it should be part of your diet. The main components of this breakfast mix can be bought already combined or you may do it yourself. Here's the basic recipe: 7 cups rolled oats, 1 cup shredded unsweetened coconut, 1/2 cup sesame seeds, 3/4 cup raw shelled sunflower seeds, 1/2 cup sliced almonds, 1 cup raw cashews, 1 cup honey, 1/2 cup safflower oil, 1 cup raisins, and 1 cup wheat germ. Mix the oats, coconut, sesame seeds, sunflower seeds, almonds and cashews together. Combine the honey and oil and pour them over the dry ingredients; mix until everything is well blended. Roast the raisins lightly in a 300-degree (F) oven for about 5 minutes, then add them, along with the wheat germ, to the mixture. Spread the cereal in a 3/4-inch layer on a cookie sheet and bake in a 325-degree (F) oven for 10 to 15 minutes. Cool the granola and refrigerate in an airtight container until you're ready to use it. With all those nutritious ingredients, it's easy to see why granola is so good and so good for you.

Of course, you can add, subtract or substitute to your own taste. For example, replace all or part of the oats with wheat, rye or barley flakes, or add different types of nuts such as walnuts, pine nuts, macadamia nuts or hazelnuts. Adding dried, powdered milk will provide a boost to the mix by providing minerals. In addition to or in place of raisins, use other dried fruits: apricots, for instance, are a good source of iron and heighten the taste. The sweetener you use may also be varied; use less of it if you add the powdered milk, which is sweet to begin with. You might try using molasses instead of honey, or add no sweetener at all and let everyone sweeten the cereal according to his own preference. To make an extra-high-protein version of granola, follow the basic method but use 2 1/2 cups wheat flakes, 1 cup soy grits, 1/2 cup powdered milk, 2 cups sunflower seeds, 2 1/2 cups peanuts, 1/2 cup chopped dried apricots, 1/2 cup safflower oil, and 1/4 cup blackstrap molasses. Try serving granola sprinkled over fruit or as a topping for puddings or cakes for dessert. Hikers and backpackers like this high-protein treat with them when camping, and if you add a bit more powdered milk to the mix you need only add water to eat it as cereal. A low-calorie mix can be made by using the basic method and these ingredients: 7 cups rolled oats, 1 cup powdered low-fat milk, 1/3 cup sunflower seeds, 1/2 cup chopped dried apricots, 1/3 cup blackstrap molasses, 1/4 cup safflower oil and 2 tablespoons water. This mixture, while high in protein, will net you only 320 calories per cup when served with 1/2 cup of skim milk. For the economy version of granola, use the basic method and this low-cost mix: 7 cups rolled oats, 3 cups wheat bran, 1/4 cup molasses and 2 tablespoons water.

If you don't want to make your own granola, there are wholesome commercially produced ones. Be sure to check the labels to make sure they aren't loaded with sugar and chemical additives. Consider granola as part of your main dishes, too. It makes an unusual stuffing or, added to soy patties or bean or nut loaves, creates a different flavor and texture. Remember to use it often since granola is packed with some of nature's finest and tastiest nutrients.

Pasta

A popular way to get some of the goodness in whole grains is to enjoy a steaming dish of whole grain pasta, either with a vegetable or cheese sauce or simply tossed with a pat of butter and a sprinkling of your favorite herbs. One cup of homemade whole wheat noodles will provide you with 9.2 grams of protein, 300 I.U. vitamin A, 0.28 mg. thiamine, 0.12 mg. riboflavin, 2 mg. niacin, 0.18 mg. vitamin B_6, 2.1 mg. iron, 0.50 mg. vitamin B_{12}, 36 mg. calcium, 220 mg. phosphorus, 560 mg. sodium, 200 mg. potassium and it tastes good, too!

When buying pasta, look for ones made with whole wheat flour for the best nutrition. There are a number of different pastas on the market made from whole wheat flour and such other ingredients as artichoke flour, soy, spinach and carrot flour. Buckwheat noodles are sold in some Oriental markets. These have an unusual nutty flavor that complements Chinese and Japanese food.

If you can't find whole wheat pasta, you can make your own, and it isn't as hard as you think. Before embarking on a noodle-making project, learning a few basic facts about the nature of flour will help you to become a successful pasta chef. Noodle dough must be somewhat elastic in order to be rolled. The gluten in the flour will provide this stretchability, but in order to take advantage of the gluten you must work the dough and then let it rest to let the gluten develop properly. In choosing flour, try to get durum whole wheat flour, as this type of wheat has the highest gluten content to begin with. In a mixing bowl, combine the flour with egg and oil in the following proportions: 1 medium egg to 2/3 cup flour and 1 teaspoon safflower oil. Add salt if you wish, up to 1/2 teaspoon, and stir everything until the dough is no longer sticky but pulls away from the sides of the bowl. If the dough is too stiff, add a teaspoonful or two of water. What you should have at this point is a very firm but not crumbly mass. Cover the bowl and allow it to sit for at least 15 minutes. This will allow the mixture to relax and is the beginning of the process of "liberating" the gluten. Now turn the dough out onto a floured board and knead vigorously, adding more flour if necessary to keep it from sticking. Knead the dough for at least 10 minutes, because the kneading action is the second step in developing the gluten. Cover the dough with an inverted bowl, and again let it "rest" for an hour or so. If you skip this step, you can still roll the dough, but it will be much harder to handle. Once the dough has rested, flour a board and get out the rolling pin. Pull off a lump of dough about the size of a tennis ball and cover the rest. Rub some flour onto the rolling pin and dust the dough with a little flour. Flatten the dough with the rolling pin and, as it gets thinner, start to pull and stretch it. You may have to sprinkle a bit more flour on the dough as you go along to keep it from sticking. The idea is to get the sheet of dough as thin as you can without tearing it. When the dough is about 1/8 inch thick, roll it up like a jellyroll, then cut the roll into ribbons. Unroll the ribbons and lay them on a floured towel to dry while you finish rolling the rest of the dough. The width of the slices you cut can be varied to give you different types of pasta, ranging from the very thin "fettucini" type to the wide bands of lasagna noodles. You may use the dough, cut into squares, to make ravioli or cannelloni for stuffing with cheese or spinach. For a change of pace, add soy or artichoke flour to the dough or sprinkle in wheat germ for a nutty flavor. Remember, however, when adding other flours that proper gluten development requires that at least half of the mixture consist of whole wheat flour. If you plan to make pasta on a regular basis, a noodle machine will be a great help. There are inexpensive models on the market that are well worth the investment in terms of the time and effort they'll spare you. Cook your homemade pasta right away or let it dry before storing in a plastic bag in the fridge. Use it within a few days for the best in taste and nutrition.

BREAD

If you eat bread every day, why not serve your family and yourself the best bread you can? Bread either can be loaded with empty calories, chemicals and sugar, or it can be bursting with whole grain goodness, full of soul-satisfying flavor, bulk and nutrients.

It's not impossible to buy good bread, but it isn't easy, either. Read the labels for the ingredients. If you can't find good bread, the only solution is to enjoy making your own. Bread making is not difficult, and bread that is hot, fresh from the oven, is incomparable. As with pasta making, knowledge of ingredients and timing are essential.

If you are thinking of making bread on a regular basis, it might make you feel better about the whole thing to know that there isn't much labor involved, although there are waiting periods between the different steps. Don't look on bread making as one long, continuous operation but a series of "labor breaks" that you can perform during the course of the day or night. Learn to be flexible in your timing; treated properly, your dough will wait for you to get to it. In fact, the biggest mistake people make is trying to rush the bread-making process. By being aware of the ingredients and how they interact, you will not fail.

Flour

The gluten in whole wheat flour is essential for well-risen bread, and when mixed with other flours provides differing tastes, textures and nutritional value. Add bean meal, soy meal or wheat germ to your loaves for added nutrition, but bear in mind that the more low-gluten substances in your bread dough, the chewier your bread will be.

Yeast

The star of the show when it comes to bread making, yeast comes as a dry powder or in cake form. The thing to remember about yeast is that it's a living organism. Don't kill it by using liquids that are too hot or deactivate it through chilling. In the beginning of your bread-making career, it would be wise to veer toward the side of not warm enough rather than too warm. Too much heat kills yeast, and dead is dead. On the other hand, if the liquid you use isn't warm enough, the yeast will just take more time to do its work.

Liquids

Milk, water, fruit juice, buttermilk and yogurt may be used in bread. Beaten eggs are added to some rich bread recipes. If a recipe calls for milk, the most convenient way to add it is in the form of powdered milk, which can be blended in with the flours. You would then add water in the amount called for instead of whole milk.

SHORTENINGS

Oil, margarine or butter may be used in all bread recipes. Butter provides a pleasant and distinctive flavor and texture. For flaky pastry, butter is best. However, some breads such as French and Italian bread taste better with oil. The more shortening a bread contains, the more tender (less crisp) the crust will be.

SWEETENERS

Yeast feeds on sugars, but you need not add sugar in making bread since whole grains contain natural sugars. In some cases, however, additional fuel for the yeast may be in order. Honey, molasses or dried fruit will provide that extra boost for the working yeast.

BREAD-MAKING TECHNIQUES

Bread making is as simple as one, two, three. When you look at any bread recipe, divide the steps into the following 3 procedures.

Proofing the yeast and mixing the dough: Two elements are at work here, the liquids that will be mixed with the yeast and the flour. The liquid mixture will consist of any combination of the following: shortening, water, milk or fruit juice, any liquid sweetening, and eggs if they are being used. First heat some of the liquid until it's about the temperature of a baby's bottle, then dissolve the yeast into it. Let this mixture sit for 10 minutes or so. By this time, small bubbles should be forming, a sign that the yeast is starting to work. If nothing happens, the yeast is dead, so throw it out and start again. This is called proofing. Now you can add the rest of the liquid to the mixture as well as sweetening and eggs if they are being used. At this point, two methods present themselves: You can mix a cup or so of flour into the liquid mixture and then cover it and let it stand for a few hours or overnight. This method requires less yeast and yields a sort of sourdough. Or you can mix in all the flour and other ingredients right away. When the dough starts to pull away from the sides of the bowl, cover the bowl with a damp towel and let it sit for at least 15 minutes (longer if you wish). This step allows the gluten in the flour to start to develop and will make kneading much easier.

Kneading and rising: Roll up your sleeves and get ready for some healthy exercise! Flour the bread board, turn out the dough, and start to knead, adding more flour if necessary to keep the dough from sticking. To fully develop the gluten in the dough, knead for at least 10 minutes, giving the bread a quarter turn every so often. When the dough is ready it will be shiny and elastic and not stick to your hands. Place the ball of dough in a lightly oiled bowl and turn it so it's coated with oil on all sides. Cover the bowl and let it sit in a draft-free spot. Now you can let it rise for the recipe's specified time or overnight. This is the first rise. When the dough has doubled in bulk, if you're not ready to proceed with the recipe, place it in the fridge and let it wait for you. If you're ready to go ahead, punch it down, knead it a few times and shape it into loaves. Cover the loaves with a damp towel and allow them to rise for at least an hour more. By then, they should have doubled once more. Once again, if you're not ready to go ahead, place the loaves in the refrigerator until you're ready for them. To determine if the dough has doubled in bulk, press it lightly with your fingertip. The depression should not fill in.

Baking: Preheat the oven and brush the tops of the loaves with melted butter or shortening for a soft crust. Bake for the amount of time specified in your recipe. To test for doneness, rap the bottom of the loaves with your knuckles. If they sound hollow, they're done.

Points To Remember When Making Bread

Don't kill yeast with liquids that are too hot, and don't try to rush things. Give yeast plenty of time to do its work.

Letting the dough relax and vigorously kneading will develop the necessary gluten in the flour to yield loaves that are light and well textured.

Be careful when adding flour to bread dough. You can always add a little more, but once you've added to much it's too late. If the dough seems too sticky at first, bear in mind that as the gluten develops, it will become more elastic and easier to handle.

Nuts, Seeds and Sprouts

Seeds and nuts should be consumed in modest amounts and as a complement to other foods, because their nutrients are similar to but more concentrated than those in grain. If you serve them for snacking, always let the nibblers do the shelling; this discourages overindulgence. Nuts also provide cozy winter evenings around a fireplace with the perfect complement to good discussion. Most seeds and nuts are a good source of protein, minerals, B vitamins and unsaturated fatty acids. They can be roasted and used in main dishes and salads. Sprouting many seeds and nuts gives the additional benefit of transforming seeds and nuts, along with beans and grains, into crunchy, tender morsels of vegetable protein that highlight a salad, stir-fry dishes and are just good nibbling.

GENERAL PROCEDURE FOR RAISING SPROUTS FROM NUTS, SEEDS, BEANS AND GRAINS

Sprouts are the best source of unsaturated fatty acids, an important source of many nutrients, and provide good amounts of protein, minerals, and vitamins A, B and E. While the vitamin and mineral content of the sprouts you grow in your indoor garden is good to begin with, the way the nutrients develop and expand as the sprout grows is truly amazing. Soybeans, for example, increase their vitamin C content by 700 percent after only 72 hours of growth. They also taste great in salads, sandwiches, main dishes and desserts. If you make it a habit to start some sprouts every week, you'll never be at a loss for the fresh taste and nourishment they give to meals. When choosing seeds for sprouting, be sure to buy seeds that have not been treated with chemicals. Check labels carefully, as some types of beans and corn seed, for example, have been dusted with a poisonous insecticide or fungicide.

You'll need an opaque, nonmetallic vessel to hold the sprouts. Plastic, china, enamel or pottery would do the trick. Choose a wide, shallow container that has a cover. If you're using a plastic container, punch some holes in the bottom. If the container you choose is glass or ceramic, punch some air holes in the lid. In any event, you must be able to drain any container without too much fuss or bother. In most cases, a little bit of seed goes a long way; start with a small amount, 1/4 cup or so. Let the seed soak in lukewarm water overnight, then drain off the water and use it to feed your houseplants. Spread the seed out in the container and cover it with a layer of damp paper toweling or cheesecloth. Put the lid on the sprouter and set it aside. At about 4-hour intervals, rinse and drain the seeds. After a while, you will know how frequently the developing sprouts need a bath. The trick is to keep them uniformly moist but not sopping wet. In a day or so, you will see the first roots come forth. From here on in, see the individual entries below for how long to let the sprouts grow and how to use them.

ALFALFA

A half teaspoon of alfalfa seed will give you enough sprouts for a very generous portion of salad, and if this doesn't seem to be enough of a bargain just consider their rich amounts of vitamin C and minerals, as well as the nutty, sweet flavor. After the sprouts have achieved their initial growth (about 1 inch long), expose them to light to let the chlorophyll develop. Then use them, instead of lettuce, on a sandwich, juice them or add them to your tossed salad.

ALMONDS

Almonds have an exceptionally high nutritional content. For a tasty nibble, try toasted almonds tossed with tamari and a sprinkle of chili powder. Use slivered almonds in stir-fry dishes to add substance and flavor, or grind whole almonds to make almond butter. Soaked overnight in milk or soy milk, drained and blended they make almond milk, which will add a great deal of subtle flavor to any dessert. Almond sprouts must be started from unshelled, fresh nuts and should be harvested when they're about 1 inch long, which takes about 4 days. Use the sprouts in salads or stir-fry dishes.

BEAN SPROUTS

The queen of sprouts is grown from mung beans, and if you're new to sprouting by all means try the mung beans first. They are easy and quick to raise, and combine so well with so many foods you'll use them often.

Soybeans make the most nutritious sprouts, but are a little more difficult to grow. They get moldy rather easily, so you must check them daily and remove any uncooperative ones. Rinse the beans at least 3 times a day and harvest them on the fourth day. It's essential to steam sprouts before using them because they contain a protein-inhibiting enzyme that heat destroys. Add them to any vegetable dish or juice them and use the liquid to enrich any soup.

Garbanzo beans, dried peas, lentils, and wheat seeds also make good crops for the indoor farmer. All can be raised according to the general instructions offered above. Sprouts can be used in salads, vegetable dishes and casseroles.

BRAZIL NUTS

On the expensive side but worth their weight in gold, Brazil nuts are a good source of protein and sulphur-containing amino acids. Serve them unshelled for snacks or add them to vegetable dishes.

CASHEW NUTS

Cashew nuts have a rich, oily flavor and make good nut butter. You can also add them to sauces along with miso paste for a unique taste. We like roasted cashews sprinkled over almost any cooked vegetable, and they add a flavorful "crunch" to any stir-fried dish.

CHIA SEED

Next to mung beans, chia seed has got to be the easiest to sprout. The tangy greens give an excellent taste accent to any salad, and if you sprout chia seed you'll find yourself nibbling a handful or so throughout the day! The sprouting directions for chia seeds are somewhat different than normal, however. On a china or other nonporous surface, place the seeds in a thin layer, cover them with warm water and let them stand overnight. By then, they should have absorbed most of the water and formed a gelatinous coating that will hold them to the sprouting surface. From here on in, just rinse several times a day until you're ready to harvest your bounty, when they're about 1/8 inch long.

CLOVER

Clover isn't just for cows, and if you're looking over a three-leaf clover sprout, eat it. Make sure to buy untreated seed and set the sprouting container on a windowsill to expose the sprouts to sunlight —to let the chlorophyll develop before harvesting. Harvest when they're 1/4 inch long. Clover sprouts are good in salads, breads and vegetable dishes.

FENUGREEK

Fenugreek seeds can be brewed into tea or used as a spice. Sprouted fenugreek should be used when the sprouts are only 1/4 inch long or they become bitter. Add them sparingly to bread dough or salads for a fresh accent.

FILBERTS OR HAZELNUTS

Use these fat, rich nuts sparingly in desserts; they make an elegant addition to tofu pudding, for example. They taste awfully good but don't contain enough protein to justify their frequent use.

FLAX

Flax is generally used only in its sprouted form; the sprouts can be grown the same way as chia seed and harvested when 1 inch long. Sprouted flax has a mild, nutty taste and is a good intestinal lubricant.

GRAIN SPROUTS

All of the grains make nutritious sprouts. (Alfalfa is covered separately.) Wheat sprouts—from wheat berries—are sweet and can be used in any dish from appetizer to dessert. For sprouting barley, use an unhulled type sold by seed companies and harvest the sprouts when they are equal in size to the grains. Use them in soups and cooked vegetable dishes. Buckwheat can be sprouted from the un-hulled groats using 1/2 inch of soil instead of paper toweling, if you prefer. Harvest the sprouts when they reach a height of 3 to 4 inches, then juice or use in salads. Try sprouting some dried corn for a change of pace. Harvest your corn crop when the sprouts are 1/2 inch long, and then use the sprouts in a salad or in bread doughs. Millet is a reliable sprouter and the tiny, tender shoots make a tangy addition to breads, salads and stir-fried dishes. Rye sprouts should be harvested when the stem is as long as the grain. Combine them with rice, add them to bread dough or juice them to gain the intestinal cleansing benefits they provide.

MUSTARD

If you raise your own mustard seed, then make your own mustard sauce by combining 6 teaspoons ground powder of the seed with 1 cup vinegar or wine and 1/4 cup corn flour and mixing to a paste. Mustard seeds are also eager sprouters, and a handful of their tangy greens will perk up any salad.

PECANS

Save pecans for a once-in-a-while break; they provide too many calories for the amount of protein they contain to be eaten often. Pecans are high in potassium and B vitamins, however, and everyone deserves a treat now and then. Serve them roasted and tossed with tamari and spices, or sautéed in butter as a garnish.

PINE NUTS OR PIGNOLIAS

Pine nuts, like pecans, should be reserved for the occasional straying off the straight-and-narrow. They taste great but aren't high in protein and have a lot of calories. Nevertheless, enjoy them now and then as a vegetable or dessert garnish.

PISTACHIO NUTS

We like them when they're served in the shell as a snack food. They can also be added to rice dishes and desserts for a colorful note. When buying pistachios, look for the kind with undyed shells.

PUMPKIN AND SQUASH SEEDS

Save the jack-o-lantern seeds and dry them for winter nibbling. They can be eaten as is or sprouted, as can squash seeds. Harvest pumpkin or squash sprouts when they're 3 or 4 days old, and use them in salads or cooked vegetable dishes. Hulled pumpkin or squash seeds can also be milled into a flour that can be added to cakes or bread dough.

RADISH SEEDS

Radish sprouts should be gathered when about 1 inch long, and their peppery flavor is a welcome addition to the salad bowl. Make sure to expose the sprouts to sunlight after their initial growth to stimulate chlorophyll development.

SESAME SEEDS

Nutritious sesame seeds can be added to almost any dish and are available hulled and unhulled. An excellent source of protein, unsaturated fatty acids, calcium, magnesium, niacin and vitamins A and E, they can be eaten raw or toasted, sprinkled on breads and vegetable dishes. Tahini, a butter made from sesame seeds that has a nutty taste, is an excellent addition to any dish containing legumes because it will complement the incomplete protein in the beans. Tahini can be added as well to sauces and milk shakes to enhance their flavor and nutritional value. Only unhulled seeds will sprout; harvest the shoots within 2 days for use in cooked dishes or beverages.

SUNFLOWER SEEDS

If you're serving these as snacks, make sure to get the unhulled type; otherwise people will gobble them up too quickly! Sunflower seeds are a rich source of protein, unsaturated fatty acids, phosphorus, calcium, iron, fluorine, iodine, potassium, magnesium, zinc, some of the B vitamins and vitamins E and D. They blend well with so many parts of nature's bounty—morning cereal, lunchtime spread, and to top off the dinner casserole. Sunflower seeds go well in bread dough, or grind them up into nut butter. Sprouted sunflower seeds should be harvested when they have just begun to bud, usually from 4 to 5 days.

Specially hulled sprouting seeds can be had from seed companies, but the husks should be rinsed off before you use the sprouts in salads, soups or casseroles.

WALNUTS

Black walnuts have almost all the vital nutrients we all require; they are rich in protein and iron—and calories. Keep them, as with all nuts, in the shell until ready for eating. Once shelled, all nuts have a tendency to dry out or become rancid. If you have your own walnut tree, the best way to remove the hard outer husk of the nut is to place the nuts on your driveway and run your car back and forth over them. When the husks have been removed, place the nuts in a paper bag and then bang them with a hammer. Let the bag sit for a day or so, then shake the nut meats from the shells. The only thing you have to do after that is to enjoy them! Walnuts make an unusual, meatlike addition to any vegetable dish. If you have a good supply on hand, don't forget to use them in bread, cookies and cakes.

Seaweed

Most Americans experience seaweed as something that gets tangled on a fishing line. Seaweed, however, is a rich source of many valuable nutrients, and it has been a staple in the Orient for ages and ages. In the Western world, seaweed eating seems limited to people "in the know" about this flavorful, nourishing food. Seaweed contains calcium, magnesium, phosphorus, potassium, iodine and sodium, but in somewhat more concentrated form than in land vegetables. Seaweed's simple structure allows it to absorb minerals in seawater through its entire surface, instead of just through a root system, as land plants do. Moreover, seaweed doesn't need the rigid cellulose structure of land plants because it is supported by water; therefore seaweeds are tender and require little cooking.

While seaweeds come in a myriad of forms, botanists classify them into 4 major groups based on color. Red kinds include dulse, purple nori, Irish moss and laver, while brown seaweed includes kelp and the wracks. Green and blue green classes include green nori and sea lettuce. Red and green seaweeds are the best sources of vitamins B_1 and B_{12}, pantothenic acid and folic acid.

Dried seaweed can be bought in health food stores and Oriental markets, and the guidelines for its storage and preparation are quite simple. The different types come packed in plastic bags and can be stored this way at room temperature indefinitely. Once the bag is opened, it's advisable to repack what you don't use in an airtight container just as you would any dried herb. Before using the seaweed, it must be "freshened" by soaking in water. Tougher kinds of seaweed should be immersed in warm or hot water, while the more tender kinds can be soaked in cool water or eaten as is. Dulse and nori, the most delicate of the seaweeds, require no freshening. Once seaweed has been freshened or cooked, it should be stored like any other cooked vegetable, in the refrigerator. Some seaweeds need to be trimmed before cooking. Wakame, for example, should be separated into two parts: the tough midrib requires simmering, but the leafy outer parts require only brief cooking, such as stir frying.

There are 6 basic methods of cooking seaweed.

Toasting

Dulse, nori and other delicate seaweeds need no presoaking but can simply be lightly toasted over low heat or on a cookie sheet in a 300-degree oven. The sheets may then be torn into strips and added to any cooked dish or used in a salad.

Powdering

Toasted seaweed can be ground into a powder, either in a blender or with a mortar and pestle, and used as a seasoning. The powder makes a nourishing substitute for salt and can be used to flavor sauces and salad dressings. If you buy prepowdered seaweed, be sure to check the label, as some brands contain MSG.

Sautéeing

Hijiki and arame, after presoaking, can be stir fried in hot oil for a minute or two and then seasoned with tamari and simmered until tender. Seaweeds prepared this way yield a savory juice that's very good served over rice.

Deep Frying

You may dip in batter and deep fry kombu strips, nori, dulse fronds and wakame strands in hot oil for a crunchy treat. The pieces should be removed from the oil as soon as they change color. Sprinkle the fried bits on top of casseroles or vegetable dishes.

Parboiling

To prepare dulse, wakame and nori for use in salads, drop the pieces into boiling water and then remove the pot from the heat after 30 seconds. Drain the leaves, wring them out, chop them and mix with your favorite dressing.

LAYERING

When cooking rice and other grains, line the bottom of the pot with kombu: it will keep the grain from sticking and also add a seafresh taste.

To help you become better acquainted with the different seaweeds, we have compiled the following information on each type and suggestions for its preparation.

KOMBU OR KELP

Dried kombu can be purchased in sheets or strands and makes a good addition to soups. To soften the sheets, soak them in hot water for 5 to 10 minutes, then cut in pieces and use in stir-fry dishes. Or soften kombu sheets slightly by wiping them with a damp cloth and then use them for wrappers in making stuffed tidbits, much the way you would stuff grape leaves or cabbage. Powdered kelp can be used as a seasoning in place of salt, but use only half as much kelp as you would salt. Kombu is a good source of iodine, vitamin B_2 and calcium.

ARAME

Dried arame comes in black, stringlike strips and has a rich, shrimpy flavor. Soften the strips with hot water before adding them to soups, salads or stir-fry dishes. Arame is an excellent source of calcium and phosphorus.

WAKAME

Fresh wakame is only to be found in Japan, but the dried variety can be found in the United States. It has 50 percent more calcium than powdered milk. Cut out the tough midrib first, then soak the fronds in hot water to soften. Wakame can be used in stir-fried dishes, in salads and all types of soup. A traditional Japanese favorite is miso soup with wakame leaves.

NORI

If you're hesitant about trying seaweed, nori should be the first type you try. The toasted sheets have a crisp texture and a nutty flavor that's quite pleasing. Nori comes in flat, paper-thin sheets and can be eaten after light toasting. Crumble toasted nori over salads or casseroles, or serve the crunchy sheets as a cocktail nibble. Nori is a good source of protein, vitamins A, B_2, B_{12} and D as well as niacin.

HIJIKI

Hijiki, a low-calorie source of vitamins A, B_1 and B_2, also contains nicotinic acid and minerals. An average portion of it will supply you with an amazing 14 times more calcium than found in a glass of cow's milk. A half cup of dried hijiki, soaked in hot water for 10 to 15 minutes, will expand to 2 cups of ready-to-cook sea vegetables. Use hijiki in salads, stir-fry dishes and soups. When mixed with rice, it makes a flavorful stuffing for dumplings or hollowed-out vegetables.

AGAR-AGAR

You could lightheartedly call this stuff "Japanese Jell-O." Agar-agar, a complex starch related to cellulose, is found in the cell walls of red agar-yielding algae. It's a good source of vitamins A, B_1, B_6, B_{12}, biotin, C, D and K. Agar-agar also aids in digestion, as well as providing a low-calorie source of bulk and nutrients in the diet. It can be used for thickening fruit and vegetable dishes or in desserts. To use it as a thickener, take 1 1/2 sticks, torn in pieces, and dissolve in a quart of liquid. (If you use the stick form, you have to simmer it for 10 minutes or so to dissolve it.) The result will be a puddinglike consistency. Use more for aspics and to replace gelatin in molds.

IRISH MOSS

Like agar-agar, this seaweed is used to thicken or gel liquids and can be added to sauces, aspics and puddings. Use 6 tablespoons of Irish moss to get a quart of liquid. Rinse it first, and soak for 10 minutes before using. Since it may have a strong taste, you may wish to rinse and soak twice before adding to dishes that have a delicate flavor.

DULSE

A red seaweed, dried dulse makes a tangy snack food or can be mixed into a salad. It can also be soaked, and then treated as any cooked green. It has a seafresh flavor that adds savor to many dishes from relishes to desserts. Try blending dulse with grains or mashed potatoes, or add it to soup. Dulse is a good source of potassium, magnesium and other minerals.

The Basics

The vegetarian larder should contain basic items that are used every day; you should exercise the same care in selecting them as you do vegetables, fruits and the other parts of your diet. You'll always want to keep on hand a supply of noodles, grains, beans and flours, but we have discussed those items already. Now's the time to look at the odds and ends that don't quite fit anywhere else.

SALT

To salt or not to salt, that may be the question. It really depends on you. There's no doubt that overconsumption of salt can lead to health problems. On the other hand, a vegetarian diet is low in natural salts to begin with. If you choose to use salt, get the natural kinds because commercial table salt is sometimes full of additives. If you eat both sea and land vegetables, the addition of iodine is not necessary. Your best choice is kosher salt. There are also good alternatives to salt. Tamari will give your food a savory flavor and provide you with protein as well. Miso can be used in much the same way. Try some gomiso, which can be purchased at the local health food store or Oriental market. You can also make it yourself if you have either a blender or a mortar and pestle. Rinse 1 cup unhulled sesame seeds and drain them. Then roast 1 level teaspoon kosher salt in a cast-iron skillet until the strong odor of chlorine is no longer released. Put the salt in the blender or mortar. Then, toast the sesame seeds in the skillet until they're a golden brown. Add them to the salt and then blend or grind the mixture until the consistency is that of a fine bran. Store your gomiso in an airtight container and use it as you would table salt.

Umeboshi plums can also be used to salt the water in which grains are cooked or used in salad dressing to add tangy flavor. These small

Japanese plums are high in citric acid and help to neutralize and eliminate some of the excess lactic acid in the body.

LEAVENINGS AND NUTRITIONAL YEAST

To bake bread daily, you want to keep some cakes of dry yeast on hand, but keep in mind that there are other leavening agents. Baking powder, used to make quick breads, is probably most familiar. Commercial baking powder is usually composed of potassium bicarbonate, calcium acid, phosphate and sodium aluminum sulphate. It destroys some of the vitamin C and B vitamins in the food you use it in and, besides that, aluminum is a known toxic agent. Better baking powder is made from plain sodium bicarbonate, although even without the aluminum it will still destroy the C and B vitamins. Make your own baking powder by using 1 part potassium bicarbonate with 2 parts cream of tartar and 2 parts arrowroot powder.

Nutritional yeast can be purchased in health food stores under the name brewer's yeast, and some supermarkets carry it as well. Brewer's yeast is very high in protein, vitamins and minerals, and is also a source for the vitamin B complex. Its low cost can give an economical but very nutritious boost to juices, soups or milk shakes. Mix some of it with butter to make a tasty topper for cooked vegetables, or add a spoonful or so to any sauce or gravy for protein enrichment and flavor.

THICKENERS

In addition to using whole wheat flour as a thickener for sauces, gravies and desserts, you can also use cornstarch or arrowroot. They will both produce a clear, gelatinous sauce of the type found in Chinese food. Arrowroot, though, should be used for more delicate sauces as it has a less noticeable flavor. Kudzu, a product made from the root of a wild, creeping plant, can sometimes be found in health food stores and can also be used to thicken any dish.

SWEETENERS

White sugar may be the most used sweetener in this country but, pound for pound, it's the least valuable when it comes to nutrition. Common table sugar has been processed to 99.9 percent sucrose and has none of the nutrients that are in raw sugar cane or raw sugar beets, except for the calories. White sugar taxes the body's digestive system and depletes its store of minerals and enzymes as the sugar is metabolized. Since white sugar is essentially an "empty" food, it would be wise to replace it with richer sugars found in natural foods. The energy you believe you get from white sugar is easily replaced with whole grains, which are an excellent source of digestible glucose. In many recipes that call for a sweetener, the natural sweetness of fruit juices is the answer. Natural maple sugar, used in moderation, is a good alternative to white sugar. Maple sugar is remarkably sweet, so in any recipe use only half as much of it as you would white sugar. Also, be sure to check the label when you buy because some maple syrups have been extracted with the use of formaldehyde or have been blended with other syrups made from refined sugar.

Perhaps the most popular alternative sweetener is honey, available in many different flavors and forms. The darker honeys are a better source of minerals and have a stronger flavor than the lighter ones. Like maple syrup, honey should be used in moderation as it is much sweeter than white sugar. You can use honey in all baked goods if you adjust the amount of dry ingredients to compensate for the fact that it's liquid. It is advisable not to use too much of any sweetener in any cooked dish since heat can be destructive to protein in the presence of sugar. When a recipe simply demands to be made with granulated sugar, try date sugar instead. It has a pleasing sweetness and the unmistakable flavor of dried dates. A versatile sweetener alternative is carob, a powder made from the dried pods of the carob tree. It comes both roasted and unroasted, with greater nutrient trace minerals present in the roasted form. A little carob goes a long way, so use it with discretion. If you use carob as a chocolate substitute, 3 tablespoons carob powder plus 2 tablespoons water or soy milk are the equivalent of 1 square unsweetened chocolate.

Ame, a syrup made from rice, is one of two grain sweeteners, the other being barley sugar. Both come in syrup and semihard forms. For a once-in-a-while treat, try making candy with either one.

Powdered milk can also be used as a sweetener in some recipes, particularly bread recipes. It contains the milk sugar lactose, which will add a naturally sweet note to any dish you make.

Some people use raw sugar or turbinado, thinking it better than white sugar. Alas, it is not. The only difference between turbinado and white sugar is that raw sugar has not been subjected to the final acid bath to make it pure white. This final step in the processing of white sugar also leaches it of its last traces of calcium and magnesium salts. Commercial brown sugar is actually made from white sugar that's been tinted brown with either burnt sugar or molasses; therefore it has nothing to recommend it over its white cousin. Molasses, on the other hand, is the one form of processed sugar that has some nutritional substance to offer. Cane or beet juice is extracted from the vegetable matter, clarified to syrup and then crystalized. The crystals are then spun in a centrifuge where more crystals are extracted from the liquid. What remains in liquid form is molasses. As the extraction process is continued and repeated, the different types of molasses are produced. The final grade is blackstrap molasses, which is most nutritious. This product contains about 35 percent sucrose and is a source of iron, calcium and B vitamins. Barbados molasses is one of the lighter extracts and has a more delicate flavor than blackstrap.

Sorghum syrup is produced in the same way as molasses, but it's made from the juice of the sorghum plant. It has a rather strong flavor and is best used in baking.

Don't neglect dried fruits as a source of natural sweetness. A small amount in any bread or cake recipe will go a long way in sweetening. Don't go overboard on nibbling dried fruit, either, because the natural sugar it contains is quite high in calories.

UNREFINED OILS

Don't begrudge the calories in the oil you put in your salad dressing. Unrefined oils are a good source of polyunsaturated fats and vitamin E. For general cooking purposes and a mild-flavored salad oil, try safflower or sunflower seed oils. Sesame seed oil has a pleasant nutty flavor and makes a good salad oil but is rather expensive for frying foods. Unrefined corn oil gives baked goods a buttery flavor, and olive oil is full and fruity in flavor; unfortunately, however, olive oil is expensive and high in calories. Mix olive oil with other oils or use it on salads only. Frankly, we think it's a waste of money to squander the fine flavor of olive oil on fried foods, where the oil's rich bouquet will just go up in smoke. Peanut and soybean oils are somewhat stronger in flavor than others and make the perfect choice for frying foods, where their distinctive flavors will not be quite so noticeable. Remember to store unrefined oils in the fridge or they'll get rancid. Throughout the recipe, whenever we call for oil but don't specify type, safflower oil is meant.

VINEGAR

White distilled or wine vinegars are the least nutritious vinegars because they have few of the naturally occurring nutrients and lack the flavor of aged vinegar. Perhaps the best and easiest to find natural vinegar is naturally aged cider vinegar, which has a wonderful, fruity bouquet and is a good source of malic acid, an aid for digestion. Oriental rice vinegar can also be found in some stores. Use it with caution, because its flavor is very distinctive. As an alternative to vinegar in salad dressings and dishes that call for mild piquancy, try lemon juice instead.

CONDIMENTS

Beyond salt and pepper, the American table seems incomplete without a few basic condiments such as ketchup, mustard and mayonnaise. As your taste for natural food develops, you will probably find that you prefer the unmasked flavors of the food you eat. In the meantime, you can safely produce your own condiments at home to avoid sugar, artificial flavors and chemical additives found in commercially produced condiments. The homemade versions taste better, anyway!

KETCHUP

Proportions for this recipe are largely a matter of taste. Start with a large can of tomato paste, then add the following ingredients: water, vinegar or lemon juice, salt, oregano, cumin, nutmeg, pepper, dried mustard powder, garlic juice and molasses. Mix well and keep refrigerated. It's not necessary to use all the ingredients, simply experiment until you achieve a "perfect" blend to your taste. It may take a little time, but you'll come up with a taste that's just right for you.

MUSTARD

If you want very hot mustard—like that served with Chinese food—simply mix dried mustard with a bit of water. It will thicken, and after 10 minutes or so the flavor will intensify to enflame your tongue. To make a milder type of mustard, pour 1 cup boiling vinegar over 1/2 cup dried mustard powder, then allow to stand for 15 minutes.

Drain off the vinegar and reserve. Pour 1 cup boiling water over the paste and allow it to stand for 15 minutes more. Repeat this process once more with boiling water, and then stir in some of the reserved vinegar until you have the consistency you want. You can then use the mustard or stir in some salt or perhaps a drop of molasses. This mustard need not be kept in the refrigerator, but do keep it covered so it won't dry out.

MAYONNAISE

Mayonnaise is easy to make if you have a blender, electric mixer or a strong arm. The homemade kind won't keep as well as the commercial kind, because it doesn't have the harmful additives and chemical preservatives. But it's so good that it won't last long, anyway. Put 1 egg and 2 teaspoons lemon juice in the blender or mixing bowl with a 1/4 cup safflower oil. Blend or mix on low speed for half a minute or beat 3–4 minutes by hand, then slowly pour in another 3/4 cup oil. If you want thicker mayonnaise, add more oil. You can season this to taste with dried mustard and salt. Do be careful to keep mayonnaise or any dish you use it with well chilled as it spoils very rapidly.

HERBS AND SPICES

Be adventurous with herbs and spices, but remember that moderation and discretion are the better part of valor when cooking. Check the package labels to make sure that the spices you buy are all flavor and no chemicals. Most dried herbs and ground spices are very concentrated, so add them gradually and keep tasting so as not to overpower your dishes. Beware the loose shaker top! We once ruined a whole batch of chili when the top, along with the whole contents of a jar of chili powder, fell into the kettle. You can always add more, but "too much" can never be taken away. Also, be aware that some spices and herbs become stronger in flavor in prolonged simmering. Some herbs and spices develop an unpleasant flavor after overexposure to heat; we have made sure to mention that in the following text. In any event, adventure and prudence make for satisfied taste buds.

Herbs

Basil: Try chewing some fresh basil or using it as a salad green. Fresh basil leaves can also be made into pesto, a robust sauce for pasta. To make pesto, whir equal amounts of fresh basil leaves with either pine nuts or walnuts in a blender. Gradually add enough olive oil to make a smooth sauce. Season to taste with salt, pepper and garlic juice, and then stir in a good handful of Parmesan or Romano cheese. Toss hot buckwheat noodles in the sauce for an Italianate treat. Dried basil has a special affinity for tomato dishes and is also good in any egg dish or salad dressing.

Bay Leaves: A little bit of these aromatic leaves goes a long way, so use them sparingly—especially when they're powdered. One-sixth of a bay leaf per quart of liquid is the rule of thumb for seasoning soups and stocks. Bay leaf also adds a fine flavor to stuffings and rice dishes.

Capers: These buds burst with flavor and are packed in jars with vinegar. Check the label to make sure no additives have been used in their preparation. Capers add piquancy to delight sauces and salad dressings. Try adding a spoonful or two of capers to your next white wine sauce for a flavor surprise!

Caraway Seed: Yes, for rye bread, but also for the enhancement of cabbage, sauerkraut, turnips or beet soup. This aromatic seed should not be exposed to prolonged heat, or else it becomes bitter. Add it to cooked foods just before they're done. And if you add it to the water when boiling cabbage, the objectionable odor is lessened.

Chervil: If you can get fresh chervil, add it to your salad. The dried form of this herb is good in sauces, salad dressings and makes the most ordinary vegetable a thing of beauty.

Coriander: In its seed form, coriander is used as an ingredient in baked goods and curries. The fresh leaves of the plant look a bit like parsley and can be used in soups, stews and casseroles. Use it more sparingly than parsley, however, because it does have a decidedly stronger taste. Coriander leaves are used to advantage in many Chinese recipes, and coriander is often called Chinese parsley.

Cumin: This versatile seed is featured in many different dishes from chili to baked goods. Cumin goes well with eggs, beans or rice and can be used in sauces and salad dressings.

Dill: Grow some fresh dill in a pot on your windowsill and enjoy its tart accent in sour cream dressings, snipped into borscht or as a garnish on your potato salad. Make dill butter by tossing a handful of the snipped herb into sizzling melted butter. This is an excellent sauce for tiny, boiled new potatoes or green beans. Dill seed can be used in all the same ways, and without it where would the pickle be?

Fennel: The leaves and roots of fennel are used as a vegetable or as an addition to salad, where their licoricelike flavor is a welcome taste accent. Fennel seeds can perk up the flavors of rice dishes, potato combinations and lentils. You can also use fennel seeds in cookies for a spicy boost or add some to your next apple pie.

Horseradish: Love it or hate it, but everyone knows that very good horseradish clears up a stuffed sinus and brings tears to the eyes. We love its pungent flavor and try to get the strongest, freshest bottled type we can. If you're lucky enough to find some fresh horseradish root, grate your own and then mix with apple cider vinegar to preserve it. Grating should be done all at once and in great quantity (stores up to 3 months in the fridge), because the fumes given off by the root will reduce you to tears faster than any onion. But it is well worth the trouble! Add some to cream sauce and serve over your favorite cooked vegetable. It's also good for cheese dips and dressings.

Marjoram: This pungent herb adds zest to tomato sauces—to any tomato dish for that matter. Add it to cream cheese, sprinkle it over green beans, use it in your salad dressings or make it part of your omelet. Vegetable and beans soups, minestrone in particular, benefit by the addition of a pinch or so of marjoram.

Mint: Fresh mint is often hard to find, so you'll be smart if you grow your own. Besides the familiar spearmint and peppermint, other mints include apple, orange, and pineapple mint, all of which can be found in seed catalogs and are worth a try. Use fresh mint leaves in tea and fruit drinks. Dried or fresh mint freshens fruit cups, cole slaw, cheese dishes and any dish made with squash.

Mustard Powder and Mustard Seed: In addition to being the base for prepared mustard, powdered mustard is a versatile seasoning that adds a zing to white sauce, cheese sauce, egg dishes, rice, lentils or cheese dip. Use mustard seed in salad dressings and homemade pickles.

Oregano: Oregano is a member of the marjoram family and can be used in the same ways. Italian dishes are characterized by the use of oregano. Add a bit of oregano to rice, lentil and bean dishes for full flavoring. We like to sprinkle some in bread dough or top the loaves with a mixture of oregano and cheese 10 minutes before they're done baking.

Parsley: Parsley is another herb worth growing in the garden or on a windowsill. It's wonderfully versatile in cooking. A bit of fresh parsley adds a lot to soup, stews, gravies, stocks or casseroles. Parsley is excellent when well washed and added to a tossed salad. At all times, parsley is flavorful without being obtrusive.

Chili Peppers, Chili Powder: This group of seasonings isn't related to the true spice pepper, which is discussed in the spice section. Chilis, and for that matter all of the vegetables we call peppers, are members of the Capsicum family. They originally caught the name "pepper" from early explorers to the New World, who likened their fiery flavor to true pepper, already being used widely in Europe. If you use fresh chilis as a seasoning, remove the seeds and veins as they are an irritant. When preparing them, be sure not to rub your eyes, and wash your hands very well afterwards. Dried red pepper flakes, available in jars, can be added to tomato and bean dishes and used in casseroles. They're also a favorite seasoning for pizza. Cayenne pepper is made from ground chilis and is very, very, very hot! Use with caution in Mexican food. Red pepper, a milder version of cayenne, can be used in the same way. Chili powder is made from a blend of red chilis and other spices. There are many variations on the market, some hot, some mild. Find your own favorite blend, but be sure to check the labels as many chili powder mixes contain chemical preservatives and MSG. If you want to mix your own chili powder, combine cayenne, paprika and garlic in a proportion that pleases you. Paprika is also produced from a member of the Capsicum family. It varies in flavor from mild to very hot. Since paprika is sensitive to heat, it should be added to food during the end of the cooking period or it will become bitter. Use it to season vegetables, cheese sauces and grain dishes. A little paprika sprinkled on top of any dish will add both color and flavor.

Rosemary: Dried rosemary adds a somewhat pungent flavor to stuffings and rice dishes. It's also good in salad dressings and in white sauce. Sprinkle some dried rosemary on top of your pizza, peas or spinach for an unusual flavor accent.

Sage: Use sage in combination with rices and other grains or to flavor soups and chowders. The unique flavor of sage also complements cheeses and adds a tang to herb bread. If you can get fresh sage, add some to the salad bowl.

Tarragon: This is one of our favorite herbs. It's slightly sweet, earthy and goes well with many different foods. Fresh tarragon makes a welcome addition to any salad bowl. Use the dried form in egg dishes, cheese dishes, mustard or any dish with mushrooms.

Thyme: This comes in whole and powdered form. For better flavor, buy whole thyme and use it in bread doughs, stuffings, gumbos and brown sauce. Some whole thyme—added to pickled beets, cucumbers or tomatoes—also adds great flavor.

SPICES

Allspice: The name for this whole berry or powdered spice is quite apt. Allspice has the flavor of a blend of cinammon, clove, nutmeg and juniper berries. Use it to enhance the flavor of soups, vegetable dishes and baked goods.

Cinnamon: Cinnamon also comes whole, in sticks, or powdered and has been a traditional favorite in baked goods. The sticks have the strongest flavor. It adds an unusual accent to fruit compotes and applesauce. We like to add some powdered cinnamon to a jar of honey and use it for a spread on breakfast toast.

Cloves: You can buy cloves whole or in powdered form, and both types stand up well in stewed fruit, chutneys and pickles. Whole cloves are easier to use since you will not have a tendency to over-season, and they can be removed before serving. The flavor of stock and bean dishes is greatly improved by adding a small onion studded with 3 whole cloves.

Curry: Curry powder is not a spice but a combination of different spices. Here again, check labels carefully because many brands of curry have artificial ingredients. You can always make your own curry, however. Make your curry suit your particular taste by experimenting. Combine all or some of the following ingredients (the first three are generally used in all curries): coriander, black and/or red pepper, cumin, fenugreek, mustard seed, powdered ginger, cinnamon and poppy seeds. Grind all ingredients with a mortar and pestle or whir them in the blender for a minute or so, then store the powder in an airtight container and usebefore the month is out. Use curry powder to enhance the flavor of bean, rice, grain and vegetable dishes and add some to cheese spreads, dips and mayonnaise.

Ginger: Both as a root and as a powder, this spice is worth its weight in gold for seasoning any stir-fry dishes. Fresh ginger root is available in Oriental markets and is expensive, but a little goes a long way. Store the fresh roots in a plastic bag in the refrigerator. For long-term storage, freeze the roots. Mince unpeeled ginger and sauté it in oil to release its flavor before adding other ingredients in any stir-fried dish. Never let it burn or it will make the food bitter. You can also extract the juice from the ginger root and add it sparingly as a seasoning to cooked dishes, fruit salads and salad dressing. Powdered ginger is used in curries, fruit dishes, pickles and baked goods.

Nutmeg and Mace: Both of these spices come from the same plant. The nutmeg is actually the "pit" of *Myristica fragrans,* and the fruit of the plant is what's used to produce mace. Both nutmeg and mace come in powdered form, but nutmeg can also be bought as a whole "nut" and then grated over foods. Mace is used primarily in fruit dishes and baked goods, while nutmeg can be used the same way and also in sauces and over cooked vegetables. We like to add some to spinach or green beans, and a pinch of nutmeg is always part of our white sauce. Nutmeg sprinkled atop eggnog or milk shakes also imparts an aromatic, nutty flavor that's quite pleasing.

White and Black Pepper: White and black pepper are not to be confused with chili peppers, which are actually members of the Capsicum family (see Chili Peppers). Pepper—black and white—comes from the berries of the tropical plant *Piper nigrum*. White pepper comes from the fully ripe berry from which the dark outer shell has been removed. It's slightly more aromatic than the black kind; however, the difference is minimal. It's hardly necessary to mention the varied ways in which pepper is used since, next to salt, it's the most familiar and popular spice. For something different, however, you might try a pinch of pepper in your special cookie dough or add some whole peppercorns to your bottle of salad dressing. For the freshest taste in pepper, buy whole peppercorns and grind them in a mill. You can also use whole peppercorns for a milder flavor when seasoning soups, stocks or gravies.

Outfitting the Kitchen and Cooking Techniques

You can be as spartan or as lavish as you like in choosing your cooking equipment, because what you buy really depends on how much you have to spend, the amount of space you have and what your cooking preferences are. There are some basics, however. Since *pots* and *pans* first come to mind when we think of the kitchen, we'll begin with them. The basic kitchen should have the following: a 1/2-quart and a 1 1/2- or 2-quart saucepan and a frying pan, all with lids, and a Dutch oven. A large stock pot, a tea kettle and extra saucepans will also come in handy. A double boiler is not completely essential, but is handy to have. Cookware with ovenproof handles can also be used in the oven.

Cookware is sold in a number of different metals, but it's essential to look for a medium- or heavy-gauge bottom on pots to insure even heating and to avoid hot spots that thin cookware is prone to have. We cannot recommend aluminum as it's under suspicion for possibly being a toxic agent. Stainless steel is a good choice; it's easy to clean and can be safely used to cook any type of food. Choose a medium or heavy gauge, or cookware with a coated bottom, though, because stainless steel is such a good conductor of heat, and the thinner types may scorch food. For even heat distribution, durability and ease of maintenance, cast-iron cookware is hard to beat, but it's heavy. It can be used in the oven as well as on the stove top. To temper cast iron before using it, grease the surface well and place the pan in a 450-degree oven for 30 minutes, then scour with steel wool and rinse. Always dry cast-iron cookware carefully before putting it away or it will rust. However, rust is easily avoided by rubbing on a light film of cooking oil with a paper towel. Some cast-iron pans never need to be washed; simply brush the pan out first and then wipe it with paper toweling. The round-bottomed Chinese wok is always cleaned this way. A wok is, by the way, a lovely and handy addition to your pot collection as its round bottom and thin cooking surface provide the rapid changes in temperature that are necessary for making stir-fry dishes.

Glass, porcelain, and enameled cooking vessels are also available and do not affect the taste, flavor or color of your food. Like cast iron, they too can do double duty in the oven if their handles are ovenproof. For those on fat-free diets or for the lazy dishwasher, Teflon-lined pans are a boon. A good, heavy-gauge kind will provide even heat and greaseless cooking with a fast cleanup.

Start with basics and add to your collection of cookware gradually. It's a mistake to buy a whole set of cookware at once, only to find out that it doesn't provide you with the right cooking surface. Make sure to look for good workmanship and durability since the pot or pan you buy today will be with you for a long time.

For *bakeware*, stainless steel, glass or cast iron is a good choice. Remember that dark surfaces absorb more heat quickly, so adjust your cooking time accordingly when using cookware that isn't white or shiny metallic. The basics of bakeware are a roasting pan or a large pan, a large casserole, a cookie sheet, 2 cake pans, 2 pie pans, a muffin tin or loaf pans and some custard cups.

As for *utensils*, you will need several mixing bowls—ceramic, plastic or ovenproof glass in different sizes is fine. The ovenproof kinds are good as they can also double as casseroles. Plastic bowls have a tendency to absorb grease since they're porous. Make sure to wash them in hot water and don't try to use a plastic bowl to whip egg whites. You will also need a measuring cup, measuring spoons, a cutting board for chopping vegetables and large cooking spoons and forks. Wooden spoons are best for mixing because they will not mar your bowls or pans or react with acid food. A spatula and a soup ladle are also essential. You will also need a strainer, a colander and a good, stiff brush for scrubbing vegetables. A collapsible steaming basket and a pair of kitchen shears will come in handy for preparing vegetables, and it's nice to have a mortar and pestle for grinding spices. Other useful items include a potato masher, funnel, tongs, an egg beater and whisk to keep your sauces smooth. If you plan to do a lot of baking, you will need an unvarnished board for kneading the dough. This board can also double as a chopping block for vegetable preparation. A flour sifter, a rubber bowl scraper, rolling pin and pastry brush will also be needed in the bakery department. A swivel-bladed vegetable parer will save you time and effort in peeling fruit and vegetables, a nutcracker—for its obvious purpose and for opening stubbornly closed jars. We save the bags and containers we get when buying food for storage. Plastic cottage cheese containers make fine small storage tubs for cooked food, and many vegetables, breads and other foods come in plastic bags that can be rinsed out and recycled.

Just as the addition of a wok will enhance your pot and pan collection, several other Oriental cooking utensils will be useful in the kitchen. Stackable bamboo steamers will expand your steaming space, and chopsticks are fine for stir-frying dishes or mixing tempura batter. A tawashi, a natural fiber brush, is good for scrubbing the wok or cleaning vegetables. A wire skimmer with a wooden handle will keep your hands cool and drain the food when you deep fry. Last but not least, if you plan to grind your own flour—we suggest you do!—invest in a hand flour mill that can also be used to grind nuts and beans.

Good, sharp *knives* are absolutely indispensable for a well outfitted kitchen. A large, heavy knife and an Oriental cleaver will be needed. Some smaller paring knives for vegetables and a bread knife would round out a basic collection. When buying knives, it's wise to also invest in a soapstone to keep them sharp and in tip-top cutting condition.

APPLIANCES

Stop and think what you will really need and just how often you will use it before you buy. We have often been the recipient of a gift for the kitchen that wound up gathering dust. It only makes sense to spend money on something you will be using on a regular basis. We use the blender every day, but we gave away the waffle iron we received as a gift because we never used it. Also choose appliances for their versatility—their ability to bake and toast, for example, at the same time.

While an electric blender will certainly ease your chores, you might not think of investing in one unless you plan to make a lot of fruit drinks. But the blender can also be used to grind nuts and beans and make breadcrumbs. When you buy a blender, look for one with a heavy-duty motor. Three speeds are enough to perform any blending chore, and forget about the flashy, 14-speed models. An electric mixer is also nice to have, and here again look for durability in the motor department and forget about "flash." You can buy mixers in both portable and counter models, but we find we use the portable most often since it's so convenient to use and easy to clean. If you like fresh juices, you might want to get an extractor since the blender cannot juice hard vegetables such as carrots. If you plan to make a lot of foods that take a long time to cook, a pressure cooker is a good buy. Choose a stainless steel model and to prevent cooking mishaps read the directions carefully before you use it. If you cook for a crowd on a regular basis and have no help in the kitchen, you might want to get a food processor. It will cut back the time you spend preparing vegetables and makes bread and pastry doughs a cinch to make. While it's true that food processors aren't cheap, if having one will motivate you to bake all your own bread, then buying one is a good investment. Just make sure to check the manufacturer's label to see if it can handle bread dough. If you make beans, soups or stews often and are short on cooking time, a slow cooker may be the answer for you. You can simmer all day without having to worry about burning food, and a slow cooker is miserly with electricity.

COOKING TECHNIQUES

The majority of the food we eat is cooked, although more of our vegetables should be eaten raw. Heat breaks down the indigestible cellulose that some foods have in overabundance. Grains and beans would be impossible to eat without cooking them first, since they're simply too hard to chew otherwise. Additionally, foods like soybeans, for example, must be exposed to heat to destroy protein-inhibiting enzymes the raw product contains.

Some cooking seals in food's natural juices, while other cooking methods are intended to draw them out, as when you make soups or broths. To cook properly, you must know what the most suitable application of heat would be for the food on hand. What follows is a brief course on how to cook.

STEAMING

Most vegetables and grains are best steamed, because steaming allows the food to retain moisture, flavor and nutrients, and the water remaining in the bottom of the steamer can be added to soups and stocks. Choose a pot with a very snug lid for steaming foods, place a steaming basket in it, then add an inch or so of water to the pot. The water should not be touching the food in the basket. Bring the water to a boil and cover the pot. The water should boil gently; you may have to add more to prevent it from boiling away. To improvise a steamer or to steam foods that might stick to the basket, use a plate balanced on a tin can.

BOILING

Boiling is the most commonly used method for cooking beans, grains and some vegetables. Stews and soups are also prepared by boiling. Actually, the food ought to be brought to a boil and then gently simmered until done. To keep the internal heat of the cooking vessel at the proper temperature and to prevent evaporation of liquids, cover the pot with a lid. Some grains, like groats and rice, may be toasted in hot fat before adding liquid to them and boiling. Pressure cooking is often used in the boiling process because it saves time, nutrients and flavor. Be careful using the pressure cooker; do not overfill it or cook foods in it that will spatter and clog the pressure release mechanism. In blanching, another hot-water cooking method, you pour boiling water over food, then rinse the food with cold water. Blanching is used to remove the skins or hulls from various foods or to prepare them for further cooking.

BAKING

Vegetables are often better baked than boiled to keep their nutritional value locked into them; however, baking vegetables is often overlooked. If you brush produce with oil before baking, you will be "oven frying" it; it will be crispy but have fewer calories than if fried. Grains can also be baked in covered cooking vessels with liquid, as can beans. For all baked goods, cakes, custards and breads, in particular, the correct oven temperature is of utmost importance. Allow your oven to preheat for 10 minutes before you put the food in, then start timing. Since oven thermometers can be off by as much as 75 degrees (F), you might want to invest in an oven thermometer.

The broiler unit of your oven or toaster oven can be used to brown food and the tops of casseroles; you may also brush sliced vegetables with oil and broil them until tender. Eggplant and squash are well cooked this way.

Some foods are particularly good wrapped and baked. Grain mixtures can be enclosed in cabbage leaves, grape leaves or cornhusks and then baked. Vegetables can be wrapped in foil as well, then baked. Some people like to bake their spuds in foil, but we believe this makes potatoes too soggy.

FRYING

Many foods are best cooked if deep fried, sautéed or stir fried. Batter-dipped vegetables fried in deep fat are succulent and juicy if the oil is at the right temperature, the basic trick for all deep frying. Don't forget that the temperature of oil will fluctuate as foods are added or taken out, and only careful regulation of the burner will give you perfect results. A deep-frying thermometer or a thermostatically controlled electric deep-fry unit is a great help for beginners. To avoid excessive spattering of fat—which is very painful on the skin—make sure the fat isn't too hot. It should never be hot enough to smoke. If a droplet of moisture comes into contact with the hot oil, it will jump out of the pan and spatter you. So be sure not to put even a drop of water in hot oil or add food to it that is wet. Either coat the food with a moisture-sealing batter, or dry the food carefully with a paper towel. Also, don't allow the cooking utensils to get wet. Harder vegetables, like cauliflower or broccoli, are best deep fried. We like to deep fry in peanut oil as it smokes the least.

Sautéeing is like deep frying, except the food is not immersed in hot fat. To sautée, add a small bit of oil or butter to the pan, and then gently brown the food in the fat. This technique is used to cook vegetables that lose a lot of moisture during cooking—like mushrooms, onions, celery—and to gently brown foods like croquettes.

To stir fry vegetables, the oil must be very hot initially—but not so hot as to smoke. In the stir-frying process, the vegetables are first seared quickly, then some liquid is added. With the addition of a cover, the vegetables are allowed to steam in the vapors of the stock or water poured in. If a vegetable combination dish is to be done, don't dump in all the vegetables at once. Instead, the ones that take longer to cook should be added first, then the others later. Sometimes tougher vegetables such as broccoli stems or large slices of carrot are blanched first, then stir fried to insure tenderness. Almost any food can be stir fried. It's faster than sautéeing or deep frying, so there's less loss of nutrients. Stir-fried vegetables are crunchier than baked, boiled or sautéed ones.

COOKING FROZEN VEGETABLES

You can use the package directions, except we find that they usually call for too much liquid. Instead, use a saucepan with a heavy bottom and a very snug lid, add some oil or butter to the pan, and then add the vegetables. A spoonful of water will be enough moisture to add if you are careful to keep the heat low. Simmer the vegetables, covered, until barely tender, season to taste and serve.

CUTTING VEGETABLES

Cook vegetables without peeling whenever possible. They should be well scrubbed before you cut them into cooking-sized portions. Some vegetables like potatoes and beets are best cooked whole, while others like turnips and parsnips must be peeled and chunked first. For stir frying, stew or casseroles, vegetables should be cut according to how long they take to cook. If you're going to stir fry peas and carrots together, for example, you would have to cut the carrots in very fine strips so that they would be done at the same time as the peas.

Planning the Vegetarian Menu

A word about good eating is the best way to start. Some people have trouble controlling eating habits, and this is as bad as it is unnecessary. Once you start to eat natural foods, you should be more in touch with your body, and any bad habits should be overcome in time. The right amounts and right proportions of the right foods will stop the incessant urge to nibble, overeat or consume foods that are nothing more than empty calories. Natural goodness means that nature takes over to do good things. Give your body and its systems time to adjust, because the systems work in a natural process. Don't feel guilty or punish yourself if things don't work out right away. In any event, don't regard food as a regimen or medicine. Natural foods as part of a balanced diet are a sensuous pleasure to be enjoyed.

It's only fair, since it's one of man's prime concerns, that the consumption of fuel to keep the body running at peak efficiency should be a sensuous pleasure, not a chore. People who really enjoy eating eat less and savor more. Chew the food slowly, taste the various flavors alone and in combination with others, enjoy the way it looks and eat in a pleasant atmosphere. Eating "on the run" or when tensions and anxieties prevail may do some small amount of good in nourishing your body but will do nothing to fuel your spirit. If you whole-heartedly make an effort to make every meal a soul-satisfying as well as body-satisfying experience, food will serve its true human function.

Whether you eat alone or with the family, present food attractively. Garnishes and contrasting colors appeal to the eyes, while contrasting textures and tastes add excitement to every meal. Planning a pleasing appearance supports the primary purpose of the meal, to achieve a nutritional balance. If you plan well and cook well, you will make your life zestier, filled with more contrasts, as well as healthier.

To those of us used to a menu of meat, vegetables and potatoes, planning the vegetarian menu may present quite a challenge. But

once the basic complementary protein foods are understood, the
endless variety of nutritious stimulation will be worth exploring. It's
actually easier to offer variety on the vegetarian menu, because most
meat and potato folk tend to ignore the diversity of whole grains
and beans. The first step is to stop thinking of the dinner plate as a
surface with three different items—an entree, and two side dishes—
and begin to imagine different foods that are nutritionally balanced
and interesting. Sometimes you may plan a menu that includes soup,
bread and salad. Other times, think of a casserole with two or three
vegetables. While there's certainly nothing wrong with a menu
centered around some vegetables prepared and served "au naturel,"
try different combinations of sauces for a change of pace. Break out
of the traditional breakfast and luncheon! Breakfast doesn't have to
be cereal, juice and toast, nor does lunch have to be a sandwich and a
piece of fruit. A bowl of hot soup with homemade bread makes a
warming breakfast on winter mornings, while fruit, yogurt and whole
grain crackers make a cooling start in summer. Pack a container of
salad in the lunchbox along with a hot or cold soup for lunch.

To get the vital nutrients you need, you must know that most foods
contain incomplete proteins, i.e., they lack some of the vital amino
acids your body needs. Fortunately, these incomplete proteins can
be teamed with other incomplete proteins that complement them to
make up for the missing amino acids. For example, a food weak in
lysine but strong in tryptophan will fortify a food deficient in
tryptophan but strong in lysine. To gain nutritional benefits of the
combination of these foods, they must be eaten in the same meal.
You will also want to make sure that your diet contains an adequate
amount of fats and carbohydrates necessary for fuel. As a rule of
thumb when meal planning, think first of how to get some complete
protein in each meal and then consider the 4 food groups and the
number of servings from each group needed daily for a complete
spectrum of the necessary nutrients.

Grains, legumes, nuts and seeds will comprise the bulk of your
diet, and everyone should get at least 6 servings daily from this food
group. Three servings from the vegetable group are a daily must, and
at least 1 of those should be a green vegetable. For vitamins, minerals
and natural sugar, eat from 1 to 3 servings of fresh fruit a day. Two
glasses of milk a day or the equivalent in other dairy products will
round out your supply of nutrients. Of the 4 food groups mentioned,
milk and dairy products provide you with the most protein, but you

must supplement this protein with the vitamins and minerals in other food groups.

Below is a list of ways to combine different food groups to come up with balanced menus to help you start thinking about how to do it.

DAIRY PRODUCTS

Since dairy products contain complete protein, they really don't require any complement. What's good about the dairy group, however, is that it can be used in small amounts to balance any meal. For instance, you can combine whole wheat and a dairy product by serving pizza with a whole wheat crust, or whole wheat bread and just butter is a winning combination. Or try combining milk and rice by serving rice pudding or rice with cheese sauce. Match up milk and potatoes with a cream of potato soup or mashed potatoes. For a real protein boost, have a glass of milk with your peanut butter sandwich.

GRAINS, NUTS AND SEEDS

This group is deficient in isoleucine and lysine and must be combined with small quantities of brewer's yeast or dairy products. A little brewer's yeast goes a long way, and you can add a small amount to many dishes without affecting their flavor.

The most common complement to grains is legumes (peas, beans and lentils). All legumes, except black-eyed peas and mung beans, are strong in lysine. Try some of the following combinations for complete protein. Corn and legumes: tortillas and refried beans, or chili and cornbread. Rice and legumes: red beans and rice; stir-fried bean sprouts and rice. Wheat and legumes: any type of bean soup served with whole wheat bread; pasta e fagioli. Nuts and legumes: snow peas or bean sprouts topped with crushed nuts; green beans with almonds. Seed and legumes: tahini with mashed chick-peas (felafel), or sesame seeds sprinkled over cooked beans.

VEGETABLES

Fresh vegetables are weak in sulphur-containing acids. To fill out the deficiency, match them with foods that are strong in these acids. That includes sesame seeds, Brazil nuts, millet, wheat, bran, mushrooms, wheat germ and brewer's yeast. Ground sesame seeds or chopped Brazil nuts are great for flavoring any vegetable dish, and millet can be added to soups. You can also complement fresh vegetables by combining them with dairy products. Cheese sauce or yogurt over cooked vegetables would serve that purpose. Or a dollop of sour cream on your baked potato could round out the amount of available amino acids you're getting.

Now that you have some of the basics for choosing and preparing food as well as for planning a menu, go on to the recipes and start cooking.

Stay healthy and *bon appétit!*

Recipes

Appetizers and Sandwiches

Nutty Cheese Spread

1 1/2 cups cottage cheese
1/2 cup chopped walnuts
1/3 cup chopped figs
3/4 cup currants
1 teaspoon cinnamon
1 teaspoon honey

Place cottage cheese in a mixing bowl. Beat briskly until it takes on a smooth texture. Add all other ingredients and mix thoroughly. A blender may also be used to combine the ingredients.

This may be used as a spread or as a filling for sandwiches. It tastes especially delicious on cinnamon raisin bread or date nut bread. ❨ Makes approximately 2–2 1/2 cups or enough for 8 "healthy" sandwiches.

❦

Cheddar Onion Spread

1/2 cup cottage cheese
1/2 cup grated Cheddar cheese
1 tablespoon Homemade Mayonnaise (p. 225)
1 small scallion, minced

In a medium mixing bowl, combine all ingredients, making sure the cottage cheese and the Cheddar are mixed well.

This spread may be served immediately after preparation. However, the flavor becomes even more delightful after the spread is chilled for an hour or so.

[113]

It may be served with crackers as an appetizer or used as a sandwich filling.

❪ Makes 1 cup, enough to fill 2 or 3 sandwiches.

❁

Cottage Cheese Spread

3 dried black figs
1/2 cup chopped walnuts
1/2 cup raisins
1/2 pound cottage cheese
1 teaspoon cinnamon
1 tablespoon molasses
1/4 teaspoon ground ginger
dash of salt

Soak the figs in 1/2 cup cool water until they become soft. Discard the water and chop the figs in a large mixing bowl. Combine the figs with the walnuts and raisins. Stir well.

While mixing, gradually add the cottage cheese. Add the seasonings and mix thoroughly.

Chill.

May be served on a slice or two of whole wheat raisin bread or scooped onto a plate with sliced fruit for a light lunch.

❪ Makes 2 sandwiches.

❁

Baba Ghanoush

3 small eggplants
3 cloves garlic
1/4 cup tahini (sesame seed paste)
juice of one lemon
1/3 teaspoon ground cumin
salt to taste
1/4 cup sesame seeds

Preheat oven to 375 degrees.

Pierce the skin of the eggplants in several places with a fork to prevent exploding. Place the eggplants in a shallow baking pan and bake until they are soft and the skin is shriveled, 45 minutes to 1 hour. Remove from the oven and cool on a plate.

When they're cool enough to handle, cut the eggplants in half and scrape the pulp from the skins. Place the pulp in a blender along with all the other ingredients, including the salt, and puree until you have a smooth mixture. You may have to puree the ingredients in several batches depending on the capacity of your blender. Refrigerate for an hour or until chilled. Then stir in the sesame seeds.

Serve with heated pita bread and alfalfa sprouts.

❨ Makes 1 to 2 cups.

❦

Baba Omgush

4 medium eggplants

1/2 cup olive oil

1 cup tahini (sesame seed paste)

1/2 cup fresh lemon juice

1 pound carrots, shredded

1 small onion, minced

4 cloves garlic, mashed

1 bunch watercress, chopped, for garnish

Preheat oven to 350 degrees.

Pierce the skin of the eggplants in several places with a fork to prevent exploding. Place them in a baking pan and bake till soft, about 45 minutes to 1 hour.

Remove them from the oven and place on a plate until they're cool enough to handle, then cut them in half.

Scoop the meat from the skin and place in a large mixing bowl. Add all ingredients except watercress; mix well.

Chill.

Garnish with watercress and serve with crackers or heated pita.

❨ Yields 2 cups.

❦

Hummus bi Tahini

1 cup dried chick-peas

juice of 2 lemons

2 cloves garlic, or more to taste

3 tablespoons apple cider vinegar

1/2 cup tahini (sesame seed paste)

2 tablespoons olive oil

salt and freshly ground pepper to taste

1/2 cup chopped fresh parsley, lemon wedges and

*   cherry tomatoes for garnish*

Soak the chick-peas overnight in enough water to cover, then drain.

Cook the chick-peas in unsalted water to cover for about 1 hour. At the end of that time they should be soft enough to mash with a fork. Pour off the cooking water and save it to add to soup stock. Let the peas cool.

Blend the chick-peas in two batches with a blender, or mash them with a potato masher or fork. Place the lemon juice, garlic and vinegar in the blender and puree, or grind them with a mortar and pestle.

Add this mixture, along with the tahini and oil, to the mashed chick-peas. Stir until very smooth; season to taste with salt and pepper.

Chill before serving. Garnish with parsley, cherry tomatoes and lemon wedges. Crisp crackers or pita bread go nicely with this.
❲ Makes 3 cups.

❦

Hummus Plus

1 cup dried chick-peas

5 cloves garlic

1/4 cup fresh lemon juice

1/2 pound onions, minced

1 bunch dill, minced

1/4 cup sesame oil

Soak the chick-peas overnight in enough water to cover. Drain.

Cook the chick-peas in unsalted water to cover for about 1 hour, or until they are soft enough to mash with a fork.

In a blender, combine the cooked chick-peas, liquid from the cooked chick-peas, garlic, lemon juice, onions, dill and sesame oil. Blend until pureed.

Chill thoroughly.

Serve as a dip with crackers or pita bread. Or use this as a sandwich spread with sprouts and tomatoes.

❨ Makes 4 1/2 cups.

❦

Zucchini Fritters

2 medium zucchini
1/2 cup whole wheat flour
1/4 teaspoon curry powder
1/4 teaspoon sesame salt
1/4 teaspoon garlic powder
1/4 teaspoon onion powder
1 egg
olive oil for deep frying

Cut the zucchini into spears. Set aside.

Combine the dry ingredients in a mixing bowl. Stir to mix.

Beat the egg in a separate small dish until frothy.

Dip each spear in the egg and then in the flour mixture; then place in an oiled and heated frying pan. Fry until brown on all sides.

❨ Serves 4.

❦

Antipasto

marinade (recipe below)
broccoli flowerettes
string beans
carrots
mushrooms
cauliflower flowerettes
celery
any other vegetable you wish totaling 2 cups

Cut the vegetables into interesting shapes and steam them separately until crisp/tender.

Place the vegetables in a flat baking dish or on a plate with high sides. Pour the marinade over the vegetables.

Chill for several hours or overnight, tossing occasionally.

Drain and serve on a bed of romaine lettuce.

❲ Makes 2 cups and will serve 4.

MARINADE

1/2 cup olive oil
1/4 cup apple cider vinegar
1 large clove garlic, pressed
1/2 teaspoon basil
1/2 teaspoon oregano
1/4 teaspoon salt

Place everything in a jar with a cover and shake well. Refrigerate the marinade if you do not plan to use it right away.

❲ Makes about 1 cup, enough to marinate 2 cups of vegetables.

You can use any marinade that was not used in the antipasto as a base for a salad dressing. Just add 1/4 cup of either vinegar or lemon juice.

❧

Guacamole

2 avocados
2 tablespoons fresh lemon juice
1 clove garlic, pressed
2 small scallions, minced fine
dash cayenne pepper
salt or tamari (soy sauce) to taste
sliced tomatoes, shredded lettuce and sprouts for garnish

Halve the avocados. Remove the pits and scoop out the pulp.

In a small bowl, mash the pulp with a fork. Add the lemon juice, garlic, scallions, cayenne pepper and salt (or tamari). Mix thoroughly.

Serve immediately with heated pita bread and garnished with tomatoes, shredded lettuce and sprouts.

❲ Makes 1 cup.

If you would like to store guacamole in the refrigerator, place the avocado pit in the center of the mixture and it will keep the guacamole from discoloring.

❦

Stuffed Avocado

1 ripe medium avocado
1/2 cup chopped celery leaves
1/4 cup chopped fresh parsley
1/4 cup fresh lemon juice
1/4 cup safflower oil
1 teaspoon honey, or more to taste
1/4 cup fresh basil, if in season, or 2 tablespoons dried
1 clove garlic
lettuce, carrot and celery sticks for garnish

Halve the avocado. Remove the pit and carefully scoop out the pulp, saving the skin.

Combine the remaining ingredients in a blender with the avocado and blend till smooth.

Fill the avocado skin with the mixture; chill.

Serve on a bed of lettuce with sliced carrot and celery sticks.

([Serves 2.

❦

Peanut Butter 'n' Celery

4 stalks celery
1/2 cup coarsely grated carrots
2 tablespoons raisins
1 1/2 cups freshly ground peanut butter

Cut each celery stalk into 3-inch lengths.

In a small bowl, combine carrots, raisins and peanut butter. Mix well.

Spread on celery.

Great for after-school snacks for children.

([Serves 6 to 12.

❧

Stuffed Celery I

1/4 pound blue cheese
plain yogurt
3 stalks celery

Mash the blue cheese in a medium-sized mixing bowl and mix in enough yogurt to make a pastry texture, leaving a few lumps.

Stuff the celery stalks with the mixture, and then cut the celery into 1-inch pieces.

Serve cold.

❲ Serves 3 to 4.

❧

Stuffed Celery II

2 bunches chives, chopped
1 large onion, minced
1 bunch scallions, chopped
1 cup celery leaves, minced
1 pound cream cheese, at room temperature
salt and pepper to taste
celery stalks
paprika

In a mixing bowl, combine the chopped chives, onion, scallions and celery leaves. Begin to blend in the cream cheese, transfer to a blender and blend first at low speed, then at high until thoroughly mixed. Or mix by hand until thoroughly blended. Season to taste with salt and pepper.

Stuff the mixture into the celery, sprinkle with paprika and serve.

❲ Makes 3 cups, enough to fill about 4 dozen celery stalks.

❧

Vegetarian Chopped Liver

1 large onion, diced
1 large green pepper, chopped
1 pound string beans, steamed and chopped

3 hard-boiled eggs, chopped

1/2 cup chopped walnuts

2 1/2 tablespoons Homemade Mayonnaise (p. 225)

salt and pepper to taste

romaine lettuce, watercress and cherry tomato for garnish

In a medium skillet, sauté the onion along with the green pepper until the onion is translucent.

Place the steamed and chopped string beans in a large mixing bowl. Add the sautéed onion and pepper. Mix in the chopped eggs. Add the walnuts and mayonnaise and blend well. Season to taste with salt and pepper.

Chill.

Served on a bed of romaine lettuce with watercress and a cherry tomato as garnish.

《 Serves 4 to 6.

❧

Curried Egg Salad

4–6 hard-boiled eggs

1 small onion, minced

2 stalks celery, diced

1/2 cup chopped parsley

1 green pepper, diced

1/2 teaspoon curry powder

1/4 teaspoon rosemary

1/2 teaspoon thyme

2 tablespoons Homemade Mayonnaise (p. 225)

slivered almonds and romaine lettuce for garnish

In a large bowl, mash the hard-boiled eggs.

Add all the other ingredients, mayonnaise last. Mix thoroughly.

Garnish with the almonds and serve on a bed of romaine lettuce.

《 Serves 4.

❦

Peanut Butter and Banana

4 slices of whole wheat cinnamon raisin bread
1/2 cup peanut butter
1/4 cup shredded unsweetened coconut
1 banana, sliced
lettuce leaves and raisins for garnish

On two slices of the bread spread the peanut butter.

Sprinkle on the coconut. Arrange the banana slices on top of the coconut.

Cover with the other slices of bread. Cut each sandwich in quarters.

Serve on a plate with a leaf of lettuce and a sprinkle of raisins for garnish.

❦ Makes 2 sandwiches.

❦

Chick-Kidney Sandwich

1/2 pound dried chick-peas
1/2 pound red kidney beans, cooked
2 medium onions, diced
3 stalks celery, diced
2 carrots, shredded
3 cloves garlic, mashed
1/2 cup sesame oil
4 pita breads
1 cup alfalfa sprouts

Soak the chick-peas overnight in enough water to cover. Drain.

Cook the chick-peas in unsalted water to cover for about an hour, or until soft enough to mash with a fork. Drain.

In a blender combine chick-peas and kidney beans. Blend till you have a smooth consistency.

Place this mixture in a large mixing bowl and add the remaining ingredients, except for the bread and the sprouts. Mix thoroughly.

Stuff the pita bread with the mixture and top with sprouts.

❦ Makes 4 sandwiches.

❧

Grilled Cheddar and Pepper Sandwich

1 cup grated Cheddar cheese
1/4 cup minced green pepper
2 tablespoons Homemade Mayonnaise (p. 225)
1/2 medium clove garlic, minced
8 slices whole wheat bread
1/4 cup melted butter

In a medium mixing bowl, mix cheese, green pepper, mayonnaise and garlic.

Spread evenly on 4 slices of bread. Top with remaining slices of bread. Brush butter on both slices of each sandwich.

Toast under broiler 4 or 5 minutes on each side.

This sandwich is particularly good with a salad of sliced raw zucchini, mushrooms, tomatoes and chopped scallions.

⟮ Makes 4 sandwiches.

Soups

Vegetable Stock

4 cups of vegetable scraps (old, soft celery and carrots, onion
skins, potato peelings, etc.)
1 bulb garlic, separated into cloves but not peeled
2 quarts water

Place everything in a large soup pot. Bring to a boil and simmer, covered, for an hour. Remove from heat and let stand until the stock is cool enough to handle.

Strain, leaving a clear broth. Discard the vegetables.

Refrigerate the stock until you are ready to use it, which should be within a week.

❦ Makes 2 quarts.

To make low-sodium vegetable stock, follow the instructions above but use only low-sodium vegetables—no spinach, celery, radishes or watercress.

❧

Barley-Millet Soup

2 tablespoons olive oil
4 leeks, sliced, including the green part
1 stalk celery, chopped
1/4 pound mushrooms, sliced
3/4 cup barley
1/2 cup millet
7 cups water, or more if necessary
2–4 tablespoons brown rice miso (a grain paste)
1/2 cup water

In a soup pot, heat the oil. Add the leeks, celery and mushrooms. Sauté over medium heat for a few minutes until the vegetables are tender, and then add the barley and millet and continue sautéeing for 5 minutes or until the barley is browned.

Add the water and bring the mixture to a boil. Simmer for 1 hour, or until the barley is tender. Add more water if necessary to keep the barley from sticking to the bottom of the pot and stir occasionally to prevent scorching.

When the barley is cooked, dissolve the miso in the 1/2 cup water and stir it into the soup. Heat just until the mixture bubbles around the edge. *Do not boil.*

Serve warm.

❨ Makes 4 to 6 large servings.

Miso is available at many health food stores and Oriental markets.

❦

Black Bean Soup

3 tablespoons olive oil
1 onion, chopped
1 stalk celery, sliced
1 1/2 cups black beans, washed very well
3 cloves garlic
6 cups Vegetable Stock (p. 124)
1 teaspoon celery salt, or more to taste
2 tablespoons whole wheat flour
1/4–1/2 cup fresh lemon juice
2 hard-boiled eggs and lemon slices for garnish

In a large soup pot, heat the olive oil and sauté the onion and celery until the onion is translucent and the celery is wilted, or about 5 minutes.

Add the black beans, garlic and vegetable stock. Bring the mixture to a boil. Cover and simmer for 3 hours, or until the beans are very tender.

Add the celery salt and the flour. (If you measure the flour into a sifter and sift it into the soup, you never have trouble dissolving it.) Remove from heat.

Transfer the mixture in batches to a blender and puree. After pureeing each batch, pour the puree into a large bowl. When you have pureed the entire mixture, return it to the pot and cook until it thickens slightly, which will take about 20 minutes to a half hour.

Stir in the lemon juice, making sure to taste the soup as you do. Some people like a more lemony flavor than others.

Chop up the hard-boiled eggs and place them in a dish to be served on the side. Garnish the soup with the lemon slices and serve.

(Makes 6 to 8 servings.

❧

Thick and Hearty Borscht

4 tablespoons olive oil
2 onions, chopped
5 beets: 3 grated, 2 chopped
1 large carrot, sliced
2 leeks, sliced (optional)
2 cups shredded red cabbage
2 cups shredded green cabbage
2 teaspoons caraway seeds
1 teaspoon salt
2 tablespoons apple cider vinegar
1 bay leaf
2 cloves garlic
2 quarts Vegetable Stock (p. 124)
2 potatoes, boiled and diced
sour cream for garnish

Heat the oil in a very large soup pot. Add all of the vegetables and cook over low heat for 10 minutes, stirring constantly, making sure all pieces get cooked. The vegetables should be tender but not over-cooked.

Add the seasonings and stock. Bring to a boil and simmer for 1 hour until everything is very tender.

Add boiled potatoes.

Serve warm with sour cream on top.

(Makes 6 to 8 servings.

🌷

Chick-Pea Soup

1 cup chick-peas
4 tablespoons olive oil
1 onion, sliced
2 carrots, sliced
1 stalk celery, sliced
1 teaspoon celery salt
1 1/2 teaspoons garlic powder
1 teaspoon parsley flakes
1 cup milk
2 tablespoons tamari (soy sauce) (optional)
1 egg, beaten
1/4 cup sour cream
1/4 cup chopped scallions for garnish

Soak the chick-peas overnight in a large soup pot with enough water to cover. Do not drain.

Then add the chick-peas (including the water they were soaking in), celery salt, garlic powder and parsley. Cover with additional water so that the water level is 1 inch above the vegetables. Bring this mixture to a boil. Cover and simmer until the chick-peas are soft, which should take about 1 1/2 hours. Remove from heat.

Transfer the mixture in batches to a blender and puree.

Return the pureed mixture to the pot and add the milk. If you would like to season the mixture further, add 2 tablespoons tamari. Slowly bring the soup to a boil over low to medium heat. When the soup begins to boil, remove the pot from the heat.

In a separate mixing bowl, mix together the beaten egg and the sour cream and then slowly stir this mixture into the hot soup.

Scatter the chopped scallions on top of the soup and serve.

❨ Makes 6 servings.

❦

Tangy Lemon Egg Soup

2 quarts Vegetable Stock (p. 124)
1/4 cup raw brown rice
4 eggs, beaten well
1/2 teaspoon tarragon
juice of 1 lemon
freshly ground pepper to taste
grated lemon rind

In a large soup pot, bring the stock to a boil and add the rice. Cover and simmer until the rice is tender, about 45 minutes.

Meanwhile, combine the beaten eggs with the tarragon and lemon juice. Allow the broth and rice to cool, then transfer in batches to a blender and puree until smooth. Return the mixture to the pot.

Bring the soup to a slow boil, then gradually add a ladle of it to the egg mixture.

Bring the soup in the pot up to a boil and then turn off the heat. Now stir in the egg mixture very slowly to thicken the soup.

Season to taste with pepper and add a dash of grated lemon rind to each bowl. Serve with a hummus sandwich for a "soup and sandwich" lunch.

This soup will not reheat well; if it's allowed to boil it will curdle.

❦

Curried Lentil Soup

1 tablespoon olive oil
1 large onion, sliced
5 cups water
1 cup lentils
4 scallions, sliced
1 celery stalk, sliced
1 carrot, sliced
1 teaspoon ground coriander
1 teaspoon turmeric
1/2 teaspoon ground cumin

1 teaspoon paprika

1/8 teaspoon cayenne pepper

1/4 teaspoon ground ginger

1 teaspoon garlic powder

1 tablespoon tamari (soy sauce)

1/2 teaspoon salt

1/4 cup chopped parsley for garnish

Heat oil in a medium-sized soup pot. Add onion and sauté until the onions are translucent.

Add water, lentils, vegetables and spices and bring to a boil. Then lower the heat and allow to simmer for about 1 hour, until the lentils are soft.

Garnish with parsley.

([Serves 4.

❧

Lentil Barley Soup

2 tablespoons safflower oil

2 cups lentils

1 cup barley

1 cup chopped onions

6–8 cups water

1 cup sliced celery

1/2 cup sliced carrots

1/2 teaspoon tarragon, or to taste

salt to taste

pepper to taste

In a large saucepan, heat the oil and sauté the lentils, barley and onion until the onion is translucent, about 5 minutes.

Add the water. Bring the mixture to a boil and then reduce the flame. Simmer for about 20 minutes or until the barley is tender.

Add the celery and carrots. Season to taste and cook for another 10 minutes or until the carrots are done.

([Serves 6.

❦

Mushroom Lentil Soup I

1 tablespoon olive oil
1 tablespoon unsalted butter
1/2 pound mushrooms, sliced
6 cups Vegetable Stock (p. 124)
1 cup lentils
1 small onion, minced
2 tablespoons tamari (soy sauce)

In a medium soup pot, heat the oil, then add the butter. When the butter has melted, add the mushrooms. Sauté until the mushrooms are soft.

Add stock, lentils, onion and tamari. Bring to a boil; lower heat and allow to simmer for 1 hour.

⟮ Serves 4.

❦

Mushroom Lentil Soup II

1 cup sliced mushrooms
3 stalks celery, chopped
3 scallions, chopped
1/4 cup parsley flakes
1 bay leaf
6 cups water
3 tablespoons olive oil
1 teaspoon garlic powder
2 cups lentils
kelp to taste
pepper to taste
12 ounces tomato sauce
1 cup mung bean sprouts

Place the vegetables, parsley, bay leaf and water in a large soup pot. Add the oil, garlic powder and lentils. Stir well. Add kelp and pepper to taste. Then add the tomato sauce. Cook over low heat for approximately 1 1/2 to 2 hours or until the lentils are tender.

About 15 minutes before the soup is done, add the bean sprouts. Store this soup in the refrigerator overnight to get its full flavor.
([Serves 6 to 8.

❧

Sweet and Sour Lentil Soup

5 cups Vegetable Stock (p. 124)
1 cup apple juice
1 cup lentils
1 carrot, sliced
1 large stalk celery, sliced
1 teaspoon garlic powder
1 teaspoon onion powder
2 teaspoons parsley flakes
2 tablespoons apple cider vinegar
1 tablespoon tamari (soy sauce), or to taste

Combine the stock and apple juice in a medium-size soup pot and bring to a boil.

Add lentils, carrot, celery, garlic powder, onion powder and parsley. Again bring the mixture to a boil, then lower heat and allow to simmer for 30 minutes.

Add vinegar and tamari. Correct the seasonings. Continue to simmer for about 20 minutes or until the lentils are soft.
([Makes 4 servings.

Green Lima Bean Soup

1 cup dried green lima beans
1/2 cup split peas
6 cups low-sodium Vegetable Stock* (p. 124)
1 bulb garlic or about 12 cloves, pressed
1/4 cup chopped fresh parsley
1/4 cup chopped fresh dill
1 large onion, sliced thin
2 teaspoons onion powder
1 tablespoon garlic powder
1/2 bunch broccoli, chopped, including the leaves
1 zucchini, sliced thin
1 yellow summer squash, sliced thin
1 bunch scallions, chopped, for garnish

Soak the lima beans overnight in enough water to cover. Drain.

Place the lima beans, split peas, stock, garlic cloves, parsley, dill, onion, onion powder and garlic powder in a medium-sized soup pot. Bring to a boil and then reduce to a simmer and cook for about 45 minutes to 1 hour, until the beans and split peas are soft.

Add the broccoli, zucchini, and yellow squash. Cook for about 10 minutes or until the broccoli and squash are tender.

Remove from the heat. Stir in the scallions.

Serve warm.

❨ Makes 4 to 6 servings.

* You may use homemade stock as long as it hasn't been made with vegetables that have a high sodium content such as spinach, celery, radishes or watercress. You might use a low-sodium vegetable powder to be sure.

Miso Tofu Soup

1 tablespoon olive oil
2 cloves garlic, pressed
1–2 carrots, sliced thin
1 large celery stalk, sliced

4 cups water

1 tablespoon parsley flakes

1 teaspoon onion powder

1/2 teaspoon oregano

1/2 pound tofu (bean curd), pressed and cubed

1/2 cup mung bean sprouts

4 scallions, sliced

4 tablespoons brown rice miso (a grain paste)

2 scallions, sliced for garnish

In a large saucepan, heat the oil. Add the garlic, carrots and celery and sauté until the garlic turns golden.

Add the water, parsley, onion powder and oregano, and allow to simmer for 10 minutes.

Now add the tofu, sprouts and scallions.

Remove 1 cup of liquid from the pot and dissolve the miso in it. Return the mixture to the saucepan and bring to a boil.

Garnish with scallions and serve immediately.

(Makes 4 servings.

Tofu can now be found in many supermarkets and Oriental markets. Miso is available in many health food stores and Oriental markets.

❧

Mushroom and Vegetable Soup

2 tablespoons unsalted butter

1/2 pound mushrooms, sliced

2 large or 4 small leeks, sliced

3 cloves garlic, pressed

4 cups low-sodium Vegetable Stock* (p. 124)

1–2 carrots, sliced thin

3 tablespoons minced fresh parsley

1 tablespoon minced fresh dill

1 cup chopped spinach (optional)

Melt the butter in a large heavy saucepan. Add the mushrooms, leeks, and garlic and sauté until the mushrooms are soft.

Add the stock, carrots, parsley and dill. Bring to a boil and then simmer for 20 to 30 minutes to allow all of the flavors to blend. At this point you may add the spinach and allow to simmer for another 3 minutes.

You can also add cooked rice or other grains or cooked beans to this soup; add them after the soup has been brought to a boil.

This soup is also good as a base for other soups, lentil, for instance.

Serve warm.

(Serves 4.

* You may use homemade stock as long as it hasn't been made with vegetables that have a high sodium content such as spinach, celery, radishes or watercress. You might use a low-sodium vegetable powder to be sure.

❦

Peanut Butter Soup

2 tablespoons unsalted butter

2 scallions, chopped

6 tablespoons peanut butter

4 tablespoons whole wheat flour

6 cups milk

1/2 cup salted peanuts and 6 sprigs parsley for garnish

In a large soup pot, heat the butter. Add the scallions and peanut butter. Cook over medium heat for 5 to 10 minutes.

Whisk in the flour and stir until the mixture becomes smooth. Gradually add the milk.

Transfer this mixture to a double boiler and cook, stirring occasionally, for 30 to 45 minutes until the mixture is smooth and heated through.

Add the peanuts and parsley as garnish and serve hot. This soup goes particularly well with yogurt, cottage cheese and fruit.

(Serves 6 to 8.

❦

Celery Potato Chowder

1–2 tablespoons safflower oil

1 small onion, chopped

1 bunch celery, chopped

3 medium potatoes, diced

2 cups water

sea salt to taste

2 tablespoons butter

2 tablespoons whole wheat flour

4 cups milk

1–2 teaspoons chives for garnish

Heat the oil in a medium-sized soup pot and sauté the onion until the onion begins to brown.

Add the celery, potatoes and water. Salt to taste. Bring the mixture to a boil, then simmer for 30 minutes.

Melt the butter in a medium saucepan and then whisk in the flour.

Gradually add the milk, stirring constantly, bringing the mixture to a boil over a low to medium heat. Stir until the mixture thickens slightly.

Add the milk-flour mixture to the celery-potato mixture and simmer until smooth and thickened.

Top with some chives and serve warm.

❪ Makes 4 to 6 servings.

This soup must be reheated carefully and not allowed to boil or it will curdle.

❦

Potato Leek Soup

1/4 cup unsalted butter

6–8 leeks, sliced, including green part

4 potatoes, sliced thin

1 teaspoon celery salt

1 tablespoon parsley flakes

6 cups water

2 cups milk

Melt the butter in a large soup pot. Add the leeks and sauté them for about 5 minutes, or until they become translucent.

Add the potatoes, celery salt, parsley and water. Cook over low heat until the potatoes are soft, which should take about 45 minutes.

Add the milk and stir well. Simmer for an additional 10 or 15 minutes until heated through, but don't allow to boil.

Serve warm.

([Makes 4 to 6 servings.

This soup can be reheated carefully if not allowed to boil, otherwise it will curdle.

❦

Turkish Spinach Soup

8 cups Vegetable Stock (p. 124)

sea salt to taste

1 large carrot, chopped or sliced thin

1 stalk celery, chopped

1 pound spinach, washed and chopped

2 tablespoons unsalted butter

2 tablespoons whole wheat flour

3 eggs, beaten

juice of 1 lemon

2 tablespoons chopped fresh parsley and 1 tablespoon chopped
fresh dill for garnish

Season the vegetable stock with the sea salt (to taste) in a large soup pot. Add the carrot and celery and cook for about 5 minutes.

Add the spinach and cook for an additional 10 minutes, or until all the vegetables are soft and cooked.

Melt the butter in a small saucepan. Whisk in the flour and stir over very low heat for 3 to 5 minutes. Add a ladle of soup and stir well. Then transfer this mixture into the larger pot containing the vegetables and the stock. Continue to simmer over low heat for about 10 minutes.

Beat the eggs in a separate bowl and add the lemon juice. Add a ladle of soup and beat well. Pour this mixture into the larger pot, stirring continuously.

Heat the soup until it is just about to boil.

Sprinkle with the parsley and the dill and serve.

([Makes 4 servings.

☙

Tofu Millet Soup

2 tablespoons safflower oil

1 onion, chopped

4 cloves garlic, pressed

1/2 cup millet

5 cups low-sodium Vegetable Stock* (p. 124)

2 teaspoons onion powder

2 teaspoons garlic powder

1 tablespoon chopped fresh parsley

1 tablespoon basil

1 teaspoon dill

1 teaspoon tarragon

1 teaspoon oregano

1/4–1/2 pound fresh green peas, shelled

1/2 pound tofu (bean curd), pressed (p. 59) and cut into
      small pieces

Heat the oil in a large heavy saucepan. Add the onion, garlic and millet and sauté until the onion is translucent and the garlic golden but not browned, about 5 minutes, stirring constantly.

Add the vegetable stock and spices. Bring to a boil, then reduce to a simmer. Cook for about 30 minutes, until the millet is just cooked.

Add the peas and the tofu and simmer about 10 minutes, until the peas are cooked. Be careful not to overcook because the peas are at peak flavor when they are just tender.

❨ Serves 4.

Tofu is available at many supermarkets now, and also at Oriental markets.

* You may use homemade stock as long as it hasn't been made with vegetables that have a high sodium content such as spinach, celery, radishes or watercress. You might use a low-sodium vegetable powder to be sure.

❦

Minestrone

1 pound white navy beans
3 tablespoons olive oil
2 cloves garlic, minced
1 cup chopped onion
1 cup chopped celery
1/2 pound spinach or escarole, washed and torn
2 carrots, sliced
6 cups water
4 cups Vegetable Stock (p. 124)
1 tablespoon salt
1 teaspoon oregano, or to taste
1 teaspoon basil, or to taste
1 pound tomatoes, peeled and chopped
1/2 cup small pasta (whole wheat)
grated Parmesan cheese for garnish

Soak the beans in a large soup pot overnight in enough water to cover them.

Heat the oil in a large skillet. Sauté the garlic, onion and celery in the oil until they are tender, about 5 minutes.

Then add the spinach or escarole and the carrots and 6 cups of water. Put a cover on the skillet and cook over low heat for 10 minutes, stirring occasionally.

After 10 minutes, transfer this vegetable mixture into the large pot containing the beans. Stir in the vegetable stock, salt, oregano and basil. Cover the pot and simmer for 1 hour, or until the beans are tender.

Add the tomatoes and pasta. Cook uncovered for 20 minutes or until the pasta is tender.

Serve warm and sprinkle with Parmesan cheese.

❡ Makes 6 to 8 servings.

❦

Vegetable Noodle Soup

1 tablespoon sesame oil
1 onion, chopped
1 carrot, sliced thin
1 small green pepper, chopped
1 stalk celery, sliced
6 cups Vegetable Stock (p. 124)
1–1 1/2 cups small pasta (whole wheat)
tamari (soy sauce) to taste
1/2 bunch broccoli, chopped
1 bunch scallions, sliced
4 tablespoons miso (soybean paste)

Heat the sesame oil in a medium-sized soup pot. Add the onion, carrots, green pepper, and celery. Sauté until all the vegetables are tender, about 5 minutes.

Add the stock and the pasta. Bring the soup to a boil, then cook for 15 minutes, or until the pasta is almost cooked.

Add the tamari and broccoli and cook for 5 minutes longer. Add the scallions.

Remove about 1 cup of liquid from the pot and dissolve the miso in it. Return the mixture to the rest of the soup and bring to a light boil.

Serve hot.

❡ Makes 6 servings.

Miso is available in health food stores and Oriental markets.

❦

Cream of Broccoli Soup

1 bunch broccoli
3 cups water, salted
1/4 cup unsalted butter
1 onion, chopped
1 teaspoon kelp
1/2 teaspoon garlic powder
1 teaspoon celery salt
1 tablespoon parsley flakes
2 tablespoons whole wheat flour
1 cup milk

Separate the broccoli stalks and cut off the flowerettes, setting aside 1 cup of the flowerettes for use later. Peel the stems and then chop them. In a soup pot, cook the chopped stems and all but the reserved flowerettes in the salted water for approximately 10 minutes, or until tender.

Place half the butter in a frying pan and sauté the onion until it is translucent. Add the onion to the broccoli as it boils. Stir the broccoli-onion mixture, then add the seasonings. Remove from heat.

Place in batches in a blender and puree. Return to the pot.

Melt the remaining butter in a separate saucepan. Whisk in the flour and then add the milk. Stir well over low to medium heat until the sauce thickens. Add this mixture to the prepared soup. Drop in the reserved flowerettes and simmer for approximately 15 minutes.

Serve warm.

❨ Makes 4 to 5 servings.

❦

Creamy Celery Soup

2 tablespoons unsalted butter
1 large onion, sliced
2 cups celery, chopped
2 ounces Vegetable Stock (p. 124)
1/2 cup milk

1/2 cup cream

2 tablespoons whole wheat flour

1 cup water

dash of kelp

dash of pepper

Melt the butter in a large soup pot. Sauté the onions, and the celery in the butter until the onions become translucent, then add all the other ingredients. Correct seasonings.

Bring to a boil; then simmer for approximately 45 minutes.

This soup may be served hot or cold.

(Serves 4.

🌷

Cream of Mushroom Soup

4 tablespoons unsalted butter

1 pound mushrooms, sliced

1 onion, chopped

2 stalks celery, chopped

3 cups water

1 tablespoon parsley flakes

1 teaspoon salt

1/2 teaspoon garlic powder

2 tablespoons whole wheat flour

1 1/2 cups light cream

Melt half the butter in a skillet and sauté the mushrooms until they are browned. Remove the mushrooms from the pan and set them aside. Sauté the onion and the celery in the butter remaining in the skillet—you may need to add a little more butter—until the onion is translucent and the celery is wilted.

Place the water in a large soup pot. Add the onion, celery, three-fourths of the sautéed mushrooms, the parsley, salt and garlic powder. Cook over low heat for about 25 minutes. Remove from heat.

Transfer the soup to a blender in batches and puree. Return it to the pot with the rest of the mushrooms.

Melt the remaining butter in a saucepan. Whisk in the flour and then add the cream, stirring over low heat until the mixture thickens. Add this mixture to the soup and stir well. Simmer for another 10 minutes or until heated through, then serve.

◖ Serves 4.

This soup can be reheated if not allowed to boil.

❦

Cream of Sweet Potato Soup

2 tablespoons unsalted butter

3 cloves garlic, minced or pressed

1 large onion, thinly sliced

2 sweet potatoes (about 1 pound), sliced

2 cups low-sodium Vegetable Stock* (p. 124)

1 bunch watercress

2 tablespoons minced fresh parsley

2 cups milk**

2 egg yolks

In a large heavy saucepan melt the butter. Add the garlic and onion and sauté over a medium heat until the garlic turns a golden brown.

Add the sweet potatoes and stock. Bring to a boil. Then turn the heat down and simmer for 10 minutes, until the sweet potatoes are soft.

Wash the watercress well. Save a handful of leaves to be used as a garnish later. Add the rest of the watercress, the parsley and the milk to the sweet potatoes and simmer for about 10 minutes.

Remove from heat. Puree in batches in blender and then return to the pot.

Heat until the first bubbles appear around the edge, and then stir in the egg yolks until they thicken the soup.

To serve, garnish with the remaining watercress.

◖ Makes 4 to 6 servings.

This soup can be reheated if not allowed to boil.

* You may use homemade stock as long as it has not been made with vegetables that have a high sodium content. You might use low-sodium vegetable powder to be sure.

** Depending on how strict your diet is, low-sodium dry milk that has been reconstituted works very well here.

🌷

Gazpacho

36 ounces tomato juice
2 green peppers, chopped
6 medium tomatoes, chopped
2 large onions, coarsely chopped
2 large cucumbers, coarsely chopped
2 canned pimientos, drained
1/4 teaspoon coarsely ground pepper
4 teaspoons tamari (soy sauce)
2/3 cup olive oil
1/2 teaspoon Tabasco
2/3 cup red wine vinegar
4 cloves garlic, split
1 cup chopped scallions

In a large mixing bowl, combine 1 cup tomato juice with half the green pepper, two-thirds of the tomatoes, half the onions, half the cucumber and 1 pimiento. Transfer to a blender and blend at high speed for approximately 1 minute. Most likely you will have to do this in several batches. Put each of the remaining chopped vegetables in a separate dish, cover and refrigerate.

Place the pureed vegetables in a large mixing bowl and add the remaining tomato juice, the pepper and tamari, olive oil, Tabasco and vinegar.

Chill, covered, in the refrigerator for at least 3 hours. Also chill the bowls and the soup tureen that you plan to use for the gazpacho.

Stir the garlic into the soup just before serving. Mix well, preferably with a wire whisk. Sprinkle the scallions on top of the soup.

Serve with the reserved chopped vegetables on the side of the plate or in separate bowls.

❡ Serves 5 or 6.

❦

Fruit Soup

1 pound mixed dried fruit (apricots, apples, figs, prunes,
     peaches, etc.)

6 cups water

2 1/2 cups apple juice

1 small cinnamon stick

2 medium apples, cored and cubed but not peeled

2 large pears, cored and cubed but not peeled

1 pint strawberries, hulled and sliced

juice of 1 lemon

2 tablespoons honey, or to taste

yogurt or sour cream and fresh mint for garnish

Combine dried fruit, water, apple juice and cinnamon stick in a large saucepan. Bring to a boil and allow to cook over medium heat for 30 minutes, then discard cinnamon stick.

Add the apples and pears. Cook for an additional 3 to 5 minutes, or until the apples and pears are just barely tender.

Add the strawberries and cook for 2 to 3 minutes more.

Remove from the heat. Stir in lemon juice and honey.

Refrigerate until well chilled—2 to 3 hours.

When serving, top with the yogurt or sour cream and a sprig of fresh mint, if available.

❨ Makes 8 servings.

❦

Chilled Cantaloupe Soup

1 teaspoon agar flakes

2 tablespoons water

1 cup orange or tangerine juice

1 tablespoon lemon juice

2 cups diced cantaloupe

sour cream for garnish

Place agar, water and 1/4 cup of the orange juice in a small saucepan. Bring to a boil, reduce heat and simmer until the agar dissolves (about 10 minutes).

Place this mixture in a blender along with the remaining orange or tangerine juice and the lemon juice as well as the cantaloupe pieces. Blend until the mixture is pureed.

Chill in the refrigerator for at least 1 hour, preferably longer.

Just before serving, return the mixture to the blender for 1 to 2 minutes.

Serve with a spoonful of sour cream on top.

([Makes 3 to 4 servings.

❦

Cold Strawberry Soup

1 pint strawberries, hulled

1 cup fruit juice (orange, papaya, apple-strawberry)

juice of 1 lemon

2 tablespoons arrowroot

honey to taste (optional)

3/4 cup sour cream

sour cream for garnish

Place three-quarters of the strawberries and the cup of fruit juice into a blender and puree. Pour the mixture into a saucepan.

Dissolve the arrowroot in the lemon juice and pour this mixture into the saucepan as well. Cook over medium heat until the mixture thickens, about 5 minutes. Remove from the heat and add honey if you like things real sweet.

Slice the remaining strawberries and fold them, along with the sour cream, into the slightly cooled mixture. Refrigerate 2 to 3 hours until well chilled.

Serve cold with a teaspoonful of sour cream on top.

([Makes 4 to 6 servings.

Stir-Fry Apples and Celery

2 tablespoons unsalted butter

2 tablespoons sesame oil

1 tablespoon lemon juice

2 cups thinly sliced celery

2 medium apples, peeled, cored and sliced thin (about 2 cups)

1/2 teaspoon salt

1/4 teaspoon pepper

Heat butter and oil in a large skillet or wok. Stir in the lemon juice and celery; fry over high heat for 5 minutes, or until almost tender.

Add the apples. Continue cooking and stirring for 5 minutes or until tender.

Sprinkle with salt and pepper.

❨ Serves 2 to 3 as an entree. Can be served hot or cold.

❦

Herb-Buttered Potatoes and Peas

1 pound potatoes, unpeeled and scrubbed

1/2 cup unsalted butter

3/4 teaspoon sea salt

1/4 teaspoon marjoram

1/4 teaspoon thyme

1/4 teaspoon pepper

1/2 bay leaf

1 pound fresh peas, steamed

In a large pot, boil the potatoes in water to cover until almost tender, about 45 minutes. Drain. Cube the potatoes and then return them to the pot.

Add the butter, salt, and the seasonings. Cover. Cook over medium heat for about 15 minutes, until the butter has melted and the flavors are blended, stirring occasionally.

Stir in steamed peas. Heat for an additional 3 to 5 minutes.
(［ Serves 4 to 6.

❦

Broccoli Almondine

1 tablespoon unsalted butter

1 cup chopped broccoli

2 scallions with 1 inch green tops, chopped

1/4 cup slivered almonds

Melt the butter in a skillet. Stir in all ingredients. Fry, stirring, until the broccoli is tender but crunchy.
(［ Serves 1 or 2 as side dish.

❦

Broccoli au Gratin

1 bunch broccoli

2 tablespoons unsalted butter

2 tablespoons whole wheat flour

1 1/2 cups white wine

1/4 pound sharp Cheddar cheese, grated

Cut the broccoli into stalks and cut the stems into bite-sized pieces. Steam the broccoli until it is just tender. While the broccoli is steaming, butter or oil a medium-size casserole. Put the steamed broccoli into the casserole.

Preheat oven to 350 degrees.

Melt the butter in a saucepan and whisk in the flour. Gradually add the white wine, whisking until well blended. Add the grated cheese while stirring constantly. Continue cooking over medium heat until the sauce thickens, about 15–20 minutes.

Pour the sauce over the broccoli. Bake for 15 minutes.
(［ Serve 4 as a main dish.

❦

Broccoli Crunch

1 bunch broccoli
2 tablespoons unsalted butter
1 cup safflower oil
1/2 cup whole wheat bread crumbs
1 cup wheat germ
2 hard-boiled eggs, chopped

Preheat oven to 325 degrees.

Steam the broccoli with the cover off until just tender. Butter a deep casserole. Put in the steamed broccoli and cover the casserole with a damp cloth to prevent the broccoli from drying out.

Heat the oil in a medium saucepan; add the bread crumbs and wheat germ and cook until golden brown. Remove from heat; stir in the eggs.

Remove the cloth from the broccoli and sprinkle the egg mixture over the broccoli. Heat in the oven till warm, about 30 minutes.

❨ Serves 4 as an entree.

❦

Broccoli Supreme

2 bunches broccoli, flowerettes only, blanched
1 cup kasha, cooked, a little firm (p. 62, but use less water)
4 teaspoons fresh lemon juice
1/2 pound ricotta salade (a brick cheese) or mozzarella
1/2 cup all-blend oil
2 cups water
1 tablespoon miso (soybean paste)
2 tablespoons Vegebase (a seasoning)
grated ricotta salade or mozzarella for garnish

Preheat oven to 350 degrees.

In a large mixing bowl, combine the blanched broccoli flowerettes, the cooked kasha, lemon juice, ricotta salade, and the oil. Mix until blended.

In a medium saucepan, heat the water, the miso and the Vegebase until everything has dissolved.

Mix together the stock and the broccoli mixture in a large roasting pan. Cover and bake until the kasha absorbs the liquid, about 30 minutes.

Serve with some grated ricotta salade or mozzarella on top.

❲ Serves 4 to 6 as an entree.

Miso is available at most health food stores and in Oriental markets. Vegebase is found in most health food stores.

❧

Golden Broccoli Supreme

1 bunch broccoli

1/4 cup unsalted butter

1/2 cup orange juice

1/2 teaspoon sea salt

1 orange, peeled and sectioned

1/2 teaspoon nutmeg

Break the broccoli into stalks and steam for 5 minutes. Place the broccoli in a shallow 1 1/2-quart casserole.

Preheat oven to 350 degrees.

Combine the butter, orange juice and salt in a small mixing bowl. Pour over broccoli. Arrange the orange sections on top; sprinkle with nutmeg. Bake for 1 hour.

❲ Serves 2 to 4 as an entree.

❧

Brussels Sprouts Creole

1 1/2 pounds brussels sprouts

1/2 cup safflower oil

1 pound onions, sliced

1 pound green peppers, chopped fine

2 garlic cloves, pressed

8 fresh tomatoes, coarsely chopped

1 cup water

rind grated from 4 lemons

basil, salt and pepper to taste

Make a cut in the base of each sprout.

In a medium saucepan, heat the oil, then sauté the onions, green peppers and garlic. When the onions are translucent, add the tomatoes, the water, brussels sprouts and the seasonings. Correct the seasonings. Bring the mixture to a boil; simmer until the sprouts are soft, about 10 minutes.

Serve as an accompaniment to an omelet or alone.

◖ Serves 4 to 6 as an entree.

❦

Stuffed Cabbage

3 quarts water, or enough to cover cabbage
1 head cabbage (1–3 pounds), cored
2 stalks celery, diced
1 cup shredded red cabbage
1 cup diced green peppers
1 cup grated Cheddar cheese
1/2 cup chopped almonds
salt and pepper to taste
sliced cheese of your choice (optional) for garnish

Preheat oven to 350 degrees.

Boil the water in a pot large enough to accommodate the cabbage. When the water is boiling, put the cabbage in and boil until the leaves are soft. Turn out into the sink and rinse with cold water.

Remove the leaves from the head, being careful not to tear them.

In a large bowl, blend together the remaining ingredients. Place about 2 tablespoonfuls in each cabbage leaf and roll up, tucking in the sides. Place the cabbage rolls in a greased baking dish and bake till warm, about 30–45 minutes.

If you wish, you may top with slices of cheese before baking.

◖ Serves 8 to 10 as a side dish.

❦

Candied Carrots

1–1 1/2 pounds carrots, sliced
3 tablespoons unsalted butter
1 1/2 tablespoons honey
1/2 teaspoon cinnamon
1/2 teaspoon nutmeg
1/4 teaspoon salt

Place the carrots in a medium saucepan with about 1/4 cup water and cook, covered, for about 15 minutes, or until the carrots are tender when pricked with a fork.

In another saucepan, melt the butter and stir in the honey. Stir the remaining ingredients into the butter and cook over low heat for 5 to 10 minutes. Pour the butter mixture over the cooked carrots, stirring well so that the carrots are all covered with the glaze.

⟨ Makes 6 to 8 servings.

❧

Cauliflower-Broccoli Dinner

2–3 tablespoons sesame oil

1 large red onion, coarsely chopped

1 clove garlic, chopped fine

1 cup tahini (sesame seed paste)

1/4 teaspoon rosemary

1/4 teaspoon pepper

1/4 cup tamari (soy sauce)

2 pounds broccoli

1 medium-sized cauliflower

2 large red peppers, sliced fine

In a medium saucepan, heat the oil and sauté the onion and garlic until the garlic is golden, about 10 minutes. Stir in the tahini; mix well. Then add the rosemary, pepper and tamari, mixing thoroughly. Bring the mixture almost to a boil. Turn off the heat, cover and allow to stand.

Meanwhile, break the broccoli into stalks and separate the cauliflower into flowerettes. Put the cauliflower into a steamer and steam 10 minutes. Add the broccoli and steam an additional 6 minutes.

To serve, mound the broccoli in the center of a platter, surround it with a row of cauliflower and then a row of red pepper. Pour the tahini-onion sauce over the vegetables.

⟨ Serves 4 as an entree.

❦

Caponata

2 small eggplants, about 1/2 pound each
salt
3 tablespoons olive oil
1 large onion, sliced thin
2 cloves garlic, minced
4 stalks celery, chopped
4 tomatoes, peeled and chopped fine
water as needed
1 tablespoon pignolia nuts (optional)
2 tablespoons capers, drained
2–3 tablespoons apple cider vinegar
salt and pepper to taste

Slice the unpeeled eggplants about 1/4 inch thick. Arrange on a plate and sprinkle with salt. Set aside for 30 minutes. Drain well and rinse with cold water. Squeeze gently to remove excess moisture and dry on paper towels.

Heat 2 tablespoons of the olive oil in a skillet and add the eggplant. Sauté until browned. Remove from pan.

Add the remaining olive oil to the frying pan and sauté the onion and the garlic until the garlic is golden brown. Add the celery, tomatoes and a little bit of water (about 2–3 tablespoons). Cover and let the mixture steam for 10 minutes. Be sure to stir occasionally.

At this point add the eggplant as well as the pignolia nuts, capers and vinegar. Season with salt and pepper to taste, and let simmer for another 10 minutes to let the flavors blend. Be careful not to burn. Serve either hot or cold. The flavor improves if you refrigerate a day or two.

❨ Serves 6 to 8 as a side dish.

❦

Mushroom Surprise

36 fresh mushrooms
1/2 bunch parsley, chopped fine
1 teaspoon garlic powder

1/2 teaspoon tamari (soy sauce)
3/4 cup ricotta cheese
1/4 teaspoon coriander

Remove the stems from the mushrooms after rinsing them carefully. Chop the stems very finely.

In a bowl mix together the chopped stems, the parsley, garlic powder, tamari, ricotta cheese, and the coriander. Spoon the mixture into the mushroom caps and transfer onto a lightly greased flat sheet or broiling pan.

Place under the broiler for approximately 5 to 10 minutes.

(Makes 3 dozen appetizers.

❦

Stuffed Mushrooms

3–5 pounds fresh mushrooms
3 cups raw wheat germ
1 cup whole wheat bread crumbs
2 eggs, beaten
1/2 cup olive oil
1 large onion, minced
1/2 cup sunflower seeds, chopped to a paste
4 garlic cloves, minced fine
1 bunch parsley, minced
1 bunch dill, minced

Preheat oven to 400 degrees.

Rinse the mushrooms and carefully break off and reserve the stems. Arrange the mushroom caps in a greased baking dish or pan.

Chop the stems very fine and combine with the remaining ingredients in a large mixing bowl. Blend together well. Fill the caps with the mixture.

Bake in oven for approximately 15 minutes.

(Serves 8 to 10 as a side dish.

❦

Grandma's Stuffed Peppers

6 green peppers

1/2 cup bread crumbs from whole wheat or seven-grain bread

1 teaspoon marjoram

1/2 teaspoon garlic

1/2 pound mild Cheddar cheese, grated

2 tablespoons chopped fresh parsley

2 eggs, beaten

2 tablespoons chopped fresh celery leaves

1 medium onion, minced

1/2 cup cooked brown rice (p. 65)

2 medium tomatoes, sliced

8 ounces tomato sauce

Preheat the oven to 350 degrees.

Cut the tops off the peppers close to the stem and remove the seeds and membranes. Parboil the peppers by placing them in boiling water to cover for about a minute. Drain and set aside.

In a large bowl, mix together the bread crumbs, herbs, cheese, parsley, eggs, celery leaves and onions. Then add the brown rice. Stuff the peppers with this mixture.

Grease a medium casserole and place the peppers in it. Next cover the peppers with the slices of tomato. Bake for 45 minutes, covered. Remove the cover and bake for 15 more minutes, then pour on the tomato sauce. Bake for 10 minutes longer until the sauce is heated.

❨ Serves 6 as an entree.

❦

Sweet Peppers and Yogurt

1–2 tablespoons olive oil

1 large sweet red pepper, coarsely chopped

1 large sweet green pepper, coarsely chopped

1 large onion, sliced thin

2 small zucchinis, sliced

1 teaspoon thyme

1 teaspoon dill weed

1/2 cup plain yogurt
Lemon Rice (p. 184), a double recipe
chopped parsley and lemon slices for garnish

Heat the oil in a heavy frying pan. Add the peppers and the onion and sauté until the onion is translucent, about 5 minutes.

Add the zucchini, thyme and dill weed and sauté for about 2 minutes, stirring. Lower heat and simmer, covered, about 5 minutes, or until the vegetables are soft.

Stir in the yogurt and remove from heat.

Arrange a double recipe of Lemon Rice on a platter and pour the vegetables on top.

Garnish with chopped parsley and lemon slices if you wish.

(Makes 3 to 4 servings as an entree.

Baked Stuffed Potatoes

2 baking potatoes, scrubbed
4 tablespoons unsalted butter
1/2 teaspoon nutmeg
salt and pepper to taste
2 egg yolks
1 egg, beaten
1/2 cup sliced almonds, sautéed in oil

Preheat oven to 400 degrees.

Pierce one end of each potato with a clean fork to allow steam to escape and prevent bursting.

Place the potatoes on a cookie sheet or in a baking pan and bake for 1 hour or until tender. (The potatoes should feel soft when gently squeezed.) Remove from the oven and cut in half lengthwise. Let cool 5 minutes.

Scoop out the flesh, being careful not to tear the shells. Set the shells aside. In a large mixing bowl, mash the potatoes well.

Add the butter and nutmeg. Season to taste with salt and pepper. Work in the egg yolks. Whip the mixture until smooth and fluffy.

Spoon the mixture back into the reserved shells. Put the filled shells on the cookie sheet or in the baking pan used to bake the potatoes, and brush with the beaten egg.

Return to the oven and bake for 10 minutes, or until nicely browned on top.

Garnish the potatoes with the sautéed almonds.

❨ Serves 2.

❦

Yogurt-Potato Casserole

6 medium potatoes, sliced and peeled

2 tablespoons sesame oil

1 medium onion, chopped

1/2 teaspoon ground cumin

1/2 teaspoon ground coriander

dash of pepper

salt to taste

1 cup plain yogurt

Boil the potatoes until tender, about 30–45 minutes.

In a skillet, heat the sesame oil and sauté the onion with all the seasonings.

Add the potatoes and mix carefully so as not to break the potatoes. Add the yogurt and mix once again. Correct the seasonings.

May be served as a side dish or an entree.

❨ Serves 4 as a side dish.

❦

Potato Kugel

4 pounds potatoes

salt and pepper to taste

2 eggs, beaten

matzo meal

Peel and grate the potatoes. Drain the liquid that accumulates from the potatoes and pour it into a small pan; thicken over a low flame. Put the liquid back into the grated potato.

Add the salt, pepper and eggs. Beat well. Then stir in enough matzo meal to make a relatively thick mixture.

Preheat the oven to 350 degrees.

Grease a medium baking pan, pour in the mixture and bake until the top becomes a golden brown, about 30 minutes.

❨ Serves 6 to 8 as a side dish.

❧

Baked Acorn Squash à l'Orange

3 acorn or table queen squash

3 tablespoons unsalted butter

1 tablespoon freshly grated orange peel

3 oranges, peeled, sectioned and seeded

Cut the squash in half lengthwise, scoop out and discard the seeds. Place the squash, cut side down, in a shallow baking dish filled with 1/4 inch of water. Bake at 375 degrees for 40 minutes.

Turn the squash; fill each center with 1/2 tablespoon butter, 1/2 teaspoon grated peel and 4 or 5 orange sections. Do not allow the water to evaporate; add more water to the pan, if necessary.

Continue baking until tender, about 20 to 25 minutes. Baste occasionally as butter melts and juice forms.

❨ Makes 6 servings.

❧

Acorn Squash with Applesauce

2 acorn squash

1 1/2 cups applesauce

1/4 cup raisins

1/2 cup chopped walnuts

1/2 teaspoon cinnamon

Preheat oven to 375 degrees.

Cut the squash in half lengthwise and remove the seeds. Put the squash in a baking pan or on a cookie sheet. Bake the squash in the oven until tender, about 45 minutes to 1 hour. Remove from oven.

Place the squash cut side up in a shallow greased casserole. Combine the remaining ingredients in a mixing bowl and then fill the squash cavities with the mixture. Bake at 350 degrees for 15 minutes.

❨ Serves 2 to 4.

❦

Tut's Treasure

1 large acorn squash
1/2 cup cottage cheese
1/2 cup chopped walnuts
3 chopped figs
1 tablespoon softened unsalted butter
cinnamon and honey to taste

Preheat oven to 350 degrees.

With a sharp knife, carefully cut the squash in half lengthwise. Remove the seeds with a spoon and discard. Place the squash on a Pyrex or stainless steel platter and bake till soft, about 40 minutes. Remove and let cool.

In a small mixing bowl, combine the cottage cheese, walnuts, figs and butter. Add cinnamon and honey to taste. Mix well.

When the squash is cool enough to handle, remove the flesh with a spoon, being careful not to tear the shells, and add it to the cottage cheese mixture. Mix well and return to the shells.

Serve chilled topped lightly with honey.

❆ Serves 2.

❦

Ronga's Butternut

2 large butternut squash
2 cups black olives, cut in half and pitted
1/2 cup Romano cheese
1/2 cup olive oil
1 bunch parsley, chopped
2 garlic cloves, diced
1/2 cup wheat germ

Preheat oven to 325 degrees.

Cut off both ends of the squash and peel with a vegetable peeler. Cut in half, remove and discard the seeds and cut the flesh into cubes 1/4 inch to 1/2 inch thick.

Grease a 9-inch baking pan, arrange the squash evenly in it. Add the olives, cheese, oil, parsley, garlic and wheat germ on top.

Cover and bake for 1 hour, or until soft. Before serving, place under a broiler for 5–10 minutes to brown.

([As an entree serves 4 to 6; as a side dish, 8 to 10.

❧

Squash Delicious

2 yellow squash
1/4 cup chopped prunes
1/4 cup slivered almonds
4 tablespoons unsalted butter, melted

Peel the squash and cube; steam the cubes until soft, about 12 minutes.

Place the squash in an oven-proof serving bowl; spoon on the prunes and almonds. Top with butter and heat in a moderate oven for 10–15 minutes, until the topping is warm.

([Serves 4 as an entree.

❧

No-Starch Spaghetti Dinner

3–4 pounds spaghetti squash
4–6 tablespoons unsalted butter

Preheat oven to 400 degrees.

Bake the spaghetti squash on a cookie sheet or in a baking pan in the oven until it's soft to the touch, about 1 1/2–2 hours. Remove from the oven and allow to cool for a few minutes.

Carefully slice the squash in half lengthwise, scoop out and discard the seeds. Spoon the "spaghetti" strands out of the shell and place in a medium saucepan. Mix in the butter and keep warm until ready to serve.

Top with sauce and serve.

([Makes 5 to 6 servings.

TOMATO SAUCE

1–2 tablespoons olive oil
3 cloves garlic, chopped fine
3 medium onions, coarsely chopped
5 large tomatoes, chopped
thyme to taste
pepper to taste
tamari (soy sauce) to taste

While the spaghetti squash is baking, make the tomato sauce. First heat the olive oil in a skillet. Add the garlic and the onion and sauté for 5 minutes, until the onion is translucent.

Add the tomatoes and thyme to taste. Bring the mixture to a boil. Reduce the heat and simmer for 40 minutes.

Add pepper and tamari sauce to taste.

(Makes 5–6 servings.

❦

Crunchy Herbed Green Beans

1 pound green beans
1 1/2 cups boiling water
2 teaspoons sea salt
1/4 cup finely minced onion
1/2 cup chopped green pepper
1/2 teaspoon marjoram
1/4 teaspoon crushed rosemary
1/2 teaspoon pepper

Snip off the ends of the green beans and steam the beans over salted water for 3 or 4 minutes or until they're tender but not overcooked— they should be crunchy.

Mix the beans, the onion, green pepper and seasonings in a large bowl. Serve hot.

(Serves 4 to 6.

❧

Italian String Beans

6 ounces string beans

1 large red pepper, diced

1 medium onion, sliced

1 1/2 tablespoons apple cider vinegar

1/2 teaspoon paprika

1/2 cup water

1/4 teaspoon dry mustard

1/4 teaspoon tarragon

In a medium saucepan, place the trimmed string beans along with the red pepper and the onion.

In a separate bowl, combine all other ingredients. Mix well. Pour the seasonings over the vegetables in the saucepan and toss to coat all pieces.

Cook over low heat until the flavors blend and the mixture is hot. Then "mangia."

❡ Makes 2 to 4 servings.

❧

Sal's String Bean Casserole

1 pound string beans

1/2 onion, chopped

1 pound almonds, chopped and sautéed in oil

1/2 pound sesame seeds, toasted

1 cup wheat germ

1 cup safflower or all-blend oil

yogurt as topping

Snip off both ends of the string beans. Steam them until tender, not soft, about 3 or 4 minutes. Chill.

Preheat oven to 350 degrees.

In a large mixing bowl, combine all the remaining ingredients. Grease a 9-inch × 9-inch baking pan or casserole. Mix the cooled string beans together with the almond mixture and spoon into the greased pan. Bake for 25 minutes. Serve warm, topped with yogurt.

❡ Serves 4.

❧

Grilled Tomatoes with Oregano

4 large or 8 small tomatoes
3 or more cloves garlic
4 teaspoons fresh oregano
salt and freshly ground pepper to taste
safflower oil

Preheat the broiler to high.

Rinse and dry the tomatoes. Do not core or peel them but cut in half and arrange the halves in a baking dish.

Cut the garlic into thin slivers. Insert the slivers at various points over the cut surface of the tomato halves. Chop the oregano coarsely and sprinkle the cut surface of the tomatoes with it. Sprinkle with salt and pepper to taste. Dribble over all with oil.

Place the tomatoes under the broiler, 4 or 5 inches from the flame, and let them broil 3 minutes or longer, until the garlic is browned and the tomatoes are soft but not mushy. Remove the pieces of garlic and serve the tomatoes hot.

❨ Makes 8 servings.

❧

Mangie Momma's Tomato

4 tomatoes
8 cloves garlic
salt to taste
1/2 pound Meunster cheese, sliced
1/2 cup olive oil
1/4 cup apple cider vinegar
1/4 cup fresh lemon juice
pepper to taste
chopped parsley and lettuce for garnish

After washing the tomatoes, slice them—(stem facing up)—being careful *not* to cut all the way through. Set aside.

To prepare garlic, mash the cloves and mix with the salt. Spread this pasty mixture with a spatula onto the sliced Meunster cheese;

place a slice of cheese in between each slice of tomato. Roll the tomato in the olive oil and wrap in Saran Wrap. Refrigerate.

After an hour or so, unwrap the tomato carefully. Combine the vinegar and lemon juice in a separate bowl. Open each slice of tomato and pour on lemon juice and vinegar and season with pepper. Garnish with chopped parsley and lettuce.

⟪ Serves 4.

❦

Stuffed Zucchini California

2 large zucchini, blanched
2 tablespoons olive oil
1 onion, chopped
1/2 cup sunflower seeds
1 cup alfalfa sprouts
1/4 cup tamari (soy sauce)
1/2 cup yogurt

Blanch the zucchini by briefly pouring boiling water over them.

Cut the zucchini in half lengthwise. With a spoon or a Parisienne knife (melon ball scooper), remove the pulp of the squash, being careful not to cut through the skin. Leave 1/4- to 1/2-inch thickness.

Heat the oil in a frying pan and sauté the onion until translucent. In a separate mixing bowl, combine the onions with the rest of the ingredients; mix well. Fill the squash with this mixture and arrange the squash on a baking sheet or in a baking pan. Bake in the oven for 5 minutes.

This dish may be eaten hot or cold.

⟪ Serves 2 as an entree, 4 if used as a side dish.

❧

Squash Stew

2 tablespoons olive oil
3 small zucchini, diced fine
1 pound onions, diced
2 stalks celery, diced
1/2 pound potatoes, peeled and sliced
3 cups tomato sauce
salt and pepper to taste
basil to taste

In a large pot heat the olive oil and sauté the zucchini, onions and celery until wilted. Add the potatoes and the sauce. Bring to a boil and allow to simmer until the potatoes are soft, about 15–20 minutes. Add seasonings to taste.

Serve warm.

(Serves 4 as an entree.

You can serve this stew on a bed of brown rice or poured over whole wheat spaghetti.

❧

Zucchini Frittata

2 tablespoons olive oil
1 small onion, sliced
1 small potato, sliced thin
2 medium zucchini, sliced
5 eggs, lightly beaten
tamari (soy sauce) to taste
4 tablespoons grated Parmesan cheese

Heat the oil in a large skillet. Place the onion and the potato in the skillet and sauté for about 3 minutes or until the onion is translucent. Then add the zucchini. Cook, stirring, until the zucchini is soft, about 20 minutes.

In a bowl, beat together the eggs, tamari and 2 tablespoons of Parmesan cheese. Pour the egg mixture over the vegetables and continue to cook over low heat. Cover the mixture until it is almost set, about 25 or 30 minutes.

Sprinkle with the remaining cheese and place under the broiler for about 1 minute just to brown the top. Serve warm.

(Serves 2 as an entree.

❦

Stuffed Zucchini Italiano

4 medium zucchini

1/4 cup chopped onion

3 tablespoons safflower oil

1 small tomato, chopped

1/2 cup shredded mozzarella cheese

1/4 cup bran

1/4 teaspoon sea salt

1/4 teaspoon oregano, crushed

dash garlic powder

Preheat oven to 375 degrees.

Cut off a slice about 1/4-inch thick from the ends of each zucchini. Chop up these slices to equal 1/2 cup. Reserve. Scoop out the center pulp of the zucchini. Reserve the zucchini shells. Sauté reserved zucchini, zucchini pulp and onion in 2 tablespoons oil in a small skillet until the onion is tender. Add the tomato, cheese, bran, salt, oregano and garlic powder. Mix well. Brush zucchini shells inside and out with the remaining oil; fill the shells with the tomato mixture. Place in a shallow baking dish. Cover and bake in the oven for 40 minutes.

(Serves 4 to 8.

❦

Italian Vegetable Stew

2 tablespoons olive oil
1 large onion, sliced thin
3 cloves garlic, pressed
1 red pepper, coarsely chopped
1 green pepper, coarsely chopped
2 carrots, sliced thin
2 small zucchini, sliced
1/2 bunch broccoli, cut into stalks
1/2 head cauliflower, cut into flowerettes
2 tomatoes, chopped
2 cups red wine
1 tablespoon honey
2 teaspoons basil
1 teaspoon oregano
2 teaspoons parsley flakes
1 tablespoon tamari (soy sauce)
1 cup grated Parmesan cheese

Heat the oil in a large skillet and add the onion, garlic, red pepper, green pepper and carrots. Sauté for 5 minutes. Add the zucchini and sauté for 2 minutes longer. Stir in the broccoli, cauliflower, tomatoes, wine, honey, basil, oregano, parsley and tamari. Cover and simmer for 25 minutes, stirring occasionally.

Place in an oiled casserole, top with Parmesan cheese and bake for 20 minutes at 350 degrees.

❪ Serves 6.

❦

Peperonata

1/2 cup olive oil
1 large onion, chopped
3 cloves garlic, thinly sliced
4 bay leaves
6 green peppers, chopped

6 tomatoes, peeled and cut in halves or quarters
1 teaspoon basil
1/2 teaspoon oregano
salt to taste

Heat the olive oil in a large skillet. Add the onion, garlic and bay leaves and sauté until the onion is golden brown. Add the green pepper and cook over high heat for almost 10 minutes or until the pepper changes color, stirring constantly.

Add the tomatoes and seasonings. Lower the heat and simmer gently for 10 to 15 minutes Serve warm.
([Serves 6 as a side dish.

❦

Grandma's Ratatouille

1 medium zucchini, sliced
1/2 red or green pepper, sliced
1/2 onion, sliced
1 small handful of string beans, chopped
1/8 teaspoon oregano
1/8 teaspoon garlic powder
1/8 teaspoon basil
1 3/4 cups tomato sauce
grated Parmesan or Romano cheese for garnish

Pour all the ingredients into a small heavy saucepan. Cook over medium heat for about 30 minutes, or until everything is tender. Stir occasionally to prevent scorching.

To serve, sprinkle on some Romano or Parmesan cheese and pour over brown rice.
([Serves 1 or 2 as an entree.

❀

Ratatouille Supreme

1 pound zucchini
1 small eggplant
1 onion, sliced
1/4 cup olive oil
2–3 cloves garlic, pressed
2 tomatoes, peeled and chopped
1 green pepper, chopped
1 teaspoon salt
1/8 teaspoon pepper
1 teaspoon basil
1 1/2 teaspoons thyme

Cut the zucchini and eggplant into 1/2-inch cubes. In a large skillet, sauté the zucchini, eggplant and onion in the olive oil for about 5 minutes, until the onion is translucent. Stir in the garlic, tomatoes, green peppers, salt, pepper, basil and thyme. Cook, covered, over medium heat for 10 to 15 minutes, or until vegetables are tender.

Serve immediately over brown rice or any other grain.

❨ Serves 4 to 6.

❀

Sautéed Vegetables

1 garlic clove, chopped
1/2 medium onion, sliced
2 tablespoons sesame oil
1 carrot, peeled and sliced
1 medium parsnip, peeled and sliced
1 red pepper, chopped
1 medium zucchini, sliced
1/2 medium eggplant, sliced
tamari (soy sauce) to taste
5 or 6 mushrooms, sliced
6–8 ounces of tomato sauce

Sauté the garlic and onion in the sesame oil in a heavy skillet. Add the carrot, parsnip, red pepper, zucchini, and eggplant. Pour in the tamari and finally add the mushrooms. Cook over medium heat for 20 to 25 minutes, mixing frequently. Lower heat and simmer for 5 to 10 minutes.

Then add the tomato sauce and simmer for an additional 5 minutes. Serve over brown rice.

(There's plenty for 2 people.

❧

Vegetable-Yogurt Surprise

1/2 cup plain yogurt

2 scallions, chopped fine

1 tablespoon tamari (soy sauce)

2 tablespoons fresh dill

2 tablespoons fresh parsley, chopped

1/4 teaspoon tarragon

1 cucumber, sliced

1 cup cauliflower pieces

1 cup broccoli pieces

Mix all ingredients, except for the cucumber, cauliflower and broccoli, in a medium mixing bowl. Arrange the cukes, cauliflower and broccoli on a plate and top with the yogurt mixture.

(Serves 4.

❦

Vegetarian Meatballs

1 cup soy grits
1 cup tomato juice
4 eggs, beaten
1/4 cup water
8 tablespoons minced onion
6 tablespoons minced green pepper
5 teaspoons tamari (soy sauce)
2 teaspoons basil
1 cup grated cheese of your choice
1/2 cup wheat germ
1/2 cup chopped walnuts
1 teaspoon salt
1/2 teaspoon pepper
oil as needed

In a large mixing bowl, combine the soy grits and juice. Mix well. Stir in the remaining ingredients and mix thoroughly. Roll the mixture into balls and place on a plate.

Heat the oil in a skillet over medium heat. Place several of the meatballs in the skillet and brown on all sides. Then drain on paper toweling.

May be served with tomato sauce, if desired.

❆ Serves 6.

Cheese

Cheese Bake

4 eggs, well beaten
2 cups milk, scalded
2 cups soft whole grain bread crumbs
1/2 pound Cheddar cheese, shredded

Preheat oven to 350 degrees.

Pour some of the beaten eggs into a small bowl. Add the milk to them, stirring constantly. Then add this mixture to the beaten eggs. Add all the other ingredients and mix thoroughly.

Pour into a greased medium baking dish and bake for about 40 minutes or until set and lightly browned on top.

(Serves 4 as an entree.

Special Soufflé

5 eggs, separated
2 cups coarsely grated Muenster cheese or Jarlsberg cheese
3 1/2 tablespoons powdered skim or whole milk
1/2 teaspoon vegetable salt

Preheat oven to 450 degrees.

Beat the egg yolks lightly in a mixing bowl. Stir in the cheese and milk powder.

Beat the whites in another bowl until soft peaks form. Fold the whites into the cheese mixture.

Spoon into an ungreased 2-cup soufflé dish and bake for 10 to 15 minutes until puffed and brown. Serve immediately.

(Serves 4.

❦

Triple Cheese Soufflé

2 tablespoons unsalted butter

2 tablespoons whole wheat flour

2/3 cup milk

1/3 cup white wine

1/4 teaspoon salt

dash cayenne pepper

1/2 cup grated Muenster cheese

1/2 cup grated mozzarella cheese

1/2 cup grated Swiss cheese

4 eggs, separated

2 scallions, minced

Preheat oven to 375 degrees.

In a saucepan, melt the butter over low heat and then whisk in the flour. Whisk until well blended. In another saucepan, bring milk to a boil, then add all at once to the butter mixture. Cook over low heat until thickened, stirring vigorously.

Whisk in wine, salt and cayenne pepper. Turn off heat and let cool for 2 to 3 minutes. Add the cheese and stir until melted. Beat in egg yolks one at a time, then stir in scallions.

Beat the egg whites until they stand in peaks, but do not overbeat. Fold the egg whites into the mixture.

Turn into a 1 1/2-quart oiled casserole and bake 30 to 45 minutes, until puffed and browned. Serve immediately.

❦ Serves 4.

❦

Cheesey Vegetable Munch

1/4 head cauliflower

1/2 bunch broccoli

2 tablespoons olive oil

2 small green peppers, chopped

1 onion, sliced thin

1 1/2 cups tomato sauce

1/2 cup grated Cheddar cheese

1/2 cup grated Muenster cheese

1/2 cup grated Swiss cheese

Preheat oven to 350 degrees.

Cut the cauliflower into flowerettes and separate the broccoli into stalks, then steam until tender, about 10 minutes. Set aside.

Heat the olive oil in a skillet and sauté the green pepper and onion until the onion is translucent and the pepper is soft. Place in the bottom of a greased casserole. Place the broccoli and cauliflower on top of this mixture. Pour the tomato sauce over all the ingredients to cover and top with the grated cheeses. Bake at 350 degrees for 25 minutes.

([Serves 4 to 6.

Green Vegetable Casserole

2 tablespoons olive or sesame oil

1 cup coarsely chopped red onion

2 cloves garlic, finely chopped

2 tomatoes, coarsely sliced

1/4 teaspoon basil

1/4 cup tamari (soy sauce)

1/4 teaspoon pepper

1 1/2 cups collard greens

1 1/2 cups chopped broccoli

1 pound asparagus

1 cup cubed Swiss cheese, 1/2-inch cubes

Preheat oven to 400 degrees.

In a large skillet heat the oil. Add the onion and garlic and sauté for 5 minutes, until the garlic is golden. Add the tomatoes and the basil; bring the mixture to a boil. Reduce flame and simmer for 40 minutes. Add seasonings.

Steam the collard greens, broccoli, and asparagus al dente. In a casserole arrange the steamed vegetables. Sprinkle with the cheese and top with the sauce. Bake for 5 minutes.

([Makes 4 servings.

❦

Broccoli Cheese Bake

1 large bunch broccoli, separated into stalks
2 eggs, beaten
1 cup ricotta cheese
1/4 cup minced green onion
1/4 cup grated Cheddar cheese
dash cayenne pepper
1/2 teaspoon salt
dash pepper
2 tablespoons unsalted butter, melted
1/3 cup wheat germ

Preheat oven to 350 degrees.

Steam broccoli until tender, about 4–5 minutes. Butter the bottom of a baking dish and arrange the broccoli in it.

In a bowl combine the eggs, ricotta cheese, green onion, Cheddar cheese, cayenne, salt and pepper. Stir until thoroughly blended. Pour this mixture over the broccoli.

In another bowl combine the melted butter and the wheat germ, then spread on top of the cheese and vegetable mixture. Bake for 25 minutes.

❨ Serves 3 to 4.

❦

Cheddar Brussels Sprouts Casserole

1 small bunch broccoli, separated into stalks
12 brussels sprouts, cut in half lengthwise
12 mushrooms, thinly sliced
1 cup grated Cheddar cheese
1 cup grated Muenster cheese
3/4 teaspoon ground coriander
1/4 teaspoon garlic powder
1/2 cup chopped walnuts
1/4 cup tamari (soy sauce)
1 red pepper, sliced into rings, for garnish

Preheat oven to 375 degrees.

Combine all vegetables in a large mixing bowl. Stir in half the Cheddar cheese and half the Muenster cheese, mixing well to distribute the cheeses evenly throughout. Add the coriander and the garlic powder; mix well. Then add the walnuts and mix thoroughly.

Transfer the mixture to a casserole. Pour tamari over the mixture and top with the remaining cheese.

Cover and bake for 45 minutes. Remove cover and bake for 5–10 minutes more just to brown the cheese slightly. Garnish with red pepper rings.

(Serves 2 to 4.

❦

Nutty Cauliflower

3 cups diced celery

8 small zucchini, cubed

1 large head cauliflower, cut into small pieces

1 cup almonds

2 1/2 cups grated Muenster cheese

2 1/2 cups grated Cheddar cheese

1/2 teaspoon salt

1/2 teaspoon pepper

1/2 teaspoon garlic powder

1 1/2 cups honey

1/4 pound unsalted butter, melted

Preheat oven to 375 degrees.

In a large bowl, combine the celery, zucchini, cauliflower and almonds. Add one half of each type of cheese and mix so that the cheese is evenly distributed throughout the mixture. Add the salt, pepper and garlic powder and mix well.

Transfer the mixture to a large baking pan. Pour the honey and then melted butter over the mixture. Top with the remaining cheese.

Cover. Bake in the oven for 45 minutes to 1 hour, or until a fork inserted into the cauliflower meets just a little resistance. Remove the cover and bake for 10 more minutes to brown cheese.

(Serves 8 to 10 people.

❦

Eggplant Parmesan Sesame

5 medium or 15 small eggplants

sprinkling of salt

3–4 cups whole wheat flour

1 1/2 cups sesame seeds

basil, oregano and parsley to taste

3 eggs, beaten with 1/4 cup cold water

1/2 gallon safflower oil, or as needed

2 16-ounce jars tomato sauce

1 pound mozzarella cheese, grated

1 pound Parmesan cheese, grated

Peel the eggplant and cut into slices 1/4 inch thick. Layer the slices on paper toweling or toweling, sprinkling salt between each layer. Place a cookie sheet or cutting board on top of the eggplant layers and add a weight to extract the bitterness. Let stand for 30–45 minutes. Rinse off the salt and wipe the slices dry.

In a medium bowl, mix together the flour, sesame seeds, basil, oregano and parsley. In another bowl, place the eggs and water. Keep a plate on the side to put the eggplant ready for frying.

Dip the eggplant slices in the egg; moisten both sides. Then dredge each slice in the flour mixture and shake off the excess flour. Put the coated eggplant slices on the plate until you're ready to fry them.

Pour oil into a large frying pan to a depth of 1 inch. Heat the oil and fry the eggplant slices until browned; turn and fry until browned on the other side. You will need to add oil from time to time to keep the slices from sticking, as the oil is absorbed by the eggplant. Be careful not to let the oil get too hot—the breading that falls off into the oil burns easily. When the eggplant is browned on both sides, put it into a warm oven on paper toweling.

Preheat oven to 375 degrees.

Spoon two ladles of tomato sauce into a large casserole. Then arrange the fried eggplant over the sauce in rows; top with a layer of mozzarella and a layer of Parmesan. Continue layering—eggplant, cheese, sauce—until ingredients are used up. Bake till the sauce bubbles, about 45 minutes.

❦ Serves 4 to 6.

❦

Eggplant Parmigiana

2 large eggplants, sliced but not peeled
1/4 cup arrowroot
2 cups whole wheat flour
2 eggs
oil as needed
8 ounces tomato sauce
grated Parmesan cheese to taste

Preheat oven to 375 degrees.

Place the sliced eggplant on paper toweling for about 20 minutes. Then boil for about 15 minutes, until tender.

Meanwhile, prepare a breading by sifting together the arrowroot and the flour. Beat the egg yolks in a medium mixing bowl. Dip each slice of the eggplant into the egg, moistening both sides, then dredge each slice in the flour mixture, shaking off the excess.

Into a deep fryer or large saucepan, put enough oil to deep fry the eggplant slices. When the oil is hot, fry the slices until browned. Remove the slices with a slotted spoon.

Arrange the eggplant in a single layer in a greased casserole. Spoon tomato sauce over the eggplant and sprinkle on some Parmesan. Continue layering—eggplant, sauce, cheese—ending with the cheese. Bake for about 45 minutes, until heated through and the cheese inside is melted.

⟨ Serves 4 to 6.

❦

Spaghetti Squash

1 spaghetti squash
1 1/2 cups grated mozzarella cheese
6 ounces tomato sauce

Preheat oven to 350 degrees.

Carefully cut the squash lengthwise with a sharp knife. Remove and discard the seeds. Place the squash, cut side up, in a baking pan and bake for 2 hours or until tender when tested with a fork.

Remove the squash from the oven and place the cheese and the sauce in the cavity of the squash. Heat until the cheese melts, about 15 minutes more.

❲ Serves 2.

❧

Cheese and Squash Supreme

1 pound zucchini, sliced

1 pound yellow squash, sliced

1 small onion, sliced thin

4 eggs, beaten

2 cups grated Swiss cheese

salt and pepper to taste

1/2 teaspoon oregano

1/2 teaspoon basil

Preheat oven to 325 degrees.

Steam the zucchini, squash and onion together 10 minutes, or until everything is tender. In a large mixing bowl, mash the vegetables together. Stir in the eggs and mix thoroughly. Next stir in the cheese, mixing until well blended. Add salt and pepper, oregano and basil.

Pour the mixture into a medium greased baking dish and place it, covered, in the oven until set, about 30 or 40 minutes.

❲ Serves 4.

❧

Swiss Squash

6 medium yellow squash

6 tablespoons unsalted butter

1 cup finely chopped onion

3 cloves garlic, minced fine

1/2 teaspoon dried thyme

1/2 bay leaf

salt and pepper

1 cup whole wheat or seven-grain bread crumbs

1 1/2 cups grated Swiss cheese

2 egg yolks, beaten

Preheat oven to 350 degrees.

Trim off both ends of the squash and cut them in half lengthwise. Scoop out the flesh from each half, leaving 1/4-inch thickness. Chop the flesh finely and reserve.

Drop the shells into boiling salted water. Simmer for 3 minutes and then drain.

Heat 4 tablespoons of the butter in a large skillet. Add the onion and cook over medium heat about 2 minutes, until translucent. Then add the chopped squash. Sauté another 10 minutes or until the squash is tender.

Meanwhile, chop together the garlic, thyme and bay leaf. Add these to the squash-onion mixture. Season with salt and pepper to taste. Cook for 5 minutes, stirring occasionally, or until dry.

Add the bread crumbs, half the cheese and the egg yolks. Stir well. Fill the shells with the mixture and sprinkle with the remaining cheese. Dot with butter. Bake for 30 minutes. Then brown for 5–10 minutes under broiler.

❨ Makes 6 to 12 servings.

Squash-Onion Casserole

4 tablespoons safflower or all-blend oil
1 medium onion, sliced
3 cloves garlic, pressed
1 tablespoon whole wheat flour
6 medium zucchini, shredded
1 cup cooked brown rice (p. 65)
2 cups grated Muenster cheese
1/4 teaspoon thyme
1/2 teaspoon oregano
1/4 cup tamari (soy sauce)
3/4 cup milk
10–12 almonds for garnish

Preheat oven to 375 degrees.

Heat 2 tablespoons of the oil in a heavy skillet.

Sauté the onion and garlic in the oil. Sprinkle in the whole wheat flour. Cook for about 5 minutes, stirring constantly. Add the shredded zucchini and cook for 5 minutes longer.

In a large mixing bowl, combine the zucchini mixture and the cooked brown rice. Stir in 1 cup of the grated cheese. Add the seasonings. Add the tamari and the milk and mix well.

Transfer all ingredients to a lightly greased large casserole. Sprinkle the other cup of cheese over the ingredients and then 2 tablespoons of oil. Garnish with almonds. Bake for 1 hour or until the squash is tender.

(Serves 8.

❦

Zucchini Parmigiana

6 medium zucchini, sliced thin

2 red or green peppers, diced

1 onion, sliced

1/4 cup tamari (soy sauce)

1/2 teaspoon garlic powder

salt and pepper to taste

14 ounces tomato sauce

4 cups grated cheese (mozzarella, Swiss or Muenster)

Preheat oven to 375 degrees.

Combine all ingredients, except for tomato sauce and cheese, in a large mixing bowl. Stir well. Transfer half of the mixture to a large lightly greased casserole. Pour one-third of the tomato sauce over the mixture. Top with one-half of the cheese. Pour the remaining mixture into the pan and then another one-third sauce, the remaining cheese and then the rest of the sauce.

Bake covered for about 1 hour or until the zucchini is tender.

(Serves 6 to 8.

❦

String Beans Ricotta

2 tablespoons olive oil

1 medium onion, sliced

1 1/2 pounds fresh string beans, cut up

1/2 cup chopped fresh parsley

1 large tomato, chopped

8 ounces tomato sauce

1 teaspoon garlic powder

1/2 teaspoon basil

1/2 teaspoon oregano

6 ounces ricotta cheese

3 cups cooked brown rice (p. 65)

Heat the olive oil in a heavy skillet. In it sauté the onion, string beans and parsley until the onions become translucent.

Add the tomato and seasonings and toss. Cook over medium heat for 10 minutes. Add the ricotta cheese and mix well. Cook over low heat for another 5 minutes, until the cheese is warmed.

Pour over brown rice and serve.

⟨ Serves 6.

Tomatoes Stuffed with Spinach and Cheese

6 medium tomatoes

salt

10 ounces fresh spinach, washed very well and drained

1/4 cup grated Parmesan cheese

1/2 cup ricotta cheese

2 eggs, beaten

1/2 teaspoon salt

1/8 teaspoon grated nutmeg

freshly ground pepper to taste

2 tablespoons unsalted butter, cut into small pieces

Preheat oven to 350 degrees.

Cut a 1/2-inch slice from the stem end of each tomato, scoop out the pulp and seeds and save for another use (making tomato sauce or Italian Stew, p. 166). Sprinkle the insides of the tomatoes lightly with salt, stand them upside down on paper towels and set aside for at least 30 minutes or until ready to stuff.

Tear the spinach into pieces. Place the spinach, the two cheeses and the eggs in a mixing bowl. Beat until well blended. Season with salt, nutmeg and pepper. Mix well again.

Stuff the tomatoes with the spinach and cheese mixture and place the tomatoes in a well-greased baking dish. Dot the tomatoes with butter and bake for about 30 minutes or until the top is browned and they are heated through.

Serve hot, warm or at room temperature.

⟨ Serves 6 as a side dish.

Beans and Whole Grains

Chick-Pea and Zucchini Curry

1 cup dry chick-peas
2 tablespoons olive oil
1 large onion, sliced
1 1/2 teaspoons turmeric
1/4 teaspoon cayenne pepper or more to taste
2 teaspoons ground cumin
1 teaspoon mustard seeds
1 1/2 teaspoons ground coriander
3/4 teaspoon cinnamon
1 clove garlic, pressed
1 or 2 thin slices of fresh ginger root
1 whole clove
1 large tomato, coarsely chopped
1 tablespoon tamari (soy sauce)
6 ounces tomato paste, thinned with 1/2 cup water
2 medium zucchini, sliced
4–5 cups cooked brown rice (p. 65)

Soak the chick-peas in water to cover overnight. Drain.

Cook the chick-peas in unsalted water to cover for about an hour, or until they are soft enough to mash with a fork. Set aside.

Heat the oil in a large skillet. When it is hot but not smoking, add the onion and all of the seasonings. Cook until the mustard seeds pop. Then add the tomato, tamari, tomato paste, and chick-peas. Stir well to mix with seasonings. Let it cook, covered with a lid, for about 15 minutes, stirring occasionally. Add the zucchini, mix well and continue to cook, covered. When the zucchini is cooked, about 10 or 15 minutes later, your meal is done. Serve over brown rice.

(Serves 4 to 6 as an entree.

❧

Black-Eyed Peas with Lemon Rice

1 cup dried black-eyed peas

5 cloves garlic

2 tablespoons olive oil

1 small red pepper, chopped

1 small onion, chopped

2 cloves garlic, minced

1 teaspoon basil

1 teaspoon oregano

1 tablespoon cilantro (Chinese parsley)

4 cups cooked Lemon Rice (p. 184)

2–3 tablespoons cider vinegar

3 scallions, chopped

Soak the black-eyed peas in water to cover overnight. Do not drain.

Add more water, if necessary, to cover the peas and add the garlic. Cook over low heat about 30 minutes or until the peas are tender.

Heat the oil in a skillet and sauté the pepper, onion and minced garlic. Stir in the seasonings, blending well, and sauté until the onion is translucent and the garlic is golden.

Add the Lemon Rice and black-eyed peas. Mix well. Add the vinegar and scallions and cook over low heat for about 5 minutes or until heated through, stirring occasionally. Serve warm.

(Serves 4 to 6.

🌸

Thick Bean Stew

1/2 cup soybeans
1/2 cup barley
8 cups Vegetable Stock (p. 124)
2 cloves garlic
1 onion, chopped
1 carrot, chopped
1 bay leaf
1/4 cup split peas
1/2 cup lentils
2 cups chopped escarole or spinach
tamari (soy sauce) to taste (4 tablespoons)

Soak the soybeans and barley overnight in enough water to cover. Drain.

Place the soybeans, barley, stock, garlic, onion, carrot and bay leaf in a large soup pot. Bring to a boil. Cover and simmer until barley and soybeans are tender, which should take *at least* 2 hours.

Add the split peas and lentils and additional water or stock as necessary to cover. Continue to cook until everything is tender, about 1/2 hour longer. Stir occasionally to prevent scorching. Then add the escarole and tamari and cook until the escarole is wilted, just a few minutes.

Serve warm.

❨ Makes 6 to 8 servings.

🌸

Lemon Rice

1 cup raw brown rice
juice of one lemon
1 teaspoon olive oil
1 teaspoon onion powder
1 teaspoon basil

Cook the rice as stated in the directions on the box (or see p. 65), but to the water add the lemon juice, olive oil, onion powder and the basil, and omit the salt indicated in the package directions.

This rice makes a great accompaniment to many dishes, such as Broccoli au Gratin (p. 147) or Sweet Peppers and Yogurt (p. 154).

❧

Grandma's Stuffed Cabbage

1 medium white cabbage

3 cups cooked brown rice (p. 65)

1 cup chopped mushrooms

1/2 teaspoon garlic powder

1/2 teaspoon oregano

1/2 teaspoon basil

16 ounces tomato sauce

Romano or Parmesan cheese (optional)

Preheat oven to 375 degrees.

Parboil the cabbage for approximately 5 minutes by placing it in a large pot of boiling water. After draining, remove the core of the cabbage and you will find each leaf comes off easily.

While the cabbage is cooling, combine the brown rice, chopped mushrooms and seasonings in a separate bowl. When the leaves are cool enough to handle, place approximately 1 tablespoon of the mixture on a leaf, then fold up carefully, tucking in the sides as you roll. Use two smaller leaves together to make the last rolls. Place the rolls, seam side down, in a shallow pan and spoon the tomato sauce over. If desired, you may sprinkle on some Romano or Parmesan cheese.

Bake for about 45 minutes or until thoroughly heated.

❦ Serves 6 to 8.

❦

Curried Cauliflower Casserole

1 head cauliflower

1 cup cooked brown rice (p. 65)

1/2 cup safflower oil

curry powder to taste

6 tablespoons unsalted butter

1/4 cup whole wheat flour

3 cups milk

1 cup cold water

1/2 pound Cheddar cheese, grated

Preheat oven to 375 degrees.

Remove the flowerettes from the head of cauliflower. Steam the flowerettes till they are still firm to the touch. Add oil and curry to the cooked rice and transfer to a 9- × 9-inch casserole. Arrange the cauliflower on top. Set aside.

In a medium saucepan, melt the butter and whisk in the flour; cook for 5 minutes. Heat the milk in another saucepan along with the water. Add the milk and water to the flour-butter mixture. Stir until the mixture thickens. Add grated cheese and stir until the cheese melts. Pour cheese sauce over the cauliflower and rice. Bake in oven for about 30 minutes.

❦ Serves 4.

❦

Paul's Peppers

1/2 cup cooked brown rice (p. 65)

1/2 cup cooked millet (p. 64)

1 stalk celery, diced

2 tablespoons chopped parsley

2 tablespoons raw wheat germ

1/4 cup safflower oil

4 large red or green peppers

ricotta cheese

Preheat oven to 350 degrees.

In a large mixing bowl, combine all ingredients except for peppers and cheese. Mix well and set aside. Cut the tops off the peppers, reserve the peppers and chop the tops coarsely. Add the chopped tops to the grain mixture and mix again.

Remove the seeds and white membrane from the peppers and stuff them with the grain mixture. Place the filled peppers in a casserole; try to pack the peppers together to prevent their falling over during cooking. Bake for 25 minutes.

Serve with ricotta cheese on the side.

❨ Makes 4 servings.

❧

Rice and Vegetables in Red Wine

2 tablespoons unsalted butter

1 cup uncooked brown rice

1 cup chopped tomatoes

4 cups (1 pound) sliced mushrooms

1/2 cup finely chopped onion

3 cups Vegetable Stock (p. 124)

1/2 cup dry red wine

2 teaspoons sea salt

1/8 teaspoon freshly ground pepper

1 cup cooked green peas

1/4 cup grated Parmesan cheese

In a large, heavy skillet melt the butter. Add the rice, chopped tomatoes, sliced mushrooms and chopped onion. Cook for about 10 minutes, stirring occasionally.

Add the vegetable stock, wine, salt and pepper. Mix well. Cover and simmer for about 45 minutes or until rice is tender and all liquid is absorbed.

Stir in peas and sprinkle Parmesan cheese on the top. Cover and heat a few more minutes, until heated through.

❨ Makes 6 servings.

Reprinted from *The Calculating Cook: A Gourmet Cookbook for Diabetics and Dieters,* copyright 1972 by Jeanne Jones. With permission of the publisher, 101 Productions, San Francisco.

❦

Algerian Couscous

1 cup chick-peas
3 cups couscous
2–3 tablespoons safflower oil
1 1/2 cups coarsely sliced onions
1 pound carrots or potatoes, peeled and sliced 1/2 inch thick
1/2 pound raisins
1 cup unsalted butter
1/2 teaspoon powdered ginger
salt and pepper to taste
2 pounds zucchini, sliced
3 pounds tomatoes, peeled and coarsely sliced
1 pound peas

Soak the chick-peas in water to cover overnight. Drain. In fresh unsalted water to cover, cook about an hour or until the chick-peas can be mashed with a fork. Set aside.

Into a large bowl pour the couscous and 3 cups of water. Let stand.

While the couscous is soaking, heat the oil in a Dutch oven or kettle and sauté the onions until translucent. Add the carrots or potatoes and about 5 cups of water. Bring to a boil and then reduce heat. Simmer for 15 minutes, until the vegetables are just tender.

If you're using a conscousier, put the couscous into the colander portion and put water into the pot to a depth of several inches. Otherwise put the couscous into a colander. Put several inches of water into the 10-quart pot and put the colander into the pot. Be sure the water doesn't touch the colander. Because you want the steam to go through the colander and not out around it, put some damp cheesecloth or a damp dishcloth around the rim of the colander to make a seal between it and the pot. Steam the couscous for 15 minutes.

Remove the cloth then take out the colander and pour the couscous into a large pan. Put in one-quarter of the butter and—with cupped hands—lift and rub the grains with the butter to separate the grains and break up any lumps.

Sprinkle the raisins over the couscous and return to the colander. Put the colander into the pot as before, sealing as before with cheesecloth or a dishcloth. Steam for another 15 minutes.

While the couscous is steaming, add the seasonings, zucchini, tomatoes, chick-peas and peas to the onion/carrot or onion/potato mixture and stir well. Simmer for 15 minutes or until ready to serve.

Remove the couscous from the colander and return it to the pan. Stir in the rest of the butter.

To serve, place about 1 1/2 cups of couscous on a plate and top with the vegetables and broth.

《 Makes 4 to 6 servings.

🌺

Italian Bulghur and Chick-Peas

1/2 cup chick-peas

1 1/4 cups raw bulghur

2 tablespoons safflower oil

1 cup sliced mushrooms

1/2 red pepper, diced

1 onion, chopped

3 cloves garlic, minced

1 1/4 cups Vegetable Stock (p. 124)

1 tablespoon basil

2 teaspoons oregano

1 bunch scallions, minced

Soak the chick-peas in water to cover overnight. Drain.

Cook the chick-peas in unsalted water to cover until tender, about 1 hour. Drain and reserve.

In a large saucepan, cook and stir the bulghur in the oil until the bulghur turns a golden brown. Add the remaining ingredients. Bring to a boil. Cover. Reduce heat. Simmer for 15 minutes.

《 Makes 4 servings.

❦

Grandma's Eggplant

1 medium eggplant, peeled
4 tablespoons safflower oil
1/2 medium onion, sliced
2 cloves garlic, minced
1/4 teaspoon oregano
1/4 teaspoon basil
1 1/2 cups cooked bulghur wheat (p. 68)
8 ounces tomato sauce
grated Parmesan or mozzarella (optional)

Preheat oven to 375 degrees.

Slice the eggplant approximately 1/4 inch thick. Brush lightly with oil, using approximately 2 tablespoons. Broil the eggplant until most of the moisture has been cooked out (3 minutes on each side should be sufficient).

In a large skillet, sauté the onion and garlic together in the remaining 2 tablespoons of oil. When the onions are translucent, stir in the other seasonings and the bulghur wheat. Cook together for 10 minutes or so to blend the flavors. Add the tomato sauce. Stir well. In a small baking pan, spoon enough sauce to make a thin layer, then make a layer of eggplant. Continue to alternate the layers, ending with tomato sauce. Top with cheese if desired and bake for 50 minutes.

❡ Serves 2 to 3 people.

You may substitute zucchini or potatoes for some or all of the eggplant.

❦

Khaloda (Algerian Eggplant)

4 tomatoes, peeled and coarsely sliced
olive oil for sautéeing
2 medium onions, sliced 1/2 inch thick
2 cloves garlic, chopped fine
1 large eggplant, sliced
1 pound okra, cut in half lengthwise

5 medium potatoes, quartered

1 teaspoon tarragon

1/2 cup water

3 green peppers, sliced 1/2 inch thick

1/2 cup sesame seeds

salt and pepper to taste

To peel tomatoes, place them in a large pot and pour boiling water over them to cover. Let them stand for 20 seconds. Then slip off the skins.

Heat the oil in a large skillet. Add the onion and sauté lightly. Mix in the garlic, eggplant, okra, potatoes, tarragon and 1/2 cup of water. Bring to a boil, then reduce heat.

Allow to simmer for 20 minutes. Add the tomatoes. Continue cooking for an additional 10 minutes. Add the green pepper, mix well and simmer for another 10 minutes. Sprinkle with sesame seeds, salt and pepper. Serve hot.

❪ Makes 4 servings.

❦

Whole Wheat Pizza with Fresh Tomatoes

1 thin slice mozzarella cheese (1 ounce)

1 slice of whole wheat bread, toasted

2 thin slices from a very ripe tomato

1 teaspoon grated Parmesan cheese

1/4 teaspoon oregano

1/4 teaspoon basil

salt and pepper to taste

Place the mozzarella cheese on the toasted bread and top with the tomato slices. Sprinkle on the Parmesan and herbs and season to taste with the salt and pepper. Place under the broiler until the cheese has melted and serve piping hot.

❪ Serves 1.

Pasta

Greek Style Pasta with Vegetables

1/4 cup olive oil

3 cups sliced zucchini, sliced 1/2 inch thick
(about 3 medium zucchini)

1/2 cup chopped onion

3 tomatoes, peeled (p. 46) and cut into large pieces

1 1/2 teaspoons mint (1 tablespoon if fresh)

1 1/2 teaspoons dill weed (1 tablespoon if fresh)

3/4 teaspoon sea salt

1 cup sour cream

1/2 pound whole wheat elbow macaroni

1/4 pound feta cheese, crumbled

Pour the oil into a large skillet and sauté the zucchini and onion until tender, about 5–8 minutes. Add the tomatoes, mint, dill and salt. Stir until mixed. Cover and simmer over low heat for 15 minutes. Stir in the sour cream. Cook just long enough to bring to a simmer again. Lower the heat to just keep the mixture warm while you make the macaroni.

Cook the macaroni as described on the package. Drain. Place the macaroni in a large bowl and pour the zucchini sauce over it. Sprinkle with the feta cheese.

⟪ Serves 4 to 6.

❧

Delicious Vegetarian Lasagna

3/4 cup chick-peas

2 tablespoons safflower oil

1 medium onion, finely diced

3 cloves garlic, chopped

20 ounces of tomato sauce

2 tablespoons water

1/2 teaspoon oregano

1/2 teaspoon basil

pinch of rosemary

1-pound box lasagna noodles (whole wheat or spinach),
cooked according to directions on package

3/4 pound ricotta cheese

1/4 pound mozzarella cheese, shredded

2 tablespoons grated Parmesan cheese

Soak the chick-peas overnight in enough water to cover. Drain.

Cook in unsalted water to cover about an hour or until tender. Drain.

Heat the oil in a large skillet and sauté the onion and garlic for about 5 minutes, until the garlic is golden, stirring occasionally.

To the skillet add the tomato sauce, water, oregano, basil and rosemary. Stir until blended, then cover the skillet and simmer for 15 minutes. Add the cooked chick-peas and stir again to mix. Cook until the chick-peas are heated through.

Preheat oven to 325 degrees.

Into a large casserole or baking pan, spoon a little of the chick-pea/tomato sauce to form a thin layer. Arrange a layer of cooked noodles on top. Spread a few tablespoons of ricotta cheese and about half of the mozzarella over the noodles. Pour half of the remaining chick-pea/tomato sauce over the cheese and layer again with the noodles. Continue to layer, ending with sauce. Sprinkle with Parmesan and cover. Bake for 30 minutes or until the lasagna is thoroughly heated.

❲ Serves 6 to 8.

❦

Mushroom Lasagna

1/2 pound whole wheat or spinach lasagna noodles, uncooked
Mushroom Sauce (p. 233)
1 pound ricotta cheese
1/2 pound mozzarella cheese, sliced
1/2–1 cup grated Parmesan cheese

Cook the lasagna noodles according to the package directions. Drain.
    Preheat oven to 325 degrees.
    In a large baking pan, casserole or lasagna pan, spread a very thin
layer of Mushroom Sauce. On top of this arrange a layer of cooked
noodles, some ricotta and mozzarella, more Mushroom Sauce and
Parmesan. Continue layering in this order, beginning with the noodles
and ending with the Parmesan. Bake for about 45 minutes or until
heated through.
    Remove from oven and let stand 15 to 25 minutes before serving.
❨ Serves 6 to 8.

    This recipe works just as well with tomato sauce.

❦

Grandma's Baked Manicotti

2 eggs, beaten
1/4 cup chopped fresh parsley
1/2 teaspoon salt
1/2 cup grated Parmesan cheese
3 cups ricotta cheese
4 tablespoons diced onion
16 manicotti shells, uncooked
32 ounces tomato sauce
2–3 tablespoons grated Parmesan cheese (optional)

Mix together the eggs and the chopped parsley in a large bowl. Add
the salt, Parmesan cheese, ricotta cheese and onion. Mix well.
    Stuff the *uncooked* manicotti shells with the mixture.
    Preheat oven to 400 degrees.

Pour half of the tomato sauce into a baking dish. Arrange the stuffed manicotti shells in the pan. Pour the remaining sauce over the manicotti and bake, covered, for approximately 20 minutes.

If desired, you may sprinkle a little Parmesan cheese over the manicotti immediately before serving.

⟨ Serves 6 to 8.

❧

Noodle and Broccoli Casserole

1/2 pound whole wheat noodles
1 bunch broccoli
1 cup cottage cheese
1/2 cup plain yogurt
2 eggs
1 teaspoon salt
1 cup grated Cheddar cheese
paprika

Preheat oven to 350 degrees.

Cook the noodles according to the directions found on the package. Drain and set aside.

Cut the broccoli into stalks and steam until tender, about 6 minutes. Set aside.

Place the cottage cheese, yogurt, eggs and salt in a blender. Blend long enough to make a smooth sauce, about 1 minute.

Arrange half the noodles in a buttered 2-quart casserole. Place the broccoli on top of the noodles. Pour about half of the cottage cheese sauce over the broccoli. Add the remaining noodles and sprinkle the grated Cheddar cheese on top. Pour the remaining cottage cheese sauce on top evenly. Sprinkle with paprika.

Bake until heated—about 30 minutes.

⟨ Serves 3 to 4.

❦

Broccoli Pasta

2 tablespoons olive oil

1 onion, chopped

1 clove garlic, crushed

1 tablespoon melted unsalted butter

1 1/2 tablespoons whole wheat flour

1 cup heavy cream

1/4 cup grated Parmesan cheese

1 bunch broccoli

1/2 pound whole wheat ziti, uncooked

dash nutmeg

salt and pepper to taste

2–3 tomatoes, cut in wedges, for garnish

In a heavy skillet combine the oil, onion and garlic and sauté for 5 minutes or until the garlic is golden. Add the butter. When the butter is melted, whisk in the flour. Then gradually stir in the cream. Cook, stirring, until thickened. Stir in the Parmesan cheese and remove from the heat.

Cut the broccoli into small pieces and then steam until tender, about 6 minutes.

Cook the ziti according to the directions on the package. Drain.

Put the broccoli and the ziti into the sauce and toss gently until everything is coated. Sprinkle with nutmeg, salt and pepper. Garnish with the tomatoes.

❦ Serves 4.

❦

Grandma's Stuffed Shells

1 1-pound box large whole wheat pasta shells

1 pound mozzarella cheese, shredded

1 pound ricotta cheese

1 tablespoon chopped scallions

1 teaspoon garlic powder

1/2 teaspoon oregano

1/2 teaspoon basil

16 ounces tomato sauce

Preheat oven to 375 degrees.

Prepare the whole wheat pasta shells according to the directions on the package. Drain.

In a separate bowl, mix together about half the mozzarella cheese, the ricotta cheese, the scallions and the seasonings. Stir until well blended.

Pour just enough tomato sauce into a shallow baking pan to make a thin layer. Carefully stuff each shell with the cheese and spice mixture using a spoon, then place each shell in the pan. Pour the rest of the tomato sauce onto the stuffed shells and then sprinkle on the remaining mozzarella cheese.

Bake for about 20 minutes or until the cheese is melted.

❨ Makes 4 to 6 servings.

※

Sesame Basil Spaghetti

1 tablespoon olive oil
4 cloves garlic, minced
1/4 cup raw sesame seeds
2 tablespoons whole wheat flour
2 cups Vegetable Stock (p. 124)
1/4 cup basil
6 tablespoons dry white wine
1 pound whole wheat spaghetti, uncooked
1 recipe Tomato Sauce (p. 160)

Heat the olive oil in a large saucepan. Add the garlic and sesame seeds and sauté until the garlic is a golden brown. Add the flour, stirring well to make sure it is mixed thoroughly. Slowly add the vegetable stock and basil until the mixture is very thick. Add the wine and cook for 4–5 minutes until you have a sauce consistency. Add the tomato sauce and stir until well blended. Cook for 5 minutes to allow the flavors to blend.

Cook the spaghetti according to directions found on the package (do not add salt) and then drain. Place in a warm bowl. Pour sauce over the spaghetti and toss lightly. Serve immediately.

❨ Makes 4 servings.

❧

Walnut Tahini Pasta

2 tablespoons olive oil
3 cloves garlic, minced
1/2 cup walnuts, chopped
2 tablespoons unsalted butter
1/2 cup tahini (sesame seed paste)
juice of two lemons
water as needed
3/4 pound whole wheat elbow macaroni, uncooked
1/2 cup Tomato Sauce (p. 160)

Heat the oil in a large saucepan. Add the garlic and walnuts and cook until the garlic turns golden, stirring constantly. Add the butter and the tahini, mixing well. Stir in the lemon juice. Add about 1/2 cup of water and mix well. Cook for approximately 5 minutes. You may have to add more water to keep it from getting too thick.

Prepare pasta according to directions on package (but do not add salt). Drain and add to the saucepan with tahini sauce. Cook for 3 minutes. To serve, top with tomato sauce.

(Serves 4.

Tofu Dishes

Butternut Tofu

1 large butternut squash
1 cake tofu (bean curd)
2 tablespoons unsalted butter
honey, molasses and salt to taste
sour cream for topping

Preheat oven to 350 degrees.

Cut the squash in half lengthwise; place cut side up on a baking sheet and bake till soft, about 45 minutes. Remove from pan and allow to cool but do not turn off oven.

After the squash has cooled, remove the pulp, placing it in a large mixing bowl and retaining the skins. Combine the rest of the ingredients with the squash pulp. Fill the squash skins with the mixture, place on the baking sheet and return to the oven until heated through.

◖ Serves 2 as an entree.

❦

Tofu Cauliflower Casserole

1 head cauliflower
3 tablespoons olive oil
1/2 pound—about 4 cakes—tofu (bean curd), pressed (p. 59)
*   and cut into cubes*
1 onion, sliced thin
3 cloves garlic, pressed
1 1/2 cups tahini (sesame seed paste)
1 tablespoon tamari (soy sauce)

Preheat oven to 375 degrees.

Break the cauliflower head into flowerettes and steam until just tender, about 10 minutes.

Grease a medium casserole with about 1 tablespoon of the olive oil and arrange in it the cauliflower and the tofu.

To prepare the sauce, heat the remaining 2 tablespoons of oil in a large saucepan. Add the onion and garlic and sauté until golden brown. Add the tahini and tamari, stirring until blended, and cook for an additional 3 to 5 minutes.

Pour the sauce over the cauliflower and tofu and bake for 20 minutes, until heated through.

⟨[Serves 4.

Tahini can be found in health food and Middle Eastern specialty stores.

❦

Herby Tofu Croquettes

4 tablespoons safflower oil
1/2 bunch parsley, chopped fine
3 stalks celery, diced fine
1 medium onion, diced
1 green pepper, diced
1/4 pound mushrooms, minced
1 pound—about 8 cakes—tofu (bean curd)
2 eggs, well beaten
3 1/2 teaspoons whole wheat flour
1/4 cup sunflower seeds
1 1/2 teaspoons tamari (soy sauce)
1 clove garlic, minced fine
1/2 teaspoon thyme
1/4 teaspoon oregano
1/4 teaspoon pepper
3/4 cup grated Muenster cheese
1/4 cup wheat germ
oil for frying
parsley for garnish

Heat the oil in a skillet until hot but not smoking and add the parsley, celery, onion, green pepper and mushrooms. While you gently sauté the ingredients in the skillet, rinse the tofu under cold water and allow the water to drain. Mash the tofu.

In a large bowl add the contents of the skillet to the tofu along with the eggs, flour, seeds and seasonings. Mix well. Stir in the cheese and then form the mixture into croquettes about 2 inches wide. Roll the croquettes in the wheat germ and chill for 30 minutes.

Heat 1/4 inch of oil in a skillet and brown the croquettes evenly.

Serve with a parsley garnish.

❨ Makes 4 dozen croquettes which serves about 12 people when served with a vegetable or salad.

The croquettes may be topped with a tomato sauce or a mushroom sauce.

❦

Mushroom and Tofu Sautéed in Miso

2 tablespoons sesame or olive oil

1 pound—about 8 cakes—tofu (bean curd), pressed (p. 59) and
*   cut into 1/2-inch cubes*

1/2 pound mushrooms, cut into thick slices

1 tablespoon brown rice miso (a grain paste)

1 teaspoon honey

2 teaspoons tamari (soy sauce)

1/2 teaspoon powdered ginger

3 cups cooked brown rice (p. 65)

Heat the oil in a large skillet or wok. Add the tofu and mushrooms and sauté until mushrooms are practically soft, almost 3 minutes.

Combine the miso, honey, tamari and ginger in a small bowl. Make sure the miso is well mixed; a fork will be helpful. Add this mixture to the mushrooms and tofu and sauté for 1 minute more. Serve hot with brown rice.

❨ Serves 3 to 4.

Miso is available in many health food stores and Oriental markets.

🌷

Tofu Orleans

16 ounces—4 cakes—tofu (bean curd)
2 cups whole wheat flour
6 tablespoons unsalted butter
3 tablespoons safflower oil
4 cloves garlic, minced
1 medium onion, chopped
1/4 cup grapefruit juice
2 tablespoons lemon rind
1/4 teaspoon cayenne pepper
1/2 teaspoon honey
1/2 teaspoon salt
1 medium green pepper, diced
1 1/2 pounds fresh mushrooms, sliced

Cut the tofu into 1-inch squares. Place the whole wheat flour on a flat plate. Dredge tofu squares in the flour so that each square is fully covered.

Melt the butter and oil in a skillet and lightly sauté the onion and garlic in it for 5 minutes. Add the floured squares of tofu and continue to sauté over medium heat until the tofu is brown on all sides, about 10–12 minutes. Add grapefruit juice, lemon rind, cayenne, honey and salt. Mix well and cover. Allow to cook covered over low to medium heat for 10 minutes.

After 10 minutes, take the cover off and add the green pepper and mushrooms. Cover and simmer for 10 minutes.

❴ Serves 4 as an entree.

🌷

Red and Green Peppers with Tofu

2 tablespoons safflower oil
1 medium onion, sliced
2 cloves garlic, pressed
1 red pepper, chopped
2 small zucchini, sliced thin

1 pound—about 8 cakes—tofu (bean curd), pressed (p. 59)
   and cut into bite-size pieces
4 tablespoons tamari (soy sauce)
4 cups cooked brown rice (p. 65)
4 scallions, sliced thin for garnish

Heat the oil in a large skillet or wok. Add the onion, garlic, and red pepper and sauté for about 5 minutes or until the vegetables are wilted. Add the zucchini, tofu and 2 tablespoons of tamari. Sauté until the zucchini is soft, 2 or 3 minutes.

Add the brown rice and the remaining 2 tablespoons of tamari and cook for about 5 minutes longer, stirring continuously. Serve warm with the sliced scallions sprinkled on top.

([Serves 4.

🌷

Soba Tofu Dinner

8 cloves garlic
1/4 cup olive oil
1/4 cup unsalted butter
1/2 pound—about 4 cakes—tofu (bean curd), pressed (p. 59)
   and cut into bite-size pieces
1 teaspoon onion powder
1/2 teaspoon salt, or more to taste
1/2 pound soba noodles
fresh chopped parsley (optional)

Cut the garlic into very tiny pieces. If your hands get sticky in the process, dip them in water and then continue chopping.

Melt the oil and butter together in a heavy skillet. Add the garlic, tofu, onion powder and salt. Cook for about 5 minutes until the garlic is golden, stirring.

Prepare the soba noodles according to label directions. Do not overcook. Drain.

Add the noodles to the garlic sauce. Allow to cook for 2 to 3 minutes. Sprinkle with parsley. Serve immediately.

([Serves 4.

Soba noodles are available in health food stores and Oriental markets.

❧

Tofu-Eggplant Parmesan

2 medium eggplants

1 cup whole wheat bread crumbs

1/4 cup sesame seeds

3 eggs

about 4 tablespoons oil for frying and greasing

20 ounces—about 5 cakes—tofu (bean curd), cut into
      1/4-inch slices

16 ounces spaghetti sauce

1 cup grated Parmesan cheese

1/4 cup mozzarella, shredded

Preheat oven to 375 degrees.

Peel the eggplant and cut into slices 1/2 inch thick.

Prepare the breading mixture by mixing together the bread crumbs and the sesame seeds on a flat plate. In a wide bowl beat the eggs.

Dip the slices of eggplant into the egg mixture then dredge in the breading. Tap to remove excess breading.

Heat about 2 tablespoons of oil in a skillet and fry the breaded eggplant slices until browned on one side, then turn and brown the other side. After all the slices have been fried, arrange them in a greased casserole. Use just enough eggplant to cover the bottom of the casserole. Next cover the eggplant layer with layers of tofu, spaghetti sauce, Parmesan and then mozzarella. Continue layering this way until the ingredients are used up.

Bake for 25 minutes or until completely heated.

❨ Serves 4.

❧

Yogurt Tofu Casserole

3–4 small onions, chopped

1/2 pound mushrooms, sliced thin

2 tomatoes, chopped

4 ounces dried mushroom soup

2 pints plain yogurt

1 1/2 pounds—about 12 cakes—tofu (bean curd), sliced
      1/4–1/2 inch thick

4 tablespoons caraway seeds

Preheat oven to 350 degrees.

In a mixing bowl, combine the onions, mushrooms, and tomatoes. Spread half of the mixture in a medium casserole.

In a separate bowl, mix together the dried soup and the yogurt. Pour approximately one-fourth of this mixture over the onion mixture. Top with one-half tofu and 1 tablespoon of the caraway seeds. Continue to layer in the same way. Bake for 30 minutes, until heated through.

(Serves 4.

❦

Tomato Tofu and Kidney Beans

1 cup dry kidney beans

2 tablespoons olive oil

1 large onion, sliced thin

3 cloves garlic, pressed

3/4 pound—about 6 cakes—tofu (bean curd), pressed (p. 59)
        and cut into bite-size pieces

6 ounces salt-free tomato paste

1 cup water

1/2 cup dry white wine

1–2 teaspoons chili powder

2 teaspoons cumin

1 teaspoon basil

1 teaspoon oregano

4 cups cooked brown rice (p. 65)

Soak the beans in water to cover overnight. Drain.

Cook the beans in unsalted water to cover for an hour or until tender. Drain.

Heat the oil in a large skillet. Add onion, garlic, and tofu. Sauté for about 5 minutes until the garlic is golden. Add the tomato paste, water, wine and spices. Stir to mix well and then simmer for about 20 minutes. Add the kidney beans and then adjust the seasonings to your own taste. Cook for another 5 minutes.

Serve over the rice.

(Makes 4 servings.

❦

Bulghur, Lentil and Tofu Casserole

3/4 cup lentils

3 cups low-sodium Vegetable Stock* (p. 124)

1 teaspoon rosemary

1 teaspoon tarragon

1 bay leaf

2 tablespoons sesame oil

1 carrot, sliced thin

4 cloves garlic, pressed

1 large onion, chopped

8 ounces—about 2 cakes—tofu (bean curd), pressed (p. 59)
    and cubed

kernels from 2 ears of corn, cooked, or 3/4 cup canned or
    frozen corn

3/4 cup bulghur wheat

1/4 pound blue cheese, crumbled

Preheat oven to 350 degrees.

In a large pot cook the lentils in the vegetable stock along with the spices for about 25 minutes until the lentils are tender. Remove the bay leaf.

While the lentils are cooking, heat the oil in a skillet. Add the carrot, garlic, onion and tofu. Sauté for 5 minutes until the onion is translucent and the carrot is soft. Add the corn and the bulghur. Stir to mix well. Remove from the heat and add the lentils and the cooking liquid. Pour into a greased casserole. Place the cheese on top, covering evenly. Bake for 20 minutes. Serve warm.

❰ Makes 4 to 6 servings.

* You may use homemade stock as long as it hasn't been made with vegetables that have a high sodium content such as spinach, celery, radishes or watercress. You might use a low-sodium vegetable powder to be sure.

🌷

Tofu à la King

2 *tablespoons unsalted butter*

1/2 *pound mushrooms, sliced*

1/2 *large red pepper, coarsely chopped*

8 *ounces—2 cakes—tofu (bean curd), pressed (p. 59) and cut into cubes*

3 *tablespoons whole wheat flour*

1 *cup Vegetable Stock (p. 124)*

1 *teaspoon marjoram*

1 *teaspoon rosemary*

2 *teaspoons each onion and garlic powder*

2 *tablespoons wheat germ*

1 *cup crumbled blue cheese*

4 *cups cooked couscous (p. 188), millet (p. 64) or your favorite grain*

Preheat oven to 325 degrees.

Melt the butter in a skillet. Add the mushrooms, red pepper and tofu and sauté until the mushrooms are soft. Stir in the flour, mixing well. Add the stock, marjoram and the rosemary, slowly stirring with a whisk. Add the onion and garlic powder. Cook until thick.

Spoon the mixture into a small casserole that has been greased and sprinkled with wheat germ. Sprinkle the cheese over the top of the mixture. Bake for 30 minutes.

Serve warm from the oven over a plate of couscous.

(Serves 2 to 3.

🌷

Sesame Tofu

1 *cake tofu (bean curd), sliced into 4 pieces*

2–3 *tablespoons whole wheat flour*

1 *tablespoon sesame seeds*

1–2 *tablespoons unsalted butter*

parsley for garnish

To reduce moisture in the tofu slices, place them on paper towels and allow them to stand for 15 minutes or so.

On a flat plate combine whole wheat flour and sesame seeds. When moisture has been reduced in the tofu, dredge in flour mixture, covering both sides of the slice.

In a large skillet, melt the butter and then add the tofu. Fry for 2 minutes on each side or until the tofu is a golden brown. If you wish, serve with soy sauce, pepper or ketchup. Garnish with parsley.

(Makes 4 slices: serves 2 as an entree. It is a tasty combination when served with brown rice.

❧

Hot Breakfast for Two

3 cups water
pinch of salt
1 cup rolled oats
2 tablespoons honey
1/2 cup raisins
1/2 cup chopped walnuts
16 ounces—about 4 cakes—tofu (bean curd), diced
4 tablespoons unsalted butter
3/4 cup milk

Boil the water in a medium saucepan. Add the salt and the rolled oats; stir well. Cook for about 5 minutes or until soft. Add all other ingredients and cook for an additional 3 or 4 minutes.

(Serves 2.

Salads

Cole Slaw

1/2 cup diced apples
3/4 cup apple cider vinegar
1 cup shredded green cabbage
1 cup shredded red cabbage
1 1/2 cups safflower oil

Diced apples should be placed in the vinegar to prevent them from browning.

In a large mixing bowl, mix all ingredients together, tossing lightly. Chill thoroughly.

It is best to allow the cole slaw to sit overnight to allow the flavors to blend well.

❲ Serves 4.

❧

Avocado Nadeau for Two

1 medium ripe avocado
lemon juice (to prevent avocado from discoloring)
1/4 cup chopped celery leaves
1 small onion, minced
1 bunch fresh scallions, chopped
1 cup alfalfa sprouts for garnish

Cut avocado in half and remove pit. Dip the cut surface of the avocado in lemon juice.

In a small mixing bowl, combine the celery leaves, onions and scallions; mix well. Fill cavity of the avocado with the mixture; chill.

Place the alfalfa sprouts on top as garnish.

❨ Serves 2.

❧

Eggplant Salad

2 large eggplants
2/3 cup safflower oil
1/2 teaspoon cumin
1/4 teaspoon marjoram
juice of 1/2 lemon
1 small red onion, chopped fine
parsley and cherry tomatoes for garnish

Preheat oven to 350 degrees.

Pierce the eggplants with a fork in several places to prevent exploding. Place them on a cookie sheet and bake for 30 minutes or until soft to the touch. Remove from oven and allow to cool.

When the eggplants are cool enough to handle, scrape the pulp from the skin and mash the pulp in a medium mixing bowl. Add all the other ingredients and mix well. Garnish with the parsley and the tomatoes.

This salad may be eaten alone, with a tossed salad, with crackers or bread as an appetizer—it can even be used as a salad dressing.

❨ Serves 3 to 4 as an entree.

❧

Tofu Apple Salad

1/2 cup raisins
1 1/2 tablespoons sesame seeds
2 tablespoons honey or maple syrup
2 apples, sliced thin
3 ounces—1 cake—tofu (bean curd)
2 large lettuce leaves
3/4 cup plain yogurt
raw wheat germ

In a large mixing bowl, gently combine the raisins, sesame seeds, honey, apples and tofu. Arrange lettuce leaves on a plate and spoon the apple mixture onto the leaves. Top with yogurt and wheat germ. ◖ Serves 2 to 3 for a light lunch.

Tofu is available in Oriental markets and some supermarkets.

❦

Chick-Pea and Bulghur Salad

1/2 cup chick-peas
2 tablespoons olive oil
1 cup bulghur wheat
2 1/2 cups Vegetable Stock (p. 124) or water
3 tomatoes, coarsely chopped
your favorite salad dressing to taste
chopped parsley and romaine lettuce leaves for garnish

Soak the chick-peas overnight in enough water to cover. Drain.

Cook the chick-peas in unsalted water to cover about an hour or until tender. Drain and put into a large mixing bowl. Set aside.

In a large, heavy saucepan, heat the oil and sauté the bulghur, stirring constantly until all of the grains are coated with the oil.

In another pot, heat the vegetable stock or water until it begins to boil. Pour it into the saucepan with the bulghur. Cover tightly and cook over low to medium heat until all the liquid is absorbed and the grains are tender, about 20 minutes.

Transfer to the bowl with the chick-peas. Refrigerate until well chilled.

Add the tomatoes and toss with the salad dressing. Garnish with the chopped parsley and serve on a bed of romaine lettuce.
◖ Serves 4.

❦

Adzuki Bean and Macaroni Salad

1/2 pound whole wheat elbow macaroni, uncooked
1 cup dry adzuki beans, cooked (p. 49)
1/4 cup sliced scallions
1 Kirby cucumber, sliced
1 or 2 carrots, sliced thin
1 recipe of the Marinade (p. 118), but omit the garlic and
     substitute 2 tablespoons of tamari (soy sauce)

Cook the macaroni according to the directions found on the package. Drain and rinse well. Place them and the cooked adzuki beans in separate bowls in the refrigerator.

While the beans and macaroni are chilling, prepare the vegetables and the Marinade. Mix all ingredients together in a large bowl, using enough of the Marinade to coat the vegetables well. Chill before serving to develop flavors.

(Serves 4.

❦

Sprouts Slaw

1 1/2 cups alfalfa sprouts
3 cups shredded cabbage
1/2 cup grated carrot
1/4 cup minced onion
salad dressing of your choice

Place all ingredients in a large mixing bowl and mix well. Just before serving, add dressing and mix again.

(Serves 4.

❦

Sprout Salad

1/2 cup raw sunflower seeds
2 or more cups salad greens, torn into bite-size pieces
1 cup alfalfa sprouts
6 or 8 radishes, sliced

1/2 cucumber, sliced
1/4 cup sesame oil
2 tablespoons apple cider vinegar
1/8 teaspoon sea salt
2 hard-boiled eggs, sliced

Toast sunflower seeds by stirring in a dry pan over medium heat for about 3 minutes. Toss together with greens, sprouts, radishes, and cucumber in a large salad bowl.

In a smaller bowl, mix oil, vinegar and salt to make dressing. Add to salad and toss again. Garnish with egg slices.
([Serves 2 to 4.

Basic Tossed Salad

3 cups chopped dandelion greens
1 1/2 cups shredded red cabbage
1 cup shredded green cabbage
1 cup chopped watercress
10 romaine lettuce leaves, torn
5 spinach leaves, torn
6 red radishes, sliced
3 scallions, chopped
2 red peppers, chopped

Place all ingredients in a salad bowl and toss with your choice of dressing.
([Serves 4.

Optional extras and toppings would be some or all of the following:

sliced or chopped hard-boiled eggs
marinated mushrooms
sliced or whole (small) fresh mushrooms
chopped, sliced or grated carrots
sliced tomatoes or tomato wedges
croutons
sesame seeds

❦

Garden Salad

1/2 head romaine lettuce

1 bunch (1 handful) fresh spinach leaves

1 full recipe Garden Salad Dressing (p. 227)

1/2 head raw cauliflower, broken into flowerettes

1 cucumber, sliced very thin

2 zucchini, sliced thin

2 stalks celery, sliced

1 green pepper, sliced thin

6 radishes, sliced thin

6 green onion tops, chopped

2 cups sliced raw mushrooms

3 large ripe tomatoes, diced

12 sprigs parsley for garnish

Early in the day, wash the lettuce and spinach and tear into bite-sized pieces. Put in the refrigerator.

Just before serving, prepare all of the other vegetables and toss them with the lettuce and spinach. Add the salad dressing and toss until all of the vegetables glisten.

Serve on chilled plates and garnish with parsley sprigs.

⟮ Serves 6 to 8.

Reprinted from *The Calculating Cook: A Gourmet Cookbook for Diabetics and Dieters*, copyright 1972 by Jeanne Jones. With permission of the publisher, 101 Productions, San Francisco.

❦

Cucumber Salad

4 cucumbers, peeled and diced

2 onions, sliced

1 cup cauliflower flowerettes

3–4 tablespoons olive oil

2 tomatoes, sliced

1/2 cup mushrooms, sliced

1 to 2 tablespoons apple cider vinegar
pinch of kelp

Place all ingredients in a large bowl. Stir gently. Chill before serving.
(| Serves 4 to 6.

❦

Sprout and Pepper Salad

1/4 cup chopped dandelion greens
1 red pepper, chopped
1 green pepper, chopped
1/4 cup chopped parsley
1/2 cup mung bean sprouts
1 cup alfalfa sprouts.

Combine all ingredients in a large salad bowl.
(| Serves 2.

❦

Right from the Garden

4 cups sliced zucchini
4 cups okra, ends trimmed
2 1/2 cups sweet corn, scraped from the ear (4 or 5 ears)
2 red peppers, chopped
1 cup chopped watercress
1/2 cup chopped parsley
1 teaspoon ground coriander
2 teaspoons rosemary
1 large green onion, chopped
2 tablespoons chopped fresh mint

Combine all ingredients in a salad bowl. Toss gently.
(| Serves 6 to 8.

❦

Spinach Salad

4 cups torn spinach
1 1/2 cups sliced mushrooms
1/2 cup slivered almonds
1/2 cup chopped parsley
1/4 cup chopped watercress
1/2 teaspoon tarragon
your favorite Italian dressing

Place all ingredients in a large salad bowl. Toss gently. Pour dressing over the vegetables. Toss again.
❨ Serves 3 to 4.

❦

Super Chef's Salad

4 romaine lettuce leaves
1/4 cup cauliflower flowerettes
1/4 cup broccoli flowerettes
1/4 cup walnuts
1/4 cup Swiss cheese, cut into chunks
1/4 cup shredded carrots
2 hard-boiled eggs, sliced
1 cup alfalfa sprouts
1/4 cup mung bean sprouts
1 tablespoon sunflower seeds
6–8 cashews or almonds
any of the other salads, such as the Four Bean Salad (p. 218) or the Vegetarian Chopped Liver (p. 120), as an additional ingredient
your favorite salad dressing

Arrange romaine lettuce at the bottom of a large salad bowl so that the leaves adorn the sides of the bowl. Combine all other ingredients neatly on top of the lettuce. Top with salad dressing.
❨ Serves 2.

🌷

Avocado-Stuffed Tomato

4 large tomatoes
salt
2 avocados, peeled, pitted and chopped
1/2 cup bran
1/2 cup chopped celery
2 tablespoons finely chopped onion
2 tablespoons finely chopped parsley
2 tablespoons lemon juice
1/2 teaspoon salt

Slice 1/2 inch off of each tomato. Remove the pulp. Chop the pulp and tops finely and then drain. Set aside.

Salt the inside of the tomato shells and turn them upside down onto toweling or paper towels to drain.

In a mixing bowl combine the chopped pulp and tops with the remaining ingredients. Spoon the mixture into the tomato shells. Chill until ready to serve.

◖ Serves 4.

🌷

Tomatoes Vinaigrette

12 thick tomato slices
1 cup olive oil
1/3 cup wine vinegar
2 teaspoons crushed oregano
1 teaspoon salt
1/2 teaspoon pepper
1/2 teaspoon dry mustard
2 cloves garlic, crushed
6 lettuce cups
minced green onion
minced parsley

Arrange the tomato slices in a square baking dish, 8 × 8 × 2 inches. Combine the oil, vinegar and seasonings in a small bowl; shake well. Spoon the dressing over the tomatoes. Cover.

Chill 2 to 3 hours, spooning dressing over tomatoes occasionally.

To serve, arrange tomato slices in lettuce cups and sprinkle with minced green onion and parsley. Drizzle each salad with a small amount of the dressing.

◖ Makes 6 servings.

❦

Pasta Salad

4 ounces whole wheat macaroni swirls, uncooked

1 cup cottage cheese

1/2 teaspoon dry mustard

2–3 tablespoons plain yogurt

1 red bell pepper, coarsely chopped

4 scallions, chopped

1 tablespoon parsley flakes

1 teaspoon dill

1 teaspoon tamari (soy sauce)

salt and pepper to taste

Cook the macaroni according to the directions on the package. Drain well and chill.

In a large mixing bowl, combine the cottage cheese, mustard, and yogurt. Add the macaroni, toss well and add the remaining ingredients. Toss again.

Serve on a bed of lettuce.

◖ Serves 4.

❦

Four Bean Salad

1/2 cup dry chick peas

1/2 cup dry black beans

1/2 cup dry kidney beans

1/2 pound fresh string beans, cut into 1-inch pieces

1–2 carrots, grated

3 scallions, sliced

1/2 green pepper, chopped
1 large stalk of celery, diced or chopped
grated Cheddar cheese

Soak the chick-peas, the black beans, and the kidney beans in separate pots in water to cover overnight. Drain.

Cook the soaked beans in unsalted water to cover for about an hour or until tender. Drain, put into separate containers and refrigerate until chilled.

Steam the string beans for 5 minutes or until just tender. Place in the refrigerator to chill.

In a large mixing bowl, combine the chilled beans and the vegetables. Pour the dressing over the mixture and refrigerate several hours or overnight. Serve on a bed of lettuce topped with some grated Cheddar cheese, or use this salad to stuff a pita along with cheese slices.

❲ Serves 6.

DRESSING

1/2 cup olive oil
1/3 cup apple cider vinegar
1 teaspoon onion powder
1 clove garlic, crushed
salt to taste
1 teaspoon basil
1/2 teaspoon oregano
1/2 teaspoon parsley flakes

Into a jar with a cover, pour all ingredients. Shake vigorously.

❦

Summer Salad

cantaloupe ring 1 inch thick, rind removed
romaine lettuce
1/2 cup cottage cheese
1/4 cup diced celery
1 tablespoon slivered almonds

Place the cantaloupe ring on several lettuce leaves and fill with cottage cheese, celery and slivered almonds.
◖ Serves 1.

❦

Carrot-Raisin Salad

1/2 cup dates, chopped
1/4 cup walnuts
1 pound carrots, grated
1/2 cup raisins
3–4 apples, diced fine
2 celery stalks, diced
1/2 teaspoon dill weed
1/2 teaspoon lemon juice
cottage cheese or plain yogurt (optional)

Combine all ingredients in a large bowl. When serving, a scoop of cottage cheese or plain yogurt may be used as a topping.
◖ Serves 4.

❦

Very Good Bean and Pea Salad

1 pound green beans, trimmed and cut into 1-inch pieces
1/2 pound green peas
1 small onion, chopped
12 black olives, sliced
4 hard-boiled eggs, chopped
salt and pepper to taste

1/2 cup Homemade Mayonnaise (p. 225)

1/2 cup salted peanuts

Mix all ingredients except for peanuts in a large salad bowl. To serve, top with peanuts.

⟪ Serves 8 to 10.

❧

Cheese-Apple Salad

2 cups cored, diced apples

8 ounces sliced Swiss cheese, cut into strips

1 cup shredded Cheddar cheese (4 ounces)

1 cup diagonally sliced celery

1/2 cup Homemade Mayonnaise (p. 225)

1 tablespoon lemon juice

1/8 teaspoon pepper

lettuce

In a large bowl combine the diced apples, cheeses, celery and mayonnaise, lemon juice and pepper. Toss to mix. Chill. Serve on a bed of lettuce.

⟪ Makes 6 to 8 servings.

❧

Tabbouli

1 cup uncooked bulghur

1/4 cup lemon juice

1/2 teaspoon salt

1/4 teaspoon freshly ground pepper

1 clove garlic, minced

1 tablespoon water

3 tablespoons olive oil

2 tomatoes, diced

4 green onions, chopped

1 cup minced fresh parsley

1/2 cup minced fresh mint leaves

24 small romaine lettuce leaves

Soak bulghur in hot water to cover for 30 minutes. While the bulghur is soaking, make the dressing.

Combine the lemon juice and salt and stir until the salt has dissolved. Add the pepper, garlic and water and mix well. Slowly stir in the oil. Put the dressing in a jar with a tightly fitted lid and shake vigorously for 30 seconds. Set aside.

Drain the bulghur thoroughly. To the bulghur add the tomatoes, green onions, parsley, and mint leaves. Pour on the dressing and toss thoroughly. Chill well.

Serve on chilled salad plates with each serving surrounded by 4 romaine leaves. Traditionally, this salad is eaten by scooping it up on the romaine leaves.

❨ Makes 6 servings.

Reprinted from *The Calculating Cook: A Gourmet Cookbook for Diabetics and Dieters*, copyright 1972 by Jeanne Jones. With permission of the publisher, 101 Productions, San Francisco.

❧

Gary's Tabooli

1 cup uncooked bulghur
1/4 cup lemon juice
1/2 cup currants or raisins
1/2 cup sunflower seeds
1 bunch scallions, chopped fine
2 bunches fresh parsley, chopped fine
1/4 cup apple cider vinegar
1/4–1/2 cup tamari (soy sauce)
Herbimare (seasoned salt) to taste
Garlic powder to taste if desired

Soak the bulghur in hot water to cover for about 30 minutes or until the water is absorbed.

When the bulghur has cooled, add the remaining ingredients and mix well.

Chill before serving.

❨ Serves 4 to 6.

Herbimare and other seasoned salts are found in many health food stores.

❦

Curry-Condiment Salad

10 walnut halves, cut into small pieces
1/2 teaspoon sea salt
1/4 cup shredded unsweetened coconut
2 heads Boston lettuce
2/3 fresh papaya, finely diced
1/2 cup Curry Salad Dressing (p. 226)

Toast walnuts as follows: Spread them thinly on a flat baking dish or cookie sheet with sides. Lightly salt them. Put them under the broiler. Watch them constantly because they burn easily. Stir them around to brown evenly. When they are golden brown, remove them from the broiler.

Toast coconut in the same manner except eliminate the sea salt. Let the nuts and coconut cool.

Wash and dry the lettuce. Tear into bite-size pieces (approximately 8 cups).

In a large salad bowl, toss the lettuce, toasted walnuts, and chopped fruit thoroughly with the curry dressing. Serve on very cold salad plates and sprinkle with toasted coconut.

❨ Makes 8 servings.

If papaya is unavailable, 1 large apple or 1 cup of chopped fresh pineapple may be substituted. Try substituting 12 crushed peanuts for the walnuts and 1/4 cup raisins for the fruit.

Reprinted from *The Calculating Cook: A Gourmet Cookbook for Diabetics and Dieters,* copyright 1972 by Jeanne Jones. With permission of the publisher, 101 Productions, San Francisco.

❦

Cold Pea Salad in the Bowl . . . Three Days Old

3 cups fresh green peas
1 cup sour cream or yogurt
1 cup green onion tops, chopped fine
1 teaspoon seasoned salt

Steam peas about 5 minutes—till they turn bright green.

Mix together the sour cream, green onion tops, and seasoned salt.

Fold into the green peas and mix thoroughly. Chill in the refrigerator for 2 days before serving.

⟮ Makes 6 servings.

Seasoned salt is available in health food stores. Some brand names are Herbimare and Spike.

Reprinted from *The Calculating Cook: A Gourmet Cookbook for Diabetics and Dieters*, copyright 1972 by Jeanne Jones. With permission of the publisher, 101 Productions, San Francisco.

❦

Semi-Tropical Fruit Cup

1/2 pint plain yogurt

1 ripe banana, sliced

1 orange, diced (a navel orange is best)

1 cup diced pineapple (or unsweetened pineapple chunks
cut in half)

dash of cinnamon and 6 mint sprigs for garnish

Put yogurt and sliced banana into the blender. Blend until smooth. Pour banana-yogurt sauce over the diced oranges and pineapple. Mix well and serve in sherbet glasses. Garnish with a sprinkle of cinnamon and mint leaves.

⟮ Makes 6 servings.

Reprinted from *The Calculating Cook: A Gourmet Cookbook for Diabetics and Dieters*, copyright 1972 by Jeanne Jones. With permission of the publisher, 101 Productions, San Francisco.

Salad Dressings, Dips and Sauces

Homemade Mayonnaise

1 egg, at room temperature
1/4 teaspoon salt
1 1/4 cups unsaturated oil (safflower, soy, peanut)
2 tablespoons lemon juice
1 tablespoon apple cider vinegar

Put the egg, the salt and 1/4 cup of the oil into a blender. Cover the container and start the blender at low speed. When the mixture is thoroughly combined and while the blender is still on, slowly pour in another 1/2 cup of oil. Then add the lemon juice and the vinegar. Add the last 1/2 cup of oil very slowly to the mixture and continue to blend until the mixture thickens. Store in the refrigerator.
⟨ Makes about 1 3/4 cups of mayonnaise.

❀

Magic Mayonnaise

1 egg, at room temperature
1/4 teaspoon dry mustard
1/2 teaspoon salt
1 tablespoon lemon juice
1 cup salad oil

Dip the egg in boiling water for 30 seconds. Put the egg into the blender with the dry mustard, salt, lemon juice, and 1/4 cup of the salad oil. Turn on low speed. Immediately start pouring in the remaining oil in a steady stream. Switch the blender to high speed for 3 or 4 seconds and then turn it off. May be stored in the refrigerator.

❲ Yields 1–1 1/2 cups.

❦

Curry Dressing

1 cup sour cream less 2 tablespoons

3 tablespoons Homemade Mayonnaise (p. 225)

1/2 teaspoon curry powder

1/8 teaspoon powdered ginger

1/4 teaspoon salt

Put all ingredients in the blender and blend until smooth.

❲ Makes about 1 1/2 cups.

❦

Creamy French Dressing

2 cups salad oil

1 clove garlic, split

2 teaspoons grated onion

1/2 teaspoon dry mustard

1/8 teaspoon pepper

1 teaspoon paprika

1 teaspoon salt

1/4 cup tomato juice

3/4 cup vinegar

1 egg white

In a mixing bowl, combine the salad oil, garlic, onion, seasonings, tomato juice and vinegar. Let stand for 1 hour; remove the garlic and discard.

Add the egg white, mixing vigorously with an electric beater (or blender). Transfer to a tightly covered jar and store in the refrigerator. ⟮ Makes 3 cups.

❧

Salad Dressing with Garlic

1/4 cup apple cider vinegar

2 teaspoons dry mustard

1 teaspoon finely chopped garlic

1 teaspoon paprika

dash of sea salt

dash of freshly ground pepper

1 cup safflower oil

Put vinegar, mustard, garlic, paprika, salt and pepper to taste in a mixing bowl. Add oil, beating with wire whisk. Chill. Serve over your favorite salad.

⟮ Makes about 1 cup.

❧

Garden Salad Dressing

1 1/2 tablespoons tarragon vinegar

1 teaspoon lemon juice

1/4 teaspoon dry mustard

1/2 teaspoon salt

3 tablespoons tomato juice

1/2 teaspoon grated onion

dash freshly ground pepper

1/8 teaspoon tarragon

5 tablespoons salad oil

1 clove garlic, quartered

Beat the vinegar, lemon juice, mustard and salt until the salt is dissolved. Add the tomato juice, onion, pepper and tarragon. Slowly add the oil and mix thoroughly. Add the quartered garlic.

Pour the dressing into a jar with a tightly fitted lid. Shake vigorously for 30 seconds. Store in the refrigerator.
([Makes 1 generous cup.

Reprinted from *The Calculating Cook: A Gourmet Cookbook for Diabetics and Dieters,* copyright 1972 by Jeanne Jones. With permission of the publisher, 101 Productions, San Francisco.

Sprout Slaw Dressing

3/4 cup plain yogurt
1/4 teaspoon sea salt
1/2 teaspoon celery seed
Sprouts Slaw (p. 212)

Mix all ingredients together in a mixing bowl. Chill, pour over sprout slaw and mix well.
([Makes 3/4 cup.

Tofu Salad Dressing

3 or 4 cakes of tofu (bean curd)
1/2 cup tamari (soy sauce)
3/4 cup oil
1/4 cup vinegar
1/2 teaspoon basil
1/2 teaspoon garlic powder
1/2 teaspoon oregano
1/2 medium onion, sliced

Mix all ingredients in a blender until creamy.
([Makes about 3–4 cups.

Tofu is available in many supermarkets and Oriental markets.

Tomato Juice Salad Dressing

1/2 cup tomato juice
2 tablespoons apple cider vinegar

1 teaspoon onion flakes
1/2 teaspoon dry mustard
1/2 teaspoon garlic powder
1/4 teaspoon salt
1/8 teaspoon white pepper
1/2 teaspoon parsley flakes
oregano, to taste

Combine all ingredients in a jar with a tightly fitting lid. Shake well. Refrigerate. Allow to marinate for 2 to 3 hours.
(Makes about 1/2 cup.

❦

Pinto Bean Dip

2 cups cooked pinto beans
1/2 onion, minced
1 clove garlic, pressed
1 chili pepper, minced
1 tomato, chopped fine
1 tablespoon tamari (soy sauce)
salt to taste

Mash the beans in a large bowl and add all of the seasonings. If you wish, you may place all ingredients in a blender and puree them.

Serve with crackers or use to fill a pita bread and garnish with sprouts for a tasty sandwich.
(Makes about 2 1/2 cups.

❦

Tamari Dip

1 cup Homemade Mayonnaise (p. 225)
1 clove garlic, pressed
2 tablespoons tamari (soy sauce)
1 tablespoon sesame oil
1 scallion, thinly sliced

Combine all ingredients in a bowl and chill for at least one hour before serving with raw vegetables of your choice.
(Makes 1 cup.

❦

Avocado Dip

2 avocados
1 or 2 finely chopped scallions
1 tomato
1–2 teaspoons Homemade Mayonnaise (p. 225) or yogurt
1 teaspoon lemon juice
1 teaspoon pineapple juice
1 sprig of parsley or watercress, chopped fine
fresh pressed garlic (optional)

Cut avocados in half. Remove the pit and the meat of the avocado. Put the meat and all other ingredients in a blender and blend well. Serve with small pieces of various raw vegetables. It's also delicious over raw cabbage.
(Makes 2 cups.

❦

Almond Sauce

2 cups almonds
2 tablespoons honey
1 tablespoon orange rind
2 tablespoons safflower oil
2 cups wheat germ
1 1/4 cups apple cider

Grind almonds in a blender. Then add the rest of the ingredients and blend until smooth.
(Makes 1 1/2–2 cups.

❦

Tofu Dip

1 small cake tofu (bean curd), pressed (p. 59) and mashed
1 teaspoon lemon juice
dash cayenne pepper
1 small scallion

1 tablespoon tamari (soy sauce)
1/2 teaspoon dry mustard

Place all ingredients in a blender and blend until smooth. You may need to add a little bit of water (up to 1/4 cup) to get the consistency you desire.
(Makes 1/2 cup.

Tofu is available in many supermarkets and Oriental markets.

❧

Mushroom Cream Hijiki

1/4 cup safflower oil
1 1/2 pounds mushrooms, sliced
1/2 pound Spanish onions, sliced
1/4 cup unsalted butter
1/4 cup whole wheat flour
1/2 cup hijiki (seaweed)
3 cups skim milk
1 cup light cream

In a large saucepan, heat the oil and sauté the mushrooms and onions briefly. Add the butter and, after it's melted, whisk in the flour. Cook over low heat, stirring, until thickened, about 5 minutes.

Prepare hijiki by soaking it in warm water. Drain. Cut into 1/2 inch strips. Add the hijiki to the mushrooms and onions.

Heat the milk and the cream in a large saucepan. Add the mushroom-flour-hijiki mixture and stir over low heat till thickening takes place.

To refrigerate this sauce, cool at room temperature with cover off or it will sour.
(Yields 1 quart of sauce.

Hijiki is available in health food stores and Oriental markets.

❦

Paul's Veggie Pesto

1 1/2 pounds shelled walnuts
1 1/2 cups fresh parsley
5 garlic cloves, peeled
1 cup water
1 cup olive oil
3/4 teaspoon salt
pinch of pepper
1 1/2 teaspoons oregano
1 1/2 teaspoons rosemary
1 1/2 teaspoons thyme
3 teaspoons basil
3/4 cup freshly grated Romano cheese

Chop the nuts and set aside.

Wash the parsley and pat dry with a towel. Remove stems. Combine parsley and all other ingredients except for nuts and cheese in a blender: puree. Remove from blender and transfer to a large mixing bowl. Add nuts and cheese. Mix well using a wooden spoon.

Serve with soups, steamed vegetables or salads.

❨ Makes about 2 pounds.

❦

Quick Tomato Sauce

1 6-ounce can tomato paste
1 cup Burgundy wine
4 cloves garlic, pressed
1 tablespoon basil
2 teaspoons oregano
1 tablespoon parsley flakes
2 teaspoons onion powder

Combine all ingredients in a small saucepan. Cook over low heat for 10 minutes. Stir occasionally to make a smooth sauce.

❨ Makes about 1 1/2 cups.

❦

Mushroom Sauce

1/4 cup unsalted butter
1 pound mushrooms, sliced thin
juice of half a small lemon (optional)
2 tablespoons arrowroot powder
1 teaspoon salt
2 1/4 cups milk

Melt the butter in a large saucepan. Add the mushrooms and lemon juice. Sauté the mushrooms until wilted.

With a whisk, blend in the arrowroot and salt. Gradually stir in the milk. Cook and stir until thickened, 5 to 7 minutes.

This sauce may be made ahead of time and refrigerated until needed.

❮ Makes about 1 1/2 cups.

Breads and Breakfasts

Easy Whole Wheat Bread

3 1/2 cups whole wheat flour
1 tablespoon active dry yeast
1 cup warm water
2 teaspoons honey
2 tablespoons molasses
1 tablespoon salt
3/4–1 cup warm water
1 tablespoon caraway seeds

Place the flour in a large bowl and put the bowl in the oven at the lowest possible setting for at least 15 minutes. This is to warm the flour and the bowl.

Sprinkle the yeast over the warm water. Add the honey and molasses. Stir to dissolve the yeast and the sweeteners. Add the yeast mixture to the warm flour. Then add salt. Stir in enough warm water to make a sticky dough.

Oil a large loaf pan and put the dough in it. Sprinkle with the caraway seeds. Let it rise for 45 minutes to 1 hour—until the dough just reaches the rim of the pan. Preheat oven to 400 degrees.

Bake for 30–40 minutes or until nicely browned. When done, the loaf should have a hollow sound when rapped on the bottom with your knuckles. Cool bread in pan for 10 minutes before removing it to cool on a rack.

❨ Makes 1 loaf.

❦

Anise Raisin Bread

1/4 cup honey
1 1/2 cups hot water
2 tablespoons active dry yeast
1 teaspoon anise seed
1/2 teaspoon ground cloves
1/4 cup safflower oil
5 cups whole wheat flour
1 cup raisins
1/2 cup melted butter

In a large mixing bowl, combine the honey and hot water. Mix well. When the water is lukewarm, dissolve the yeast in it. Add the spices and oil to the water. Stir after each addition.

Pour 3 cups of flour into the water and combine thoroughly. Add 1 more cup of flour and mix again. Add the rest of the flour slowly, controlling the consistency of the dough so that it is moist and flexible. The dough must be workable and not stick to the bowl.

Knead dough at least 10 minutes, then transfer it to an oiled bowl. Cover with a damp cloth and let the dough rise in a warm place for an hour or until it doubles in size.

Punch dough down. Knead in the raisins. Return the dough to the bowl, put in a warm place and let it rise again for 45 minutes.

Punch down again and then turn dough onto a flat surface. Cut dough carefully in half with a knife. Shape into 2 loaves forming smooth tops and place on a greased cookie sheet. Let rise for 20 minutes or until doubled in bulk.

Preheat oven to 350 degrees. Bake for 40 to 60 minutes. After loaves have started to brown (about 1/2 hour after being in the oven) brush tops with melted butter. When the bread is done the loaves should make a hollow sound when rapped on the bottom with your knuckles.

❦ Makes 2 loaves.

❧

Yeasted Banana Cornbread

1 1/2 tablespoons active dry yeast

1/2 cup warm water

2 tablespoons honey

1 cup cornmeal

3/4 cup whole wheat flour

1/4 cup soy flour

3/4 teaspoon salt

2 medium bananas

3 tablespoons safflower oil

2 eggs, beaten

Dissolve the yeast in the water and add the honey. Set aside this mixture while you prepare the rest of the ingredients.

Combine the cornmeal, whole wheat flour, soy flour and salt in a mixing bowl.

In another bowl, mash the bananas (to equal 1 cup) and to them add the oil and the eggs. Stir well. Add the banana mixture to the yeast. Now combine the liquid and dry ingredients, stirring to mix well.

Pour into a greased 8-inch-square pan. Let the dough rise in a warm, draft-free spot (like a kitchen cabinet) for 30 minutes. Bake at 350 degrees for 30 to 35 minutes until a toothpick inserted into the center comes out clean.

❲ Makes 1 cornbread.

❧

Cinnamon Bread

3/4 cup boiling water

1/2 cup rolled oats

1/4 cup honey

2 tablespoons unsalted butter at room temperature

1 teaspoon cinnamon

1 tablespoon active dry yeast

1 cup lukewarm water

5–6 cups whole wheat flour

Pour the boiling water over the oats in a large bowl and let the mixture stand for 30 minutes. Add the honey, butter and cinnamon.

In a separate bowl, dissolve the yeast in the warm water and allow to stand for 5 minutes. Add the yeast to the oat mixture. Next beat in about 3 cups of flour. When the flour has been worked in, add another cup of flour. When this has also been thoroughly worked in, add flour gradually as needed to make a medium-soft dough.

Turn onto a floured board and knead until smooth, about 10 minutes. Place the dough in a clean, buttered bowl, then turn to butter the top. Cover with a towel and let it rise in a warm place until it doubles in bulk, about 1 hour.

Turn onto a floured surface and knead again. Divide and shape the dough into two loaves and place in well-oiled 9 × 5 × 3 loaf pans. Cover and let rise until doubled in bulk, about 45 minutes.

Preheat the oven to 400 degrees and bake loaves for 5 minutes, then lower the temperature to 350 degrees and bake for 40 minutes longer or until loaves sound hollow when tapped on the bottom with your knuckles.

❪ Makes 2 loaves.

❧

Corn and Raisin Bread

1 tablespoon active dry yeast
1 teaspoon honey
1 1/2 cups warm water
3 tablespoons oil
1 tablespoon salt
3 tablespoons molasses
1 teaspoon ground cloves
1 1/2 cups whole wheat flour
2 cups cornmeal
1/2 cup raisins

In a large mixing bowl, combine the yeast, honey, and water. Let stand for 5 minutes. Then add the oil, salt, molasses and cloves to the yeast.

Stir in about 1/2 cup of whole wheat flour and 1/2 cup cornmeal and beat well. Continue adding whole wheat flour and cornmeal gradually, beating until the dough is elastic. The dough should be very hard to beat toward the end. Let it rise for 1 hour.

Meanwhile, soak raisins in boiling water to cover for 3 minutes and then drain well. Stir down the batter and add the raisins. Place in an oiled loaf pan and let rise for 50 minutes.

Preheat oven to 350 degrees.

Bake for 1 hour or until a tester inserted into the center comes out clean.

(Makes 1 loaf.

❦

Cottage Cheese Oatmeal Bread

1/2 cup hot water

2 cups (1 pound) cottage cheese

1 teaspoon onion powder

3 tablespoons unsalted butter

2 teaspoons salt

2 eggs

2 tablespoons honey

3 1/2 cups whole wheat flour

2 tablespoons active dry yeast

1 cup rolled oats (oatmeal)

2 tablespoons dill seed

Place water, cottage cheese, onion powder, butter, salt, eggs, and honey in a blender and blend until smooth. Place 2 cups of flour and yeast in a large bowl and add blended mixture to it. Beat until very smooth, about 2 minutes. Stir in oats, dill and 1 1/2 cups flour. Turn into oiled bowl. Cover and let rise until double in bulk, approximately 1 hour.

Punch down and place in an oiled loaf pan and let rise for 45 minutes. Bake at 350 degrees for 35 minutes or until the loaf sounds hollow when tapped on the bottom with your knuckles.

(Makes 1 loaf.

❦

Oatmeal Raisin Bread

1 tablespoon active dry yeast

2/3 cup warm water

2 tablespoons honey

1/4 cup milk powder

2 tablespoons oil

1/2 teaspoon salt

1 egg, beaten

2/3 cup rolled oats (oatmeal)

2 cups whole wheat flour

1/2 cup raisins

1 egg and water to be used as egg wash

Sprinkle yeast over the warm water and add the honey. Stir to dissolve and let sit for 5 minutes. Add the milk powder, oil, salt and egg to the yeast mixture, mixing well. Mix in the oats and 1 cup of flour, beating until thoroughly incorporated. Continue stirring in flour gradually as needed to form a dough that is easy to knead.

Turn the dough onto a floured surface and knead until smooth and elastic, about 10 minutes. Place in an oiled bowl and then turn the dough so that all sides are coated. Cover with a towel and let stand in a warm place until doubled in bulk, about 1 1/2 hours.

Punch dough down and knead in raisins.

Preheat oven to 375 degrees.

Shape dough into a round loaf. Then make an egg wash by beating an egg with a little bit of water. Brush the top of the loaf with the wash. Place the loaf on an oiled cookie sheet to rise. Let rise 1 hour in a draft-free spot (inside a kitchen cabinet).

Bake for 25 minutes until nicely browned and the loaf sounds hollow when rapped on the bottom with your knuckles. Cool on rack before slicing.

(Makes 1 loaf.

❦

Onion Bread

1 cup low-sodium Vegetable Stock* (p. 124)

1 tablespoon honey

1 tablespoon active dry yeast

2 cups whole wheat flour

1 small onion, minced

1/2 teaspoon dried dill weed

Heat the stock in a saucepan until warm. Transfer the stock to a large bowl. Add the honey and stir to dissolve. Add the yeast and stir to dissolve. Add flour, minced onion, and dill weed. Mix well with a large wooden spoon. When the batter is smooth, cover the bowl with a towel and let the dough rise in a warm place until it triples in bulk, about 45 minutes.

Preheat oven to 350 degrees.

Stir down and beat vigorously for a few minutes. Then turn into a greased loaf pan. Let stand for about 10 minutes in a warm place before putting into the oven. Bake about 1 hour or until the loaf sounds hollow when tapped on the bottom with your knuckles.

❲ Makes 1 loaf.

* You may use homemade stock as long as it has not been made with vegetables that have a high sodium content. You might use low-sodium vegetable powder to be sure.

❧

Rye Bread

1 tablespoon active dry yeast

3/4 cup warm water

3/4 cup milk

1 tablespoon honey

2 teaspoons salt

2 tablespoons oil

2 tablespoons caraway seeds

2 cups rye flour

2–3 cups whole wheat flour

1 egg for wash, beaten

In a large mixing bowl, dissolve the yeast in the water. Allow to sit for 5 minutes. Add the milk, honey, salt, oil and caraway seeds to the yeast and stir well.

Blend in the rye flour and 2 cups of whole wheat flour, then gradually add the rest of the whole wheat flour as necessary to make a dough that is easily kneaded. Knead for 5 minutes until smooth and elastic.

Place the dough in an oiled bowl, turn to coat all sides and let rise for 1 1/2 hours.

Punch down, knead, and shape into a loaf. Brush with the beaten egg. Let rise for another 30 minutes.

Preheat oven to 375 degrees.

Put the loaf on an oiled cookie sheet and bake for 35–40 minutes, until the loaf sounds hollow when tapped on the bottom with your knuckles.

❨ Makes 1 loaf.

❧

Nut Brown Triticale Loaf

2 tablespoons active dry yeast

2 cups warm water

1 tablespoon blackstrap molasses

1/4 cup safflower oil

2/3 cup dry milk powder

1 tablespoon salt

1/2 cup soy flour

2 1/2 cups whole wheat flour

3 cups triticale flour

Dissolve the yeast in the warm water along with the molasses. Allow this mixture to sit until it bubbles, about 5 minutes. Add the oil, milk powder and salt. Combine the soy flour, whole wheat flour and triticale flour and stir into the yeast mixture. Do not knead now. Let the dough rise, in a covered bowl, until doubled in bulk.

Now turn it out onto a floured board and knead until smooth and elastic. Add more flour as necessary to keep the dough from sticking to the board. Form the dough into a ball, replace in the bowl and let rise until doubled in bulk again.

Punch the dough down, knead briefly and form into 2 loaves. Place the loaves into oiled loaf pans and let them rise until doubled.

Preheat oven to 350 degrees.

Bake loaves for 50 to 60 minutes. When done, they should be golden brown and sound hollow when tapped with your knuckles.

❨ Makes 2 loaves.

For a chewier bread, omit the second rising.

❦

Soy-Enriched Wheat Berry Bread

2 tablespoons active dry yeast
1/2 cup warm water
2 1/4 teaspoons honey
3/4 cups very hot (but not boiling) water
1 1/2 tablespoons safflower oil
1 tablespoon salt
2 1/2 cups whole wheat flour
1/4 cup dried milk powder
1/4 cup soy flour
1/2 cup cooked wheat berries
unsalted butter, melted

Dissolve the yeast in the warm water along with 1/4 teaspoon of honey. Let this mixture stand until it bubbles, about 5 minutes while you combine the hot water with the oil and two tablespoons of honey. Pour this mixture into the yeast mixture and add the salt. Add one cup of the whole wheat flour and beat until very smooth. Sift the remaining flour, the dry milk powder and soy flour into another bowl and then stir it into the yeast mixture along with the wheat berries.

Turn the dough out onto a floured board and knead for 10 minutes. Allow the dough to rise for 20 minutes, then punch it down, knead it once again and allow it to rise for an additional 10 minutes.

Form into a loaf and place in an oiled pan. Brush the top of the loaf with melted butter and place the pan in a loose plastic bag.

Refrigerate for at least two hours, though you may keep it chilled for up to 12 hours before baking.

Allow the dough to stand at room temperature for at least 30 minutes before baking in a preheated 350-degree oven for 50 minutes. The bread should sound hollow when rapped on the bottom with your knuckles.
⟨ Makes 1 loaf.

❦

Simple Brown Bread

2 cups whole wheat flour
1/2 cup wheat germ

1 teaspoon baking soda
1/4 teaspoon salt
1/2 cup molasses
1 1/2 cups buttermilk
1/2 cup raisins

In a mixing bowl combine the flour, wheat germ, baking soda and salt. In a separate bowl, mix together the molasses and the buttermilk. Add this mixture to the flour mixture. Stir in the raisins. Bake in a greased loaf pan at 350 degrees for 50 minutes or until a tester inserted into the center comes out clean.
❧ Makes 1 loaf.

❀

Buttermilk Cornbread

2 1/2 cups cornmeal
1/2 teaspoon baking soda
1 teaspoon salt
2 eggs, beaten
3 tablespoons oil
2 cups buttermilk

Combine the cornmeal, baking soda, and salt in a mixing bowl. In another bowl, mix together the beaten eggs, the oil and the buttermilk. Stir in the dry ingredients and mix until you have a smooth batter. Pour into an 8-inch-square pan that has been well greased.

Preheat oven to 400 degrees.

Bake for 35 minutes, or until a tester inserted into the center comes out clean.
❧ Makes 1 loaf.

❦

Variety Cornbread

1 cup yellow cornmeal

1/2 cup whole wheat flour

1 teaspoon salt

3 teaspoons baking powder

1 tablespoon honey

1 egg

3 tablespoons safflower oil

1/4 cup milk

1/2 teaspoon curry powder and/or

1/2 cup cooked corn kernels and/or

1 teaspoon celery seed and/or

1 tablespoon finely chopped fresh basil or
    1/2 teaspoon dried basil

Preheat oven to 450 degrees.

Combine the first 4 ingredients in a mixing bowl and stir in the honey, egg, oil and milk. The batter should be medium thick, so you may have to add a bit more milk. Add any or all of the variations and stir well. Pour into a well-greased loaf pan and bake for 30 minutes. The bread is done when a tester inserted in the center comes out clean.

❦ Makes 1 loaf cornbread.

❦

Date Nut Bread

2 tablespoons unsalted butter

1/2 cup honey

1 egg

1 teaspoon almond extract

1 1/2 cups whole wheat flour

1/4 teaspoon salt

1/4 teaspoon baking soda

2 teaspoons baking powder

1/2 cup buttermilk

1 cup chopped dates

1/2 cup chopped walnuts

Preheat oven to 350 degrees.

Cream the butter and honey until fluffy, preferably using an electric mixer. Add the egg and beat well. Add the almond extract and beat again.

In a separate bowl, combine the flour, salt, baking soda and baking powder. Then add this dry mixture to the butter and honey mixture alternately with the buttermilk. Fold in the dates and the walnuts.

Bake in an oiled loaf pan for 50 to 60 minutes, until a tester inserted into the center comes out clean.

⁅ Makes 1 loaf.

❧

Irish Soda Bread

1/4 cup butter

2 tablespoons honey

2 eggs

4 cups whole wheat flour

1 teaspoon salt

2 teaspoons baking powder

2 teaspoons baking soda

2 tablespoons caraway seeds

1 1/2 cups buttermilk

1/2 cup raisins

Preheat oven to 375 degrees.

Cream the butter and the honey in a large mixing bowl. Beat in the eggs.

In a separate bowl, sift together the flour, salt, baking powder and baking soda, and then add the caraway seeds. Add the buttermilk to the creamed mixture alternating with the flour mixture. Work the raisins in with your hands.

Turn the dough onto a floured surface and knead for about 1 minute. Form dough into a round loaf and place it in a greased 1 1/2-

quart casserole. Make a slash with a sharp knife across the top of the bread. Bake for 60 to 70 minutes. Cool in casserole dish for 10 minutes and then turn onto rack to cool completely.

(Makes 1 loaf.

If you don't have a round casserole, just knead in enough flour to make the dough stiff enough to hold a shape. Make into a round loaf and bake on a greased cookie sheet. Reduce cooking time by about 15 minutes.

❦

Lemon Tea Bread

1/2 cup unsalted butter

1/3 cup honey

2 teaspoons grated lemon peel (optional)

2 cups whole wheat flour

3 teaspoons baking powder

1/2 teaspoon baking soda

1 teaspoon salt

2 eggs

3/4 cup water

2 tablespoons lemon juice

Preheat oven to 350 degrees.

Cream together butter, honey, and lemon peel in a large bowl with an electric mixer.

In a separate bowl combine the flour, baking powder, baking soda and salt. Add the eggs one at a time to the creamed butter, beating well after each addition. Combine the water and lemon juice. Add the flour to the creamed mixture alternating with the lemon/water. Pour into a greased loaf pan. Bake for 1 hour or until a toothpick inserted into the bread comes out clean.

(Makes 1 loaf.

❦

Whole Wheat Sunflower Seed Bread

2 eggs

1 cup milk

1 tablespoon safflower oil

1/4 cup honey

1/4 cup molasses

3 cups whole wheat pastry flour

2 teaspoons baking powder

1 teaspoon salt

1/2 cup toasted sunflower seeds

1/2 cup currants or raisins

1 tablespoon sesame or poppy seeds

Preheat oven to 350 degrees.

Combine the eggs, milk, oil, honey and molasses in a large mixing bowl. Beat until blended.

In another bowl, combine the flour, baking powder and salt. Pour the dry ingredients into the egg and milk mixture. Beat well, then fold in the sunflower seeds and currants. Pour into a greased loaf pan and sprinkle with the sesame or poppy seeds. Bake for 1 hour until the top is golden brown.

❡ Makes 1 loaf.

❧

Sweet Zucchini Bread

1 cup honey

1 cup safflower oil

2 eggs

1 teaspoon vanilla

2 cups shredded raw zucchini (with skin)

3 cups whole wheat flour

2 teaspoons baking soda

1/2 teaspoon baking powder

1 teaspoon cinnamon

1 teaspoon powdered ginger

1 teaspoon ground cloves

1/2 teaspoon salt

1 cup walnuts, broken into pieces

Preheat oven to 325 degrees. Then grease two 9 × 5 × 3 loaf pans.

Blend honey, oil, eggs, vanilla and zucchini in a bowl.

In another bowl sift together the flour, baking soda and the baking powder. Add the spices and the salt. Then add the dry ingredients to the zucchini mixture. Mix well. Fold in the walnuts. Mix well and turn into loaf pans and bake for 1 hour or until a toothpick inserted into the bread comes out clean. Cool for 20 minutes before removing from the pan.

(Makes 2 loaves.

❦

Blueberry Biscuits

2 cups whole wheat pastry flour
1 tablespoon baking powder
1/2 teaspoon sea salt
1/3 cup safflower oil
2/3 cup milk
1/2 teaspoon cinnamon
1 teaspoon vanilla extract
1 cup blueberries, stems removed

Into a large mixing bowl, sift together the flour, baking powder and salt. Add the oil. The mixture will not be smooth. Add the milk, cinnamon and vanilla. Mix well until you are able to shape the dough into a ball. Knead several times. Work the blueberries into the dough carefully.

Roll out the dough until it is about 1/2 inch thick. Using either a biscuit cutter or a glass, cut out the biscuits. (If you are using a glass be sure to use the open end and dip it in flour to prevent the dough from sticking to it.) Grease a cookie sheet. Place each biscuit on the sheet so that the biscuits touch.

Preheat oven to 400 degrees.

Bake for 12–15 minutes.

(Makes 10–12 biscuits.

❦

Whole Wheat Popovers

3 eggs
1 1/2 cups milk
1 cup whole wheat flour
3/4 teaspoon sea salt
3 tablespoons unsalted butter, melted

Preheat oven to 475 degrees.

Combine eggs, milk, flour and salt in a mixing bowl and beat vigorously for about 2 minutes. Add butter.

Grease muffin tin with oil and place in oven for 2 minutes. Remove muffin tin from oven. Fill each cup three-quarters full and bake for 15 minutes. Turn oven temperature down to 350 degrees and bake 25 minutes longer until golden brown.

(Makes 12 muffins.

❧

Apple Muffins

2 cups whole wheat flour

5 teaspoons baking powder

1/2 teaspoon salt

1 egg

1 cup milk

*3/4–1 cup chopped cored apples (leave the skin on if the
    apples aren't waxed)*

2–4 tablespoons honey, depending on the sweetness of the fruit

1/4 cup unsalted butter, melted

Preheat oven to 375 degrees.

In one bowl combine the flour, baking powder and salt.

In a second bowl beat the egg and then add the milk and fruit. Mix.

In a third bowl pour desired amount of honey. Melt the butter and add it to the honey, stirring until it is mixed thoroughly. Then combine the flour mixture with the milk mixture and then add the butter mixture. Mix thoroughly.

Fill each muffin cup three-quarters full and bake for 25 minutes, until golden brown.

(Makes 12 muffins.

Any fruit may be used, i.e., blueberries, peaches, raisins, etc.

✿

Banana Bran Muffins

1 egg, beaten
1/4 cup milk
1/4 cup safflower oil
1 cup mashed banana (about 2 medium bananas)
1 cup whole wheat flour
2 teaspoons baking powder
1/2 cup bran
1/2 teaspoon sea salt
1/3 cup honey

Preheat oven to 400 degrees.

Combine egg, milk and oil in a mixing bowl and mix well. Stir in the banana.

Combine the dry ingredients in a separate bowl. Add the dry ingredients to the egg mixture. Add honey. Mix just until the dry ingredients are moistened. Pour the batter into a greased muffin tin until the cups are two-thirds full. Bake about 20 minutes, until the tops are golden brown.

❨ Makes 12 muffins.

✿

Currant Bran Muffins

1 cup whole wheat flour
3/4 cup bran
3/4 teaspoon baking soda
1 cup buttermilk
1 egg
1/4 cup honey
1 tablespoon oil
1/4 cup currants

Preheat oven to 350 degrees.

Combine flour, bran and baking soda in a large mixing bowl and mix well.

In another bowl combine the buttermilk, egg, honey and oil. Add the liquid ingredients to the dry ingredients and stir only enough to moisten flour mixture. Add currants. Mix well. Spoon into well-greased muffin tin filling each cup two-thirds full. Bake for 20 to 25 minutes until the muffins are golden brown.

❨ Makes 12 muffins.

❦

Bran Muffins

1 cup whole wheat flour
3/4 cup bran
1/8 teaspoon salt
3/4 teaspoon baking soda
1 tablespoon honey
1 cup buttermilk
1 egg, beaten
1/4 cup molasses
1 tablespoon safflower oil

Preheat oven to 350 degrees.

In a large mixing bowl combine the flour, bran, salt and baking soda. Mix well.

In a separate bowl combine the honey, buttermilk, egg, molasses and oil. Mix thoroughly. Add this mixture to the dry ingredients, and beat until the mixture is just moistened. Spoon into a greased muffin pan, filling each cup three-quarters full.

Bake for 20 to 25 minutes, until the tops begin to brown.

❨ Makes 12 muffins.

❦

Three-Grain Muffins

1/3 cup cornmeal
1/3 cup soy flour
1 cup whole wheat flour
3/4 teaspoon salt
1 teaspoon baking soda
1 egg, beaten
1 cup yogurt
1/3 cup unsalted butter
2 tablespoons honey

Preheat oven to 350 degrees.

Combine the cornmeal, soy flour, and whole wheat flour together with the salt and baking soda in a large mixing bowl.

In a separate bowl mix together the egg and the yogurt. Beat thoroughly. Melt the butter and mix the honey in it, stirring to dissolve the honey. Pour the yogurt mixture into the flour mixture. Stir in the butter and mix only enough to moisten.

Pour into a greased muffin pan until each cup is two-thirds full and bake for 25 minutes or until brown.

❨ Makes 12 muffins.

❧

Gary's Magic Muffins

1 cup whole wheat flour

2 cups bran

1/2 cup safflower oil

1/3 cup honey

2/3 cup molasses

1 cup water

1 teaspoon vanilla

1/4 teaspoon allspice

1/4 teaspoon nutmeg

2 bananas, mashed

1/2 cup raisins

1/4 cup chopped pecans

1 teaspoon salt

Preheat oven to 350 degrees.

Combine all ingredients in a mixing bowl; mix well until blended. Pour the batter into a greased muffin tin until each cup is two-thirds full.

Bake for 30–45 minutes, until the tops are golden brown.

❨ Makes about 12 muffins.

❧

Corn Muffins

2/3 cup cornmeal

1 cup whole wheat flour

1 teaspoon baking soda

1 teaspoon onion powder

1/2 teaspoon dill weed

1 egg, beaten

1 cup plain yogurt

2 tablespoons honey

1/2 cup safflower oil

Preheat oven to 350 degrees.

In a bowl combine the cornmeal, flour, baking soda, onion powder and dill weed.

In another bowl, mix together the egg, yogurt and honey. Make sure the honey is mixed throughout the egg and the yogurt. Add the egg mixture to the dry ingredients. Mix only enough to moisten. Stir in the oil.

Pour the mixture into a buttered muffin tin so the cups are two-thirds full and bake for 25 minutes or until done.

⟨ Makes 12 muffins.

Whole Wheat Muffins

2 cups whole wheat flour

2 teaspoons baking powder

1/2 teaspoon salt

1 egg, beaten

1/4 cup safflower oil

1 1/2 cups milk or water

Preheat oven to 400 degrees. Grease muffin tins.

In a medium mixing bowl, combine all dry ingredients. In another mixing bowl, beat together the egg, oil and milk. Fold the liquid ingredients into the dry ones quickly and only until the flour is moistened. Spoon the batter into the muffin tins to fill the cups two-thirds full.

Bake 20 minutes, until the tops begin to brown.

⟨ Makes 12 muffins.

❦

Cheese Crisps

1 cup grated sharp Cheddar cheese

1/4 cup unsalted butter

1/4 teaspoon salt

1/2 cup whole wheat flour

In a large mixing bowl, combine the cheese, butter and salt. Add the flour and mix thoroughly. Roll into small balls. Place the balls on an oiled cookie sheet and flatten.

Bake at 400 degrees for 5 to 8 minutes. Do not let the edges get brown. Tastes great warm or cold.

❨ Makes about 2 1/2 dozen.

❦

Granola

6 cups rolled oats (oatmeal)

1 cup shredded unsweetened coconut

1/2 cup sesame seeds

3/4 cup raw, shelled sunflower seeds

1/2 cup sliced almonds

1 cup raw cashews

2 tablespoons sunflower meal

2 tablespoons almond meal

2 tablespoons sesame meal

1 cup wheat germ

1 cup honey

1/2 cup safflower oil

1 cup raisins

Preheat oven to 325 degrees.

Mix the dry ingredients together in a large bowl. Combine the honey and oil and pour them over the dry ingredients. Mix until everything is well blended.

Spread the cereal in a shallow baking pan. Cook for 10 minutes. Then add the raisins and cook for an additional 5 minutes.

Allow the granola to cool. Store it in an airtight container—such as an old mayonnaise jar—until you're ready to use it.

Serve with milk, yogurt or as a topping.

(Makes about 8 1/2 cups of granola.

❧

Crunchy Granola

3 cups uncooked rolled oats (oatmeal)

1/2 cup wheat germ

2 cups unsweetened coconut

1/4 cup bran

1/2 cup sunflower seeds

1/4 cup safflower oil

1/2 cup honey

1/2 cup apple juice

1/2 cup cashews

1/2 cup walnuts

1/2 cup almonds

1/2 cup raisins

2 teaspoons cinnamon

1/2 teaspoon nutmeg

Preheat oven to 250 degrees.

Mix together in a large bowl the oats, wheat germ, coconut, bran and sunflower seeds. Mix well.

In a small dish, combine the oil and the honey then add to the oat mixture. Then add the apple juice gradually.

Lightly grease a large baking pan with oil. Transfer the mixture to the baking pan, spreading it evenly over the pan. Place it in the oven and bake for 1 1/2 hours. It is important to stir the mixture every half hour or so.

Turn off the oven and, while the granola is still in the oven, stir in the raisins. Sprinkle the cinnamon and nutmeg over the entire mixture, and let the cereal cool in the oven.

Store in a jar with a tight cover.

(Makes about 6 cups.

❦

The Everything Breakfast

4 ounces of plain yogurt
2 ounces of your favorite kefir milk (liquid yogurt)
3 tablespoons raisins
1/4 cup walnuts, broken into pieces
1/4 cup almonds, broken into pieces
2 teaspoons cinnamon
1/4 cup Granola (p. 254)
1 banana, sliced
1 apple, sliced

Mix all ingredients in a bowl. There's enough for two to enjoy.

❦

Gary's Favorite Topping

1 8-ounce can frozen orange concentrate
1 cup ultrapasteurized heavy cream
*1/2 pound pitted cherries or strawberries (frozen may be used if
    out of season)*

Put all ingredients into a blender and whip until firm, about 1 1/2–2
minutes. Refrigerate until ready to use. Good on pancakes, waffles,
french toast—just about anything.
❦ Makes about 2 cups of topping.

❦

Whole Wheat Pancakes

3/4 cup whole wheat flour
3 eggs
1/2 cup cottage cheese
1/2 cup plain yogurt
1 teaspoon baking powder
1 teaspoon baking soda
fruit or tofu may be added

Blend all ingredients together. Pour onto a hot greased grill. Cook until bubbles appear on top. Turn and cook on the other side.
❴ Makes enough for 4.

❦

Baked Apple Pancake

3 eggs

3/4 cup milk

3/4 cup whole wheat flour

1/2 teaspoon salt

7 1/2 tablespoons unsalted butter

1 pound apples, washed, peeled, cored and thinly sliced

2–4 tablespoons honey (optional)

cinnamon

nutmeg

honey (1 tablespoon)

Preheat oven to 450 degrees.

Place eggs, milk, flour and salt in a blender and blend until smooth.

In a heavy 12-inch, oven-proof skillet, melt 1 1/2 tablespoons butter. As soon as it becomes hot, pour the batter in and put the skillet in the oven. After 15 minutes, lower the temperature to 350 degrees and cook for another 10 minutes. If the pancake puffs up while cooking just pierce it with a fork.

To prepare apples, sauté them in 4 tablespoons of butter until they are just soft. Add the honey and cinnamon and nutmeg to taste.

When the pancake is ready, slide it onto a plate. Pour apple filling on one half and then fold over the other side.

In a small dish combine the honey and 2 tablespoons melted butter. Pour over the pancake. Serve warm.

❴ Serves 2 to 4.

Desserts

Applesauce

5 pounds apples
1 1/2 cups cranberries
1/2 cup raisins
1/4 cup grated orange peel
1 cup honey or more to taste

Peel, core and quarter the apples. Put the apples and cranberries into a Dutch oven or kettle and cover with boiling water. Cook over low heat until the fruit is soft but not mushy, 10–15 minutes.

Pour off the water and puree the apples and cranberries in a blender or food mill. Stir in the raisins and orange peel and honey to taste and enjoy.

Keep refrigerated.

❦ Makes 3 quarts.

🌷

Nutty Apple Slices

1 medium apple
1 tablespoon lemon juice
1 tablespoon cream cheese
1/2 cup cottage cheese
2 tablespoons finely chopped pecans
1/4 teaspoon cinnamon

Do not peel the apple but core and slice it. Toss the apple slices in a small bowl with the lemon juice.

In another bowl, blend together the cream cheese, cottage cheese, and nuts. Spread the slices of apple with the cheese mixture. Arrange on a flat plate. Sprinkle with cinnamon. Refrigerate. Serve cold.
⟮ Serves 1 or 2.

❧

Baked Apple Fruit Medley

4 large baking apples (Rome Beauty)
1 cup finely diced dried figs
1/2 cup finely diced dates
1 medium Bartlett pear, peeled and minced fine
1/4 cup finely chopped walnuts
1/2 cup finely diced orange sections (remove seeds before dicing)
1/2 cup toasted wheat germ
4 teaspoons honey
cinnamon to taste
4 tablespoons unsalted butter

Core the apples and enlarge the core hole somewhat for the filling. Peel 1 inch of skin from the top.

In a medium mixing bowl, combine all the remaining ingredients except the butter. Mix well until thoroughly blended. Stuff the apples with the mixture.

Preheat oven to 375 degrees.

Place a pat of butter atop the stuffing, place the apples on a baking sheet and bake for 20 minutes. Serve warm or chilled with heavy cream.
⟮ Makes 4 servings.

❧

Apricot Roll

2 pounds dried Turkish apricots
1/2 pound black mission figs
1/2 pound chopped raisins
1/2 cup chopped dried apples
1/4 cup chopped almonds
1/4 cup chopped walnuts

Chop the apricots to a paste with a greased knife to prevent the apricots from sticking to the knife. Set aside the chopped apricots in a medium mixing bowl.

Combine the remaining ingredients in another bowl. Stir to blend.

On a large piece of greased wax paper, evenly spread the apricots with a spatula. Then place the chopped mixture onto the apricots and distribute evenly. Roll into a log, using the wax paper to lift the apricots, and then peel off the wax paper. Refrigerate till firm, about 2–3 hours.

Slice with a very sharp knife dipped in hot water before serving.
❲ Serves 10 to 12.

❦

Banana Peach Compote

2 cups water

2 cups apple juice

1 cup dried fruit (raisins, apples, figs, etc.), chopped

2 1/2 cups pureed bananas

2 1/2 cups pureed raw or cooked peaches

nutmeg, cloves, allspice to taste

yogurt or sour cream (optional)

In a large saucepan, combine the water and the apple juice. Add the dried fruit and place over medium heat. When the mixture begins to boil, lower the heat and allow to simmer for about 20 minutes.

Remove from the heat and add the banana and peach purees. Mix well. Stir in spices to taste.

Top with some yogurt or sour cream before serving either hot or cold.
❲ Serves 4 to 6.

❦

Ordinary Oranges

4 large seedless oranges

1 pint heavy cream (not ultra-pasteurized)

1/2 cup frozen orange concentrate

honey to taste

salt to taste

fresh mint for garnish

Cut oranges in half. Remove pulp; save pulp and shell. Chop the pulp finely and set aside.

In a large mixing bowl, whip the cream at low speed. Beat in the orange concentrate. Continue beating as you gradually pour in the honey and salt. Increase speed as the cream begins to hold its shape, but don't overbeat or you'll get butter. Beat only until the cream forms soft peaks or can hold its shape.

Fold in the orange pulp and mix gently. The mixture must be firm. Fill the orange shells with the cream and chill.

Garnish with fresh mint leaves.

⟨ Serves 8.

❦

Pears Baked with Cream

2 tablespoons unsalted butter

3 tablespoons honey

1 1-inch piece of vanilla bean, slit (or 1 teaspoon vanilla extract)

4 ripe pears, peeled, cored and quartered

6 tablespoons heavy cream

Melt the butter in an ovenproof skillet. Stir in the honey and vanilla bean or extract. Stir till blended. Arrange pears in the skillet and cook over low heat for 15 minutes, turning the pears once or twice.

Preheat oven to 350 degrees.

Add the cream and cook for 3 minutes longer. Place the skillet in the oven and bake for 5 minutes. Serve hot.

⟨ Serves 4.

❦

Pears with Raisin Stuffing

1/2 pound raisins

1 cup water

2 large Bartlett pears

1/2 cup honey

cinnamon to taste

3 tablespoons orange rind

In a small mixing bowl, combine the raisins and water. Let the raisins soak until they puff, about 10 minutes. Drain.

Cut the pears in half lengthwise. Remove the center and stem as well as the seeds. Remove the pulp of the pear, being careful not to tear the skin.

In a large mixing bowl, chop the pear pulp with the raisins. Add the honey and cinnamon and stir well to mix. Stuff the mixture into the pear shells. Sprinkle with orange rind. Serve immediately or chill and serve.

❡ Serves 2 to 4.

❧

Pretty Parfait

1 cup fresh pineapple (if canned, use unsweetened and drain)
1 cup papaya
raspberries, fresh or frozen (without sugar)
raisins and walnuts for garnish

Place the pineapple in the blender and puree. Pour the puree into a bowl. Puree the papaya the same way.

Using a parfait glass or any clear dessert glass or cup, pour in pineapple till the glass is one-quarter full. Now pour or spoon in papaya puree till the glass is half full. Continue layering.

Top with fresh raspberries and the raisins and walnuts. Serve as is or chill and serve—chilling improves the flavor.

❡ Makes 4 to 6 parfaits.

❧

Tropical Delight

4 chopped dates
1 papaya, peeled and sliced
2 bananas, peeled and sliced
unsweetened coconut, optional

Place all ingredients in a blender and puree. Pour into dessert cups. If you wish, top with a sprinkle of unsweetened coconut. Chill before serving.

❡ Serves 4 to 6.

❦

Almost Mocha Whipped Cream

2 cups heavy cream (not ultra-pasteurized)
honey to taste
1 teaspoon molasses
cinnamon to taste

In a large mixing bowl, whip the cream using the low speed on the mixer. Fold in the honey, molasses and cinnamon. Gradually increase the speed as the cream starts to hold its shape. Do not overbeat. ⟮ Makes about 2 cups.

❦

Crunchy Whole Wheat Pastry Pie Crust

2 cups whole wheat pastry flour
1/2 cup sunflower seed meal
1/4 teaspoon salt
1/2 cup unsalted butter, chilled
5 tablespoons ice water (more or less)

Combine the flour, sunflower seed meal and salt in a mixing bowl.

Cut the butter into 1/2 inch patties and add the patties to the dry ingredients. Use two knives or a pastry blender to incorporate the flour and butter until you have pea-sized particles. Do not work the dough with your fingers as your body warmth will cause the dough to become too sticky.

Add the ice water a bit at a time. (The amount you use will depend on the natural moisture of the flour, the temperature of the butter and the heat in your kitchen.) You should only add enough to make a dough that will hold together when you gather it up into a ball.

Turn the dough out onto a piece of canvas or thick cotton or a counter that you have dusted with flour. Divide the dough in half if you're making 2 bottom crusts. If you are making a 2-crust pie, use a slightly larger portion of dough for the bottom .crust. First pat the portion of dough you are using into a rough circle. Then start to roll it, turning the cloth to achieve a neat, circular shape. Pick up the cloth and invert the dough over the pie pan. Trim and flute the edges. Prick the dough with a fork so it will not buckle during baking. Chill for 30 minutes and then bake in a preheated 425-degree oven for 5 minutes.

Use the baked shell with any filling you wish. If you are making a 2-crust fruit pie, simply chill the shell and the rolled top first, then fill with fruit and bake according to recipe directions.

(Makes 2 9-inch pie shells or 1 double-crust pie.

❦

Apple Pie

2 pounds baking apples, washed, peeled, cored and sliced

1/2 cup honey

juice of 1 lemon

2 teaspoons cinnamon

1 teaspoon mace

1 double 9-inch pie shell, unbaked (p. 263)

2 tablespoons unsalted butter

In a large mixing bowl, mix together the apple slices, honey, lemon juice, cinnamon and mace. Pour into the pie shell. Dot with the butter.

Roll out the dough for the top crust and place on top of the apples. Pinch the edges together and then prick the top with a fork.

Bake at 350 degrees for 35–45 minutes or until top is browned and bubbles of juice do not burst.

(Serves 8.

❦

Organically Grown Apple Pie

6 cups sliced but not peeled apples (McIntosh or Rome Beauty)

1/4 to 1/2 cup raisins or sweet dried cherries

1/4 cup maple syrup

1/4 cup orange juice

1 teaspoon each cinnamon and ground cloves

1 9-inch or 10-inch pie shell (p. 263)

unsalted butter

Preheat oven to 400 degrees.

In a large bowl mix together all the ingredients except for the pie shell, butter and about 2 cups of the sliced apples. Put the mixture into the shell, then arrange the reserved apple slices on top in petal fashion, starting in the center and working toward the outer edge until you cover the whole pie. Dot well with butter. Bake for 45 minutes.

❡ Makes 1 pie or approximately 8 servings.

❧

Banana Cream Pie

3 tablespoons honey

1/4 teaspoon salt

4 tablespoons arrowroot

2 cups milk

2 eggs, well beaten

1/4 teaspoon lemon extract

3 bananas, peeled and sliced

1 9-inch baked pie crust (p. 263)

In a heavy saucepan, stir together the honey, salt and arrowroot. Add the milk and stir well. Place over low heat and stir constantly until the mixture thickens.

Remove from the heat and continue to stir. Add the eggs. Return to the stove and cook for about 8 minutes longer until the mixture thickens. Continue to stir as the mixture cooks.

Remove from the heat and stir in lemon extract.

Place a layer of sliced bananas over the bottom of the pie crust. Pour half of the cream filling over the bananas. Follow with another layer of bananas and the other half of the cream filling. Allow to cool. Then place in the refrigerator to chill before serving.

❡ Makes about 8 servings.

❦

Banana Yogurt Cheese Pie

1 cup rolled oats (oatmeal)
1/2 cup chopped pitted dates
2 tablespoons safflower oil
8 ounces cream cheese, at room temperature
2/3 cup plain yogurt
1 teaspoon vanilla extract
2 tablespoons honey
1 banana, mashed, or 1/2 cup other fruit, mashed or pureed

Place the oats and chopped dates in a blender and grind until the oats are broken into pieces and are mixed well with the dates. Add the oil and blend again until mixed thoroughly. Press into an 8-inch pie plate.*

Combine the cream cheese, yogurt, vanilla and honey in a large bowl and beat until very smooth or blend in a blender until smooth. Stir in the mashed banana. Pour into the pie shell and refrigerate several hours or until it sets. This pie doesn't have a very solid consistency but it's delicious.

❲ Makes 1 pie or about 6 servings.

* You may use a whole wheat pie crust, instead (p. 263).

❦

Carob Cream Pie

1 tablespoon agar-agar flakes
3/4 cup milk
1/4 cup honey
1/4 cup carob powder, sifted
2 tablespoons coffee beverage (Pero)
1/8 teaspoon salt
1 cup heavy cream
1 9-inch pie shell, baked (p. 263)

In a heavy medium saucepan combine the agar-agar, the milk, honey, carob powder, Pero and salt and stir well until mixed. Bring to a boil and then cook over low heat, stirring, for about 5 minutes or until the flakes dissolve.

Remove from heat and place in the refrigerator for about 5 minutes or until slightly thickened.

Whip the cream until it holds its shape. Fold in the carob mixture and mix gently. Pour into the pie shell and chill for at least 1 hour before serving.

(Serves 8.

❧

Coconut Custard Pie

2 cups milk

3 eggs, beaten

4 tablespoons honey

1 teaspoon vanilla

1 cup unsweetened coconut

1 9-inch pie shell, unbaked (p. 263)

Preheat oven to 450 degrees.

Mix the milk, eggs, honey and vanilla together in a large bowl. Make sure they are mixed well. Stir in the coconut. Pour into the pie shell. Bake for 10 minutes. Then turn oven down to 300 degrees and bake for 30 minutes longer or until a toothpick inserted into the custard comes out clean.

(Serves 8.

❧

Lemon Coconut Pie

4 egg yolks

1/2 cup honey

1 tablespoon agar-agar flakes

1/3 cup lemon juice

2/3 cup water

1 teaspoon lemon extract

4 egg whites, stiffly beaten with 1/4 teaspoon salt

1/2 cup shredded and toasted unsweetened coconut

1 9-inch whole wheat pie shell, baked (p. 263)

mint leaves for garnish

Combine the egg yolks, honey, agar-agar flakes, lemon juice and water in a saucepan. Cook over medium heat until the mixture comes to a boil. Simmer very slowly for about 5 minutes, stirring constantly with a wire whisk, until the flakes are dissolved. Stir in the lemon extract and chill the mixture in the refrigerator until it begins to thicken.

To beat the egg whites into really stiff peaks, make sure they are cold, the bowl is chilled and there is no trace of grease in the bowl or on your beaters.

Fold the egg whites into the lemon mixture along with the toasted coconut. Pile into the baked pie shell and chill for 2–3 hours before serving. Fresh mint leaves make a tasty and pretty garnish.

❖ Makes 8 servings.

❦

Peanut Pecan Pie

2 cups blackstrap molasses
pinch of salt
1 tablespoon whole wheat pastry flour
2 tablespoons unsalted butter, melted
1/2 cup shelled pecans
1/2 cup raw, unsalted peanuts
4 eggs, well beaten
1 8-inch pie shell, unbaked (p. 263)

Preheat oven to 350 degrees.

Grind the nut meats or put them into the blender until pulverized. Pour into a medium mixing bowl. Add all the other ingredients and stir until well combined. Pour the mixture into the pie shell and bake for 45 minutes, until well browned on top. Allow the pie to cool before serving.

This is very good topped with a small scoop of vanilla ice cream.

❖ Makes 1 pie or 6 servings.

❦

Pumpkin Carrot Pie

1 cup mashed cooked pumpkin (see below)
1/2 cup mashed cooked carrot
1/2 teaspoon cinnamon

1/2 teaspoon powdered ginger

nutmeg and mace to taste

dash salt

1 cup milk

1/2 cup cream or half and half

1 9-inch pie shell, unbaked (p. 263)

To make mashed cooked pumpkin, cut a pumpkin in half and scoop out the seeds (save them for toasting later). Put the halves of the pumpkin on a lightly oiled baking sheet and bake in a 450-degree oven until tender, about 45 minutes. Scoop out the flesh and mash before using. Any leftover pumpkin can be frozen for use in other recipes.

Combine all the ingredients using an electric mixer or egg beater and pour the mixture into the pie shell. If you wish a crispier crust, prebake the pie shell at 350 degrees for 10 minutes first. Bake the pie with the filling in it for 45 minutes at 350 degrees and allow it to cool before serving.

([Makes about 8 servings.

❦

Heather's Gutsy Tofu Pumpkin Pie with Wheatberry and Sunflower Crust

CRUST

3/4 cup 3-day sprouted wheatberries

3/4 cup sunflower meal

1 tablespoon safflower oil or butter

2 tablespoons whole wheat flour or more

Blend sprouted wheatberries and sunflower meal together with oil or butter. Add flour as necessary to hold the mixture together. Transfer to a 9-inch pie plate and press the mixture in evenly with your hands. Set aside.

FILLING

3 tablespoons barley malt or 2 tablespoons honey

1 16-ounce can pumpkin filling (sugar free)

1/2 cake tofu (bean curd)

1 egg (optional)

1/4 teaspoon cinnamon

1/4 teaspoon ground cloves

1/4 teaspoon allspice

1/4 cup shredded unsweetened coconut

Preheat oven to 350 degrees.

Pour all ingredients into a blender and blend well. Pour into the pie shell and bake for about 30 minutes, until set. Be sure not to overbake.

❨ Makes 1 9-inch pumpkin pie that serves 6 to 8.

Tofu is available in Oriental markets and some supermarkets.

❦

Mock Pumpkin Pie

CRUST

1/4 cup sesame oil

3 tablespoons boiling water

1 cup whole wheat pastry flour

1/2 teaspoon lecithin granules

1/4 teaspoon salt

Mix the liquid ingredients together in a bowl.

In another bowl, combine the dry ingredients. Pour the liquid ingredients into the dry. Blend together. Form into a ball and press into place in a 9-inch pie plate. Bake for about 5 minutes at 375 degrees.

FILLING

1 large squash, peeled and cubed, about 2 cups

1–1 1/2 cakes of tofu (bean curd)

2/3 cup maple syrup

1/2 teaspoon salt

1 teaspoon nutmeg

1/2 teaspoon cinnamon

1/2 teaspoon ground ginger

2 tablespoons soy margarine or unsalted butter

Place squash in about 4 cups of boiling water. Simmer for about a half hour until you have a thick, runny sauce. Add the rest of the ingredients and mix in a blender or with a fork till combined.

Pour the filling into the crust and bake in a preheated oven at 350 degrees for 1 hour or until a toothpick inserted into the filling comes out clean.

(Serves 6 to 8.

Tofu is available in Oriental markets and some supermarkets.

❀

Strawberry Yogurt Pie

1 1/2 cups plain yogurt

3 eggs, beaten

1/4 cup unsalted butter, melted

1/2 cup honey

1 1/2 teaspoons vanilla extract

pinch of salt

1 9-inch pie shell, unbaked

2 1/2–3 cups whole strawberries

2 tablespoons arrowroot

1 tablespoon water

Combine yogurt, eggs, butter, 1/4 cup of the honey, vanilla and salt in a mixing bowl. Beat until very smooth. Pour this mixture into the unbaked pie shell and bake at 400 degrees for 10 minutes, then 325 degrees for 35 to 40 minutes. Remove from oven and allow to cool for 1 hour.

Wash the strawberries and separate the soft, ripe ones from the firm ones. You will need about 2 cups of soft strawberries and 1 cup of firm ones. Slice the firm ones in half and reserve. Mash the soft ones in a saucepan and add 1/4 cup honey to them. Place on the stove and bring to a boil over low-medium heat.

Dissolve the arrowroot in the water in a small dish and pour into the boiling strawberries. Stir. Cook for just about a minute, stirring constantly.

Arrange the sliced strawberries on top of the cooled pie. Then pour the cooked strawberries over them. Make sure to cover the pie with the cooked strawberries evenly. Refrigerate for 3 to 4 hours before serving.

(Serves 8 to 10.

❦

Basic Tofu Pie

5–6 medium cakes tofu (bean curd)
1/2 cup rice syrup (or maple syrup)
1/2 cup maple syrup
1/4–1/3 cup sesame oil or safflower oil
1 tablespoon soy margarine
1/2 teaspoon sea salt
1–2 tablespoons fresh-squeezed lemon juice
1/2 cup carob powder (optional)
1/2 cup unsweetened shredded coconut (optional)
1 tablespoon vanilla extract (optional)
1 9-inch pie shell, unbaked

Place the tofu in a thick dish towel and gently squeeze the water from it until it has the consistency of cream cheese. Place tofu in a blender and gradually add remaining ingredients (including the optional ones if you decide to use them). Add each ingredient little by little to the tofu until they are all blended together and you have achieved a smooth creamlike consistency. Add the filling to the pie crust and bake in a preheated oven at 350–375 degrees for approximately 45 minutes or until a toothpick inserted into the filling comes out clean.

(Makes 8 servings.

Tofu is available in many supermarkets and Oriental markets.
Rice syrup is found in Oriental markets and some health food stores.

🌸

Carob Cream Cake

2 1/2 cups whole wheat flour
2 teaspoons baking soda
1/2 teaspoon salt
1/4 cup carob powder, sifted to remove lumps
2 tablespoons instant coffee beverage (Pero)
1/2 cup boiling water
1 cup unsalted butter, softened
1 cup honey
4 eggs, separated
1 teaspoon vanilla extract
1 cup buttermilk

In a mixing bowl, sift together the flour, baking soda and the salt.

In another bowl, place the sifted carob powder and coffee and pour in the boiling water, stirring to dissolve all lumps.

In a larger bowl, cream the butter and the honey until very light. Add the egg yolks, one at a time, beating well after each addition. Add the vanilla and the carob water. Mix well.

Then add flour mixture and buttermilk alternately and mix until just blended.

In another bowl beat the egg whites until stiff. Gently fold into the batter. Bake in a well-greased tube pan at 350 degrees for 70 minutes or until a toothpick inserted into the cake comes out clean.

❲ Makes 16 servings.

❧

Carrot Dream

1 cup honey

1 cup unsalted butter

4 egg yolks, beaten

1 teaspoon vanilla extract

2 cups whole wheat flour

1 teaspoon baking soda

1 teaspoon salt

1 cup light cream or half and half

4 egg whites

2 cups grated carrots

1 teaspoon cinnamon

1/2 cup shredded unsweetened coconut

Preheat oven to 350 degrees.

Cream the honey and butter together in a large mixing bowl. Add the egg yolks one at a time and the vanilla. Beat well after each addition.

Sift the dry ingredients together in another bowl and add alternately with cream to the honey mixture. Mix well.

Beat the egg whites until they form peaks and fold into the batter. Add the grated carrots. Mix well.

Pour the batter into a greased 9-inch × 16-inch pan. Sprinkle with cinnamon and coconut. Bake 45 minutes to 1 hour, or until a tester inserted into the center comes out clean.

❲ Serves 10 to 14.

❧

Geranium Carob Cake

1 1/2 cups unsalted butter, softened

1 cup maple syrup

6 eggs

1/2 teaspoon salt

2 1/2 cups whole wheat pastry flour

1/2 cup soy flour

2 teaspoons baking powder

1/2 cup unsweetened carob powder
1 cup milk
1 teaspoon vanilla extract
1 cup chopped pecans
1/2 cup carob chips
1/2 cup raisins
1/2 cup chopped, dried apricots
16 large, clean geranium leaves (from an unsprayed plant)

Cream the butter as you gradually add the maple syrup. As you continue to beat the mixture, add the eggs, one at a time, beating well after each addition.

Combine the salt, the flours, the baking powder and the carob powder in a separate bowl. Alternating with the milk, add the dry ingredients to the egg mixture. The batter should be quite smooth. Add the remaining ingredients, with the exception of the leaves.

Preheat oven to 325 degrees.

Grease a 9-inch tube pan and press the leaves against the sides so as to cover the entire surface. Gently pour in the batter, being careful not to disturb the leaves. Bake the cake for 1 1/2 hours. When done, it should spring back when lightly pressed with your fingertip. Allow the cake to cool and then turn it out on a plate. Remove the leaves and serve as is, or top with scoops of ice cream.

❰ Makes 10 to 14 servings.

Carob chips are sold in health food stores.

❦

Nutty Carrot Cake

2 1/2 cups whole wheat pastry flour

1 teaspoon baking powder

1 teaspoon baking soda

1 teaspoon salt

1 1/2 teaspoons cinnamon

1 1/2 teaspoons ground nutmeg

4 eggs

1/2 cup honey

1/2 cup blackstrap molasses

1 cup safflower oil

2 1/2 cups coarsely shredded carrots

1 cup raisins

1 cup coarsely chopped pecans or raw peanuts

1/2 cup finely chopped dates

Preheat oven to 375 degrees.

Combine the flour and other dry ingredients in a medium mixing bowl.

Beat the eggs and honey together with an electric mixer or a wire whisk until the mixture is light and fluffy. Gradually beat in the molasses and oil and then add the dry ingredients, continuing to beat until you have a smooth batter. Stir in the carrots, raisins, nuts and dates. Pour into a well-greased 9-inch tube pan and bake for 70 minutes. The cake is done when the top springs back when pressed lightly.

After removing the pan from the oven, allow the cake to cool for 10 minutes. Then loosen it gently with a spatula, turn it out and allow it to cool on a wire rack before serving.

❲ Makes 12 to 14 servings.

❦

Cheesecake

CRUST

2/3 cup wheat germ

2/3 cup whole wheat flour

1/4 cup unsalted butter

1/2 teaspoon vanilla extract

2/3 cup cashew meal, or other nut meals

1 1/2 tablespoons honey

In a mixing bowl, mix together the wheat germ and the whole wheat flour. Beat in the butter. Then add the vanilla, cashew meal and the honey. Use your hands to combine.

Press into the bottom and sides of an oiled 9-inch spring form pan. The crust will be very thin.

FILLING

6 eggs

1 cup sour cream

1 1/2 pounds cream cheese

1 teaspoon vanilla extract

1 teaspoon honey

Place all ingredients in a blender and blend until smooth. Pour into the crust and bake at 300 degrees for 2 hours.

Remove from the oven. Let it stand for 5–10 minutes before placing in the refrigerator to chill. Chill at least 6 hours before serving. ([Makes 10 servings.

❧

Apricot Tofu Cheesecake

8 ounces plain yogurt

16 ounces—2 large cakes—tofu (bean curd)

4 eggs

5 tablespoons unsalted butter, melted

8 ounces cream cheese

3/4 cup honey

4 tablespoons arrowroot

1 teaspoon almond extract

1 teaspoon vanilla extract

1/4 cup chopped dried apricots

Preheat oven to 350 degrees.

Mix all ingredients except for the dried apricots in a bowl. Then transfer to a blender in batches and blend until smooth. (There will be too much to put into the blender all at once.) Blend the apricots with the last batch. Pour the batches into a 9-inch spring pan that has been greased well.

Bake for 1 1/2 hours or until set. Then allow the cake to remain in the oven with door ajar 1 inch for 1 hour.

❴ Makes 1 9-inch cake that serves 10 to 14.

Tofu is available in many supermarkets and Oriental markets.

❦

Fruitcake

3/4 cup honey

1 1/4 cups unsalted butter

3 eggs

1 teaspoon salt

1 teaspoon baking powder

1 1/2 cups chopped pecans

1 cup chopped dried peaches

1/2 cup chopped dried papaya

1 1/2 cups currants

3/4 cup chopped dates

2 1/2 cups whole wheat flour

2 1/2 tablespoons lemon rind

1 cup plain kefir milk (liquid yogurt)

1 teaspoon baking soda

1 teaspoon cinnamon extract

Preheat oven to 350 degrees.

In a large bowl, cream together the honey and the butter, then beat in the eggs one at a time. Add the salt and baking powder and mix well. Set aside.

In another bowl combine the pecans, peaches, papaya, currants and dates. To this combination add 1/2 cup flour. Set aside.

In a small bowl combine the lemon rind, kefir milk, baking soda and cinnamon extract. Pour this mixture into the creamed mixture alternately with the remaining flour. Fold in the fruit-nut mixture. Mix well. Pour into a greased 9-inch spring pan.

Bake for 1 1/2 hours. It will be done when you stick a toothpick in and it comes out clean. Allow the cake to cool outside the oven for 15 minutes before removing from the spring pan.
(Serves 10 to 14.

Kefir is available at health food stores.

❧

Oatmeal Cake

1 cup rolled oats (oatmeal)
1 1/4 cups boiling water
1/2 cup unsalted butter, softened
1 cup honey
2 tablespoons molasses
2 eggs
1 3/4 cups whole wheat flour
1/2 teaspoon salt
1 teaspoon baking soda
1 1/4 teaspoons cinnamon
1 1/2 teaspoons nutmeg
1 1/2 teaspoons vanilla extract

Place the oatmeal in a mixing bowl. Pour the boiling water over the oatmeal and let it stand while preparing the rest of the batter.

In a large bowl, cream the butter until light and fluffy, pour in the honey and molasses slowly. Beat well. Add the eggs one at a time, beating well after each egg.

Stir in the flour and the remaining ingredients. Stir in the oatmeal. Mix thoroughly. Pour into a greased 9 × 5 × 3 loaf pan.

Bake at 350 degrees for about 1 hour or until a toothpick inserted into the cake comes out clean.
(Serves 8 to 10.

❦

Perfect Poundcake

3 cups whole wheat flour
2 teaspoons baking powder
1 1/2 cups unsalted butter
2 teaspoons almond extract
1 cup honey
11 eggs, separated

In a small bowl sift together the flour and the baking powder.

Cream together the butter and the almond extract in a large mixing bowl until soft and smooth, and then gradually add 2/3 cup honey. Beat until smooth. Add the egg yolks one at a time, beating hard after each addition. Mix in flour mixture thoroughly.

In another bowl, beat the egg whites until they are stiff and gradually add 1/3 cup of honey. Beat hard until you have a smooth meringue. Fold into creamed batter very gently, making sure to hide all egg white patches. Pour into a well greased 9-inch tube pan. Bake at 325 degrees for 80 minutes or until a toothpick inserted into the cake comes out clean.

❡ Serves 16 to 20.

Remember to break the eggs 1 at a time into a small dish. That way any accidents won't affect more than 1 egg.

❦

Spice Raisin Cake

1/2 cup raisins
water
2 eggs
1 cup unsalted butter
1 teaspoon vanilla extract
1 cup honey
1/8 teaspoon almond extract (optional)
dates (optional)
pinch of salt
1 3/4 cups whole wheat flour

1/2 teaspoon baking powder

1/2 teaspoon baking soda

1 teaspoon cinnamon

1 teaspoon nutmeg

1/4 teaspoon ground cloves

Preheat oven to 300 degrees.

In a small saucepan, boil the raisins in water to cover for 20 minutes.

Blend together the eggs, butter, vanilla and honey. If you wish to use the almond extract and/or the dates, add them at this time. Set aside.

Sift together in another mixing bowl the salt, flour, baking powder, baking soda, cinnamon, nutmeg and cloves. Pour the dry ingredients into the egg mixture, stirring continuously. Mix in raisins while they're still hot.

Pour the batter into an 8 × 8 baking pan and bake in the oven for 40 minutes or until a toothpick inserted into the cake comes out clean. ❴ Serves about 8.

❦

Whole Wheat Jelly Roll

butter for basting

3/4 cup whole wheat pastry flour

1 teaspoon baking powder

1/4 teaspoon salt

4 eggs, separated, at room temperature

1/4–1/2 cup honey

1 1/2 teaspoons vanilla extract

1/4 cup carob powder

*1 8-ounce jar of unsweetened apricot, cherry or any of your
     favorite preserves*

Preheat oven to 375 degrees.

Line a 10 × 15 jelly roll pan with waxed paper. Baste with butter.

In a mixing bowl, mix together the pastry flour, baking powder and salt.

Beat the egg whites in another bowl until they are stiff but not dry. Set aside.

In a large mixing bowl, beat the egg yolks until they are lemon colored. Add the honey and stir until it dissolves. Add the vanilla. Sprinkle the flour mixture over the egg yolks, then gently fold the egg whites in only until the flour becomes incorporated with the rest of the mixture. Pour into the pan and spread evenly. Bake for 12–15 minutes. Remove from the oven and invert cake on a cotton cloth dusted with the carob powder. Roll the cake up with the cloth. Let the cake cool.

Unroll the cake, spread the jam on it and then roll again without the cloth. Trim the ends and slice 1/2 inch thick. Place in the oven at 375 degrees for 20–30 minutes.
(Serves 8 to 10.

❦

Carob Brownies

2 eggs, beaten
1/2 cup honey plus 2 tablespoons
1/4 cup safflower oil
1/2 teaspoon vanilla extract
1 cup whole wheat flour
1/4–1/2 cup carob powder
1/2 teaspoon salt
2/3 cup chopped walnuts

Beat together in a large mixing bowl the eggs, honey, oil and vanilla.

In a separate bowl sift together the flour and the carob powder. Add the salt. Combine the wet and the dry ingredients. Mix well. Then add the nuts.

Pour the batter into an oiled 8-inch square pan. Bake at 350 degrees for 35 minutes. Remove from the oven and cut into squares.
(Makes 16 brownies.

❦

Carob Pecan Fudge

1 cup pecan halves
1 cup toasted unsweetened coconut
3/4 cup carob powder
1/2 cup honey
1/2 cup carob syrup

1 cup nonfat dry milk
1 teaspoon vanilla extract
3/4 cup peanut butter
1 cup carob chips

No cooking required. Set aside the pecans and the toasted coconut. Mix all the other ingredients together in a large bowl. Form into patties. Roll in toasted coconut and top each with a pecan half. ⟨ Makes 15 to 20 patties.

Carob chips can be bought at most health food stores.

❦

Coconut Date Bars

1/2 cup honey
1/4 cup unsalted butter, softened
1/2 cup whole wheat flour
1 egg
1/2 teaspoon vanilla
2 tablespoons wheat germ
1/4 teaspoon salt
1/2 teaspoon baking powder
1/4 cup coconut
1/2 cup chopped dates
1/2 cup chopped walnuts

In a bowl, cream together 1/4 cup of the honey, the butter and the flour. Press into a greased 8-inch square pan. Bake for 15 minutes at 375 degrees.

Mix the remaining honey with the rest of the ingredients in the order listed above in a large mixing bowl. Mix thoroughly. Spread this mixture over the warm mixture in the pan. Bake at 375 degrees for 20 minutes. Cut into squares as soon as you remove it from the oven.

⟨ Makes 16 bars.

❧

Ginger Cookies

1/4 cup safflower oil
1/4 cup honey
2 eggs
1/2 cup molasses
2 1/2 cups whole wheat pastry flour
1/4 teaspoon salt
1/4 teaspoon nutmeg
1 teaspoon cinnamon
3 teaspoons powdered ginger
1/2 cup sunflower seeds

Beat the oil and the honey together in a large mixing bowl. Add the eggs one at a time and then the molasses, beating well after each addition.

In a separate bowl, combine the flour, salt, nutmeg, cinnamon, ginger and sunflower seeds. Add these dry ingredients to the liquid mixture, stirring well. Drop by the teaspoonful onto a greased cookie sheet. Bake at 350 degrees for 10–15 minutes or until brown around the edges.

❲ Makes 2 1/2 dozen.

❧

Hazelnut Butter Cookies

1 cup unsalted butter, softened
1/4 cup honey
1 teaspoon almond extract
2 cups whole wheat flour
1 cup hazelnuts, chopped fine

Cream the butter with the honey in a large mixing bowl until very smooth and fluffy using electric beater. Add the almond extract. Mix well. Add the flour and the nuts.

Place in the refrigerator to chill for 2 hours or more.

Shape into logs or crescents and place on a greased cookie sheet. Bake at 350 degrees for 15 minutes in a preheated oven. Cool on rack.

❲ Makes approximately 6 dozen.

❦

Peanut Butter Cookies

2 1/2 cups whole wheat flour

1 teaspoon baking soda

2 teaspoons baking powder

1/2 cup unsalted butter, softened

1/2 cup safflower oil

1 cup honey

1/4 cup wheat germ or bran

2 eggs

1 cup peanut butter (if unsalted, add a scant 1/2 teaspoon salt)

2 teaspoons vanilla extract

1/2 cup chopped roasted peanuts

In a mixing bowl, combine the flour, baking soda and baking powder. Set aside.

In a large mixing bowl, cream the butter, oil and honey together. Add the rest of the ingredients in the order listed above. Mix well and then add the flour mixture.

Drop by teaspoonfuls onto an ungreased cookie sheet. Bake at 350 degrees for 10–15 minutes or until the edges just start to brown.
❆ Makes 6–7 dozen.

❦

Nutty Chews

CRUST

1/2 cup unsalted butter

1 1/3 cups sifted whole wheat flour

Cream the butter and the flour together and then pat evenly into a greased 9 × 12 pan. Bake for 10 minutes at 350 degrees.

FILLING

2 *eggs*
1/2 *cup honey*
1 *teaspoon vanilla extract*
2 *tablespoons whole wheat flour*
1/2 *teaspoon salt*
3 *crushed bananas*
3/4 *cup walnuts*
1 *cup carob chips*
1 *cup unsweetened coconut*

Mix all ingredients together adding walnuts, carob chips and coconut last; spread on top of the baked crust. Place in the oven and bake for 20 minutes at 350 degrees. When cool, cut into squares.
(Makes 9 to 12 squares.

Carob chips can be bought at most health food stores.

❦

Nutty Candy

3/4 *cup honey*
1 *cup salt-free peanut butter*
3–4 *tablespoons carob powder*
1 *cup sunflower seeds*
1/2 *cup chopped roasted almonds*
1/2 *cup chopped roasted walnuts*

Place honey, peanut butter and carob powder in a heavy medium saucepan. Cook over low heat. Stir to mix well, raising the heat if you feel it is necessary to blend more thoroughly. Add the seeds and the nuts. Mix very well. Turn into an 8-inch-square pan. Refrigerate for 1 hour.

Remove from the refrigerator and cut into small pieces and then refrigerate again.
(Makes about 3 dozen pieces.

✿

Sour Cream Raisin Cookies

2/3 cup unsalted butter
3/4 cup honey
1 teaspoon vanilla extract
2 eggs
2 1/2 cups whole wheat flour
1 teaspoon baking powder
2 teaspoons baking soda
1/2 teaspoon salt
1 cup sour cream or yogurt
1/2–1 cup raisins
1/2 cup chopped walnuts

Cream the butter, honey, and vanilla together in a large bowl. Add the eggs one at a time, beating vigorously after each addition.

In a separate bowl, sift together the flour, baking powder, baking soda and salt. Add this dry mixture to the butter mixture alternately with the sour cream. Stir in the raisins and the walnuts. Place teaspoonfuls of the batter on an ungreased cookie sheet and bake at 350 degrees for 12–15 minutes.

❆ Makes 3 to 4 dozen.

✿

Sunflower Banana Cookies

1/2 cup sunflower seeds
1/4 cup sesame seeds
1/4 cup rolled oats (oatmeal)
1 large banana (1/2 cup mashed)
1 egg, beaten
1 tablespoon safflower oil
2 tablespoons honey
1/3 cup whole wheat flour

Place seeds and oats in a blender and grind into a meal.

Mash the banana in a medium bowl and mix in seeds and oats.

Add the rest of the ingredients. Place teaspoonfuls of batter on a greased cookie sheet. Bake at 350 degrees for 20 minutes.
([Makes 12–15 cookies.

❧

Graham Crackers

3 cups whole wheat flour
3/4 teaspoon baking soda
1 teaspoon baking powder
1/2 teaspoon salt
3 tablespoons unsalted butter, softened
1/4 cup honey or molasses
2/3 cup whey powder (milk powder)
1/2 cup cream or milk
1 teaspoon vanilla extract
3 tablespoons oil

Sift together the flour, baking soda, baking powder and salt in a large mixing bowl.

In another bowl, cream together the butter and the honey until fluffy and then add the whey powder, cream, vanilla and oil. Mix well. Pour the butter mixture into the flour mixture. If the dough is too dry you may add 1/4 cup water to the dough. The dough should be just moist enough to roll out.

Roll the mixture between two sheets of wax paper. Peel off the paper and turn over onto a well-greased, floured cookie sheet. Score the dough into squares with a knife. Decorate the squares with a fork or a knife if you wish. Bake at 350 degrees for 10 or 15 minutes, until browned.
([Makes 3 to 4 dozen.

❧

Almond Pudding

4 egg yolks
1/4 cup honey
1/2 pound blanched almonds, ground fine
4 egg whites, beaten until stiff

In a mixing bowl, beat the egg yolks until they are thick and lemon-colored. Add the honey and beat until the mixture is frothy, about 4 minutes more. Stir in the almonds, then fold in the egg whites.

Turn the pudding into a buttered medium baking dish. Bake for 30 minutes or until thoroughly heated.

Serve warm or chilled.

(Serves 4.

❦

Apricot-Peach Custard

1/2 cup fresh apricots, pitted

2 cups peach kefir milk (liquid yogurt)

3 eggs

1/2 teaspoon vanilla extract

1/2 teaspoon cinnamon

1/4 teaspoon nutmeg

1/2 cup maple syrup

1/2 cup raisins

slivered almonds for garnish

Place all ingredients in a blender and blend until smooth. Pour into a greased casserole. Bake for 1 hour at 350 degrees. You may top the custard with additional raisins or slivered almonds. Refrigerate until chilled.

(Makes 4 to 6 servings.

Kefir milk is found in many health food stores.

❦

Bananaberry Pudding

2 cups fresh blueberries

2 bananas, peeled

4 figs chopped

2 nectarines, pitted and sliced

1 cup plain yogurt

2 tablespoons chopped almonds

In a blender, puree the blueberries, the bananas and the figs until you have a smooth mixture. Transfer the mixture to a shallow baking pan. Arrange the nectarine slices on top of the blueberry mixture. Spread the yogurt on top of the nectarine slices. Sprinkle with the almonds and serve.

❨ Makes 6 to 8 servings.

❧

Banana Coconut Gel

3 cups piña colada (juice available in health food stores)
1 tablespoon agar-agar flakes
2 ripe bananas, peeled and sliced

Pour the piña colada into a saucepan and heat until just simmering. Sprinkle the agar-agar over it and cook for 5 minutes until the agar-agar is dissolved. Remove from the heat and refrigerate for 5 minutes until it begins to thicken. Drop in the banana slices and pour into serving glasses.

Refrigerate for 1 hour or more before serving.

❨ Serves 6.

Other combinations might be apple-loganberry juice with apple slices, grape juice with apple slices, or mango juice with orange pieces.

Piña colada juice is available in many supermarkets and health food stores.

❧

Blueberry Pudding

2 cups blueberries
2 cakes tofu (bean curd), cut into 1/2 inch slices
3 tablespoons honey
1/2 teaspoon vanilla extract
dash of cinnamon

Reserve some blueberries for garnish.

Combine all other ingredients in a blender and puree for 30–45 seconds. Pour into 4 dessert cups and garnish with reserved blueberries.

Chill before serving.

❨ Serves 4.

You may substitute any fruit you like for the blueberries.
Tofu is found in Oriental markets.

❦

Coconut Maple Custard

5 egg yolks, beaten until lemon-colored

1/2 cup maple syrup

3 cups milk, scalded

1 teaspoon vanilla extract

1/2 cup shredded unsweetened coconut

In a bowl mix all ingredients thoroughly. Pour into 6 custard cups. Place in a large baking pan that has been filled half way with boiling water. Place in a 375-degree oven for 35 minutes or until set. ⦅ Makes 6 servings.

To scald the milk, heat the milk until it comes to a simmer.

❦

Cranberry Fruit Mold

4 1/2 cups cranberries (frozen or fresh)

5 tablespoons apple juice

4 teaspoons agar-agar flakes

2 cups fresh pineapple (or a 1-pound can of unsweetened
*   pineapple, drained)*

1 cup raisins

3 apples, peeled, cored and diced

1 cup assorted dried fruits

1/2 cup assorted seeds (sesame, sunflower, pumpkin)

2 teaspoons grated lemon rind

Wash and pick over cranberries. If using frozen cranberries, allow them to defrost before using. Put the cranberries into a large saucepan and add the apple juice. Cook over medium heat for 10–15 minutes.

Dissolve the agar-agar in about 2/3 cup of water in a small saucepan. Bring the water to a boil then simmer over low heat until the flakes are dissolved. Remove from heat and allow to cool.

Add the remaining ingredients to the large pot. Mix well. When the agar-agar has cooled, add it to the cranberry mixture. Mix well.

Pour into a 2-quart mold and chill until firm. Unmold before serving by *briefly* dipping mold into hot water, then inverting onto a plate.

❡ Serves 10 to 14.

❦

Date Pudding

4 cups milk
1/2 pound dates, pitted
2 tablespoons maple syrup
4 tablespoons arrowroot
2 eggs

Place all ingredients in a blender and blend briefly until the dates are coarsely chopped. Pour into a large heavy saucepan and cook over low heat, stirring frequently, until the pudding thickens, about 20 minutes. Pour into dessert glasses and refrigerate until chilled. If you prefer, you may also serve warm.

❡ Serves 4 to 6.

❦

Rice Pudding

2 cups cooked brown rice (p. 65)
1/2–1 cup raisins
3 cups milk, scalded
1/4 cup honey
3 eggs, well beaten
1/4 teaspoon salt
1 teaspoon cinnamon
1/2 teaspoon vanilla

Mix all ingredients together in a large mixing bowl. Then pour into a 2-quart casserole that has been greased. Bake at 325 degrees for 1–1 1/4 hours. When a knife inserted into the center comes out clean, the pudding is done.

❡ Serves 6 to 8.

To scald the milk, heat the milk until it comes to a simmer.

❦

Strawberry Pudding

2 cups whole strawberries, hulled

2 cups milk

1/2 cup honey or to taste

3 tablespoons arrowroot

2 eggs

Reserve several strawberries for garnish.

Place all other ingredients in a blender and blend well. Pour the mixture into a heavy saucepan and cook over low heat, stirring constantly, until thick, about 20 minutes.

Now pour the mixture into small pudding dishes and top each with a whole strawberry.

Chill.

❬ Serves 4 to 6.

❦

Strawberry Yogurt Gel

3 cups apple-strawberry juice

1 tablespoon agar-agar flakes

1 cup plain yogurt

1 cup sliced strawberries

1–2 tablespoons honey (optional)

Heat the apple-strawberry juice and the agar-agar in a saucepan until it boils. Simmer over low heat for about 5 minutes or until the flakes are dissolved. Refrigerate for another 5 minutes until the mixture begins to thicken.

In a mixing bowl, combine the yogurt, strawberries and honey. Mix well. Pour the thickened apple-strawberry juice into the yogurt mixture and mix thoroughly. Transfer to dessert glasses and refrigerate until firm.

❬ Makes 6 servings.

❦

Blueberry Jam

3 cups blueberries
1/2 cup honey
2 tablespoons lemon juice
dash of cinnamon
dash of nutmeg

Combine all ingredients in a medium saucepan and bring to a boil. Boil for approximately 20 minutes. It is important to stir occasionally to prevent the jam from scorching. Pour into a clean jar and put into the refrigerator. The jam will thicken when cool.

Keep refrigerated.

❧ Makes 2 cups.

Beverages

Apple-Date Shake

1/3 cup dates, pitted
1 teaspoon cinnamon
dash of nutmeg
8 ounces apple juice
1/2 banana, peeled

Combine all ingredients in blender. Cover and blend on high speed until smooth.
⟮ Serves 1.

🌷

Banana Split

1/4 cup strawberries
1/4 cup walnuts
1/2 cup cold milk
1 banana, peeled
1 scoop carob ice cream

Put all ingredients except for ice cream in the blender. Cover and blend on high speed. After the ingredients have been thoroughly mixed, pour into a sherbet or dessert glass and top with the ice cream.
⟮ Serves 1.

Carob ice cream is available in some supermarkets and health food stores.

❦

Bubbling Low-Calorie Fruit Punch

5 Red Zinger tea bags
2 cups boiling water
1/4 teaspoon nutmeg
2 teaspoons cinnamon
10 whole cloves
1/2 cup lime juice
1 teaspoon orange rind
2 quarts carbonated mineral water
lemon slices for garnish

In a large pitcher, combine the tea bags, water and spices. Let the mixture stand for 5 or 10 minutes. Remove and discard the tea bags. Stir in the lime juice and orange rind. Refrigerate until chilled.

When chilled and ready to serve, pour in the mineral water. Garnish each glass with a slice of lemon and serve.
(Makes about 14 servings.

❦

Carob Nut Shake

1/4 cup raisins
2 teaspoons carob powder
1 cup cold milk
6 almonds

Place all ingredients in the blender. Cover and blend on high speed until creamy smooth.
(Serves 1.

❦

Delicious Egg Nog

1 tablespoon honey
1 egg
1/4 teaspoon vanilla extract
1 cup milk
dash of cinnamon

dash of nutmeg

2 ice cubes

Mix all of the ingredients in a blender. Cover and blend on high speed until all the ice is chopped.
([Serves 1.

❧

Energy Drink

4 tablespoons tahini (sesame seed paste)

2 tablespoons sunflower seeds

2 tablespoons pumpkin seeds

1/2 tablespoon honey

1 1/2 cups alfalfa sprouts

Combine all ingredients in a blender. Cover and blend on high speed until creamy.
([Serves 1.

❧

For Those Cold Nights ...

1 quart apple juice

1 orange, sliced but not peeled

1 teaspoon cinnamon

1/4 teaspoon nutmeg

Place all ingredients in a large pot. Heat over medium heat to the almost-boiling point, then allow to simmer for 5 to 10 minutes. Serve hot.
([Serves 4 to 6.

❦

Gary Null's Sure-Fire Energy Lifter

your favorite fruit—1 apple, 1 peach—whatever is in season
2 tablespoons soya powder
2 tablespoons nonfat dry milk
4 egg yolks or 2 whole eggs
1 teaspoon cod liver oil
2 teaspoons lecithin
1 teaspoon bee pollen
1 teaspoon ginseng powder
6 ounces apple juice

Remove the core from or pit the fruit and quarter it. Place all the ingredients in a blender. Cover and blend on high speed till well mixed.   .
❴ Serves 1.

All of the dry ingredients in this recipe can be found in health food stores.

❦

Hawaiian Delight

2 tablespoons plain yogurt
2 bananas, peeled
1/2 cup unsweetened pineapple juice
12 almonds
2 dates, pitted

Mix all ingredients in a blender. Cover and blend on high speed until creamy.
❴ Serves 1.

❦

Head Start

1 cup cold milk
1 apple, peeled and sliced
1/4 cup sunflower seeds
1 tablespoon lecithin

1 tablespoon brewer's yeast
touch of honey

Put all ingredients into a blender. Cover and blend on high speed until creamy smooth.
◖ Serves 1.

Lecithin and brewer's yeast are available in health food stores.

❧

Ice Cream Float

2 scoops of your favorite honey-sweetened ice cream
1/2 cup fresh strawberries
10 ounces carbonated mineral water

Place the ice cream and the strawberries in a blender, cover and blend on high until creamy. Pour into a large glass and stir in the mineral water.
◖ Serves 1.

You can find honey-sweetened ice cream in health food stores and in some supermarkets.

❧

Milkless Super Energy Drink

1 tablespoon lecithin
1 banana, peeled
1/4 cup raisins
1/3 cup sesame seeds
1 teaspoon cinnamon
3/4 cup water
2 ice cubes

Put all ingredients in a blender. Cover and blend on high speed until all ice has been chopped.
◖ Serves 1 or 2.

Lecithin is available in health food stores.

❦

Mint Julep

1/2 cup apple juice
4 cups unsweetened pineapple juice
1/2 cup lemon juice
1 1/2 cups grapefruit juice
mint leaves for garnish

Mix apple juice, pineapple juice, lemon juice and grapefruit juice in a large pitcher. Stir well. When serving, garnish with a sprig of mint.
⟪ Serves 4 to 6.

❦

Morning Wake-Up

1 cup cold milk
1 tablespoon lecithin
1 tablespoon wheat germ
1 banana
1/2 tablespoon sunflower seeds
1/2 teaspoon vanilla extract
1/2 teaspoon cinnamon

Combine all ingredients in a blender. Cover and blend on high speed till creamy.
⟪ Serves 1.

Lecithin is available in health food stores.

❦

Orange Energy Nog

1 cup fresh-squeezed orange juice, chilled
1 egg
1 tablespoon honey
2 ice cubes

Combine all ingredients in a blender. Cover and whir about 1 minute on high speed until frothy. Serve immediately.
⟪ Makes about 1 1/2 cups.

🌷

Low-Calorie Orange-Pineapple Fizz

1 cup carbonated mineral water
1/2 cup orange juice
1/2 cup unsweetened pineapple juice
1 teaspoon lemon juice
4 sprigs mint for garnish

Mix all ingredients together, except for the mint, in a large pitcher. Stir. Serve in chilled glasses and garnish with the mint.
⟮ Serves 4.

🌷

Low-Calorie Peach Melba

2 peaches
1 cup apple juice
1/4 cup nonfat dry milk
3 ice cubes
2 cinnamon sticks for garnish

Remove the pit from the peaches. Slice them and put into a blender along with the apple juice and nonfat dry milk. Add 3 ice cubes. Blend for approximately 3 minutes until the ice cubes have been completely chopped. Pour into chilled glasses and serve with the cinnamon stick as a garnish.
⟮ Serves 2.

🌷

Pineapple Tofu Breakfast Drink

3 ice cubes
1 cup pineapple chunks
1/2 teaspoon cinnamon
2 cakes tofu (bean curd)
1/2 cup cold milk
1/2 tablespoon honey

Mix all ingredients in the blender, cover and blend on high speed until the ice cubes are chopped and the mixture is smooth and creamy.
(Serves 1.

Tofu can be found in Oriental markets and some supermarkets.

❦

Sesame-Coco-Cooler

6 cups water
4 tablespoons honey
1 cup sesame seeds
1/2 cup shredded fresh coconut
mint leaves for garnish

You will have to do this in two batches. Place half the water, honey and sesame seeds in the blender and blend at high speed until smooth. Then do the second batch, with the coconut meat added. Strain the mixture and chill before serving in tall glasses with a mint leaf garnish.
(Serves 5 to 6.

❦

Special Summer Smoothie

1/2 cup strawberries
1/2 cup apple juice
1 banana
1 peach, pitted and sliced

Place all ingredients in a blender, cover and blend until thoroughly blended and smooth.
(Serves 1.

❦

Super Shake

1/2 cup unsweetened pineapple juice, chilled
1/2 cup unsweetened grapefruit juice, chilled
1/2 cup buttermilk
1/2 cup raspberries or strawberries (frozen and thawed if you
*   are unable to get fresh)*

1 tablespoon wheat germ
4 ice cubes

Combine all ingredients in a blender container. Run on high until smooth and well blended.
([Serves 2.

❦

Yogurt-Fruit Juice Drink

1 cup plain yogurt
1 cup fresh orange juice
1 banana
1/4 teaspoon cinnamon
dash of nutmeg
2 ice cubes

Put all ingredients in a blender and blend until smooth and ice is crushed. The more ice, the thinner the drink.
([Serves 1 or 2.

List of Suppliers

American Oriental Grocery
20736 Lahsor Road
Southfield, Michigan 48075
  Chinese and Middle Eastern specialties

Casso Brothers
570 Ninth Avenue
New York, N.Y. 10036
  Middle Eastern specialties; $25 minimum order

Chico San, Inc.
P.O. Box 1004
Chico, California 95926
  Rice syrup, soy sauce, sesame seeds, soybean paste

East West Journal Mail Order
233 Harvard Street
Brookline, Massachusetts 02146
  Grains and beans, cereals and noodles, seeds and nut butters, soy products

Star Market
3349 North Clark Street
Chicago, Illinois 60657
  Chinese specialties

Walnut Acres
Penns Creek, Pennsylvania 17862
  All kinds of staples, including flours and peanut butter. Write for free catalog.

Western Dietary Products
P.O. Box 552
Bellevue, Washington 98009
  Vegetable broth powder, salt-free

To the best of our knowledge, the names and addresses listed above are correct. We cannot be responsible for any change of address or change in mail-order policy.

Index

Acorn Squash
  with Applesauce, 157
  à l'Orange, 157
  Tut's Treasure, 158
Adzuki beans, 49
  and Macaroni Salad, 212
Agar-agar, 86
Alfalfa Sprout(s), 77
  Energy Drink with, 297
  Salad, 212, 215
  Slaw, 212; Dressing for,
    228
Allspice, 97
Almond(s), 77; sprouts, 77
  -Carob Shake, 296
  Cauliflower with, 175
  Pudding, 288
  Sauce, 230
Ame, 90
Anise-Raisin Bread, 235
Antipasto, 117
Appetizers, 113-121
Apple(s), 15-16
  and Celery, Stir-Fry, 146
  -Cheese Salad, 221
  -Date Shake, 295
  -Fruit Medley, Baked,
    259
  Juice, Hot Spiced, 297
  Muffins, 249
  Pancake, Baked, 257
  Pie, 264
  -Tofu Salad, 210
  Slices, Nutty, 258
Applesauce, 258
  with Acorn Squash, 157
Appliances, 102-103
Apricot(s), 16
  -Peach Custard, 289
  Roll, 259
  -Tofu Cheesecake, 277
Arame, 85
Arrowroot, 89
Artichokes, 26-27
Asparagus, 27-28
Avocado, 16
  Dip, 230
  Guacamole, 118
  Nadeau for Two, 209
  Stuffed, 119
  -Stuffed Tomato, 217

Baba Ghanoush, 114
Baba Omgush, 115
Bakeware, 101
Banana(s), 16-17
  -berry Pudding, 289
  -Bran Muffins, 250
  -Coconut Gel, 290

Cornbread, Yeasted, 236
Cream Pie, 265
  -Peach Compote, 260
and Peanut Butter, 122
Split, 295
  -Sunflower Cookies, 287
  -Yogurt Cheese Pie, 266
Barley, 62; sprouts, 79-80
  -Lentil Soup, 129
  -Millet Soup, 124
Basil, 94
  Spaghetti with Sesame
    Seeds and, 197
Bay leaves, 94
Bean curd. See Tofu
Bean(s), 48-51
  Salad, 218
  Stew, Thick, 184
  See also individual types
    of beans
Bean Sprouts, 78
  and Pepper Salad, 215
Beet greens, 28-29
Beet(s), 29
  Borscht, 126
Belgian endive, 36
Berries, 17-18
  See also individual types
    of berries
Beverages, 295-303
Biscuits, Blueberry, 248
Black Bean(s), 49
  Four-Bean Salad, 218
  Soup, 125-126
Blackberries, 18
Black-Eyed Peas (Cow
  Peas), 50
  with Lemon Rice, 183
Black Raspberries, 18
Blender, electric, 102
Blueberry, 17
  Biscuits, 248
  Jam, 294
  Pudding, 289, 290
Blue Cheese, 8
  Celery Stuffed with, 120
Borscht, 126
Boysenberries, 18
Bran Muffins, 250, 251
Brazil nuts, 78
Bread, 72-75
  Anise Raisin, 235
  Blueberry Biscuits, 248
  Cinnamon, 236
  Corn. See Cornbread
  Cottage Cheese Oatmeal,
    238
  Date Nut, 244
  Irish Soda, 245
  Lemon Tea, 246

Oatmeal Raisin, 238
Onion, 239
Rye, 240
Soy-Enriched Wheat
  Berry, 242
techniques for making,
  74-75
Triticale Loaf, 241
Whole Wheat, 234, 242,
  246
Zucchini, Sweet, 247
See also Muffins
Breakfast, 108, 208, 256,
  301
Brick cheese, 8
Brie, 7
Broccoli, 29-30
  Almondine, 147
  au Gratin, 147
  Casserole, 195
  -Cauliflower Dinner, 151
  Crunch, 148
  Pasta, 196
  Soup, Cream of, 140
  Supreme, 148, 149
Brownies, Carob, 282
Brussels Sprouts, 30
  -Cheddar Casserole, 174
  Creole, 149
Buckwheat, 62-63; 80
Bulghur, 68
  and Chick-Peas, Italian,
    189
  and Chick-Pea Salad, 211
  Lentil and Tofu Casserole
    with, 206
  Tabbouli, 221, 222
Burdock, 30
Butter, 4-5, 95
Buttermilk, 10
  Cornbread, 243
Butternut Squash, 158, 199
Butter spreads, 4-5

Cabbage, 30
  Borscht, 126
  Cole Slaw, 209
  Sprouts Slaw with, 212
  Stuffed, 150, 185
Cake
  Carob, 273, 274
  Carrot, 274, 276
  Cheese, 276, 278
  Fruit, 278
  Oatmeal, 279
  Pound, 280
  Spice Raisin, 280
Camembert, 7
Candy, Nutty, 286

Cantaloupe Soup, Chilled, 144
Capers, 94
Caponata, 152
Caraway Seed, 94
Carob, 90
  Brownies, 282
  Cake, 273, 274
  Cream Pie, 266-267
  -Nut Shake, 296
  -Pecan Fudge, 282
Carrot(s), 31
  Cake, 274, 276
  Candied, 150
  -Pumpkin Pie, 268
  -Raisin Salad, 220
Cashew Nuts, 78
Casserole
  Bulghur, Lentil and Tofu, 206
  Cauliflower, Curried, 186
  Cheddar Brussels Sprouts, 174
  Green Vegetable, 173
  Noodle and Broccoli, 195
  Squash-Onion, 179
  String Beans, Sal's, 161
  Tofu Cauliflower, 199
  Yogurt-Potato, 156
  Yogurt Tofu, 204
Cauliflower, 31-32
  -Broccoli Dinner, 151
  Casserole, 186, 199
  Nutty, 175
Cayenne pepper, 96
Celery, 32
  Apples and, Stir-Fry, 146
  and Peanut Butter, 119
  -Potato Chowder, 134
  Soup, Creamy, 140
  Stuffed, 120
Chard, Swiss, 32
Cheddar Cheese, 8
  Casserole, 171, 174
  Cauliflower with Almonds and, 175
  Crisps, 254
  -Onion Spread, 113
  Vegetable Munch, Cheesey, 172
Cheese(s), 5-8, 170-181
  -Apple Salad, 221
  Cake, 276, 277
  Casserole, 171, 174
  cottage. *See* Cottage cheese
  making your own, 5
  Soufflé, 171, 172
  Tomatoes Stuffed with Spinach and, 181
  Zucchini Parmigiana, 180
  See also individual cheeses
Cherries, 18
Chervil, 94

Chia Seed Sprouts, 78-79
Chick-Peas (Garbanzo Beans, or Ceci), 50
  Bulghur and, Italian, 189
  and Bulghur Salad, 211
  -Kidney Bean Sandwich, 122
  Four-Bean Salad, 218
  Hummus bi Tahini, 116
  Hummus Plus, 116
  Soup, 127
  and Zucchini Curry, 182
Chicory (Curly Endive),33
Chili Peppers, 96
Chili Powder, 96
Chinese Parsley (Coriander), 94
Chocolate, carob as a substitute for, 90
Cider Vinegar, 92
Cinnamon, 97
  Bread, 236
Clover Sprouts, 79
Cloves, 97-98
Coconut, 19
  -Date Bars, 283
  Pie, 267
  -Sesame-Cooler, 302
Cole Slaw, 209
Collard Greens, 33
Compote, Banana Peach, 260
Condiments, 92-93
Cookies,
  Ginger, 284
  Hazelnut Butter, 284
  Peanut Butter, 285
  Sour Cream Raisin, 287
  Sunflower Banana, 287
Cooking techniques, 103-106
Cookware, 100-101
Coriander, 94
Corn, 33-34
  Dried, 63
  Muffins, 252
Cornbread, 236, 237, 243, 244
Corn Flour, 63
Corn Oil, 91
Cornmeal, 63
Corn Sprouts, 80
Cornstarch, 89
Cottage cheese, 5-7
  dressing, 7
  making your own, 6-7
  -Oatmeal Bread, 238
  Spread, 113, 114
Couscous, 68
  Algerian, 188
  Tofu à la King with, 207
Cow Peas (Black-Eyed Peas), 50
  with Lemon Rice, 183
Crackers, Graham, 288

Cranberries, 19
  -Fruit Mold, 291
Cream, 261, 263
Cream Cheese Pie, 266
Crème Fraîche, 10
Croquettes, Tofu, 200
Cucumber(s), 34-35
  Salad, 214
Cumin, 95
Currant(s)
  -Bran Muffins, 250
  in Nutty Cheese Spread, 113
Curry Powder, 98
Custard, 289, 291

Dairy Products, 3-10
  menu planning and, 109
  See also Butter; Buttermilk; Cheese; Cream; Sour Cream; Yogurt
Dandelion Greens, 35
Date(s)
  -Apple Shake, 295
  -Coconut Bars, 283
  -Nut Bread, 244
  Pudding, 292
Date Sugar, 90
Deep frying, 105
Desserts, 258-294
Dewberries, 18
Diabetic recipes
  Candied Carrots, 150
  Cold Pea Salad, 223
  Curry-Condiment Salad, 223
  Curry Dressing, 226
  Garden Salad, 214
  Garden Salad Dressing, 227
  Italian String Beans, 161
  Mayonnaise, 225
  Semi-Tropical Fruit Cup, 224
  Tabbouli, 221
Dill, 95
Dips, 114-116, 118, 229-230
Dressings. *See* Salad Dressings
Drinks, *See* Beverages
Dulse, 86-87

Egg(s), 11-14
  -Lemon Soup, Tangy, 128
  Nog, 296-297
  Omelets, 13-14
  Poached, 13
  Salad, 121
  See also Soufflé
Eggplant(s), 35-36
  Algerian (Khaloda), 190
  Baba Ghanoush, 114
  Baba Omgush, 115
  Caponata, 152

Grandma's, 190
Parmesan, 176, 204
Parmigiana, 177
Ratatouille Supreme, 168
Salad, 210
Endive, Belgian, 36
Endive, Curly (Chicory),
33
Energy Drink, 297, 299
Energy Lifter, 298
Escarole, 36

Farmer's Cheese, 6
Fennel, 95
Fenugreek, 79
Feta, 7
Fiddlehead Ferns, 25
Filbert(s) (Hazelnuts), 79
-Butter Cookies, 284
Flax Sprouts, 79
Flour, 61
buckwheat, 63
corn, 63
rye, 66
triticale, 66
whole wheat, 67-68
See also Whole
Wheat
Food processor, 103
French Dressing, Creamy,
226
Frittata, Zucchini, 164
Frozen Vegetables,
cooking, 105-106
Fruit(s), 15-23
-Apple Medley, Baked,
259
Cake, 278
Cup, Semi-Tropical, 224
dried, as sweeteners, 91
Mold, Cranberry, 291
Punch, Bubbling, 296
Soup, 144
See also individual fruits
Frying, 105
Fudge, Carob Pecan, 282

Garden Salad, 214
Garden Salad Dressing, 227
Garlic, 36
Salad Dressing with, 227
Gazpacho, 143
Gel
Banana Coconut, 290
Strawberry Yogurt, 293
Ginger, 98
Cookies, 284
Gluten, Wheat, 67, 68
Gomiso, 88
Gorgonzola, 8
Graham Crackers, 288
Graham Flour, 67
Grains, 61-62
menu planning and, 109
See also individual grains
Grain Sprouts, 79

Granola, 68, 254, 255
Grapefruit, 19
Grapes, 19
Great Northern Beans, 49
Green Beans, 29
Crunchy Herbed, 160
and Pea Salad, 220
Green Peas. *See* Peas
Green Peppers. *See*
Peppers, Sweet
Gruyère, 8
Guacamole, 118

Hawaiian Delight, 298
Hazelnut(s) (Filberts), 79
-Butter Cookies, 284
Herb(s) (herbed), 93-97
Hijiki, 86
Mushroom Cream, 231
Honey, 90
Horseradish, 95
Hummus bi Tahini, 116
Hummus Plus, 116
Hyperactive Recipes
Candied Carrots, 150
Italian String Beans, 161
Mushroom Surprise, 152
Nutty Cheese Spread,
113
Semi-Tropical Fruit
Cup, 224
Tabbouli, 221
Hypertensive Recipes. *See*
Salt-Free Recipes
Hypoglycemic Recipes
Almond Pudding, 288
Almond Sauce, 230
Avocado Dip, 230
Avocado-Stuffed Tomato
Salad, 217
Baked Acorn Squash à
l'Orange, 157
Banana Bran Muffins,
250
Broccoli Almondine, 147
Cheese-Apple Salad, 221
Cheese and Squash
Supreme, 178
Creamy French Dressing,
226
Crunchy Herbed Green
Beans, 160
Golden Broccoli
Supreme, 149
Grilled Cheddar and
Pepper Sandwich, 123
Grilled Tomatoes with
Oregano, 162
Herbed Buttered Pota-
toes and Peas, 146
Nutty Apple Slices, 258
Orange Energy Nog, 300
Peanut Butter and
Celery, 119
Salad Dressing with
Garlic, 227

Special Soufflé, 171
Sprouts Slaw, 212
Sprout Slaw Dressing,
228
Squash Delicious, 159
Stir-Fry Apples and
Celery, 146
Stuffed Zucchini, 165
Summer Salad, 220
Super Shake, 302
Tomato Juice Salad
Dressing, 228
Tomatoes Stuffed with
Spinach and Cheese,
181
Tomatoes Vinaigrette,
217
Very Good Bean and
Pea Salad, 220
Whole Wheat Muffins,
253
Whole Wheat Pizza,
191
Yogurt Drink, 303

Ice Cream Float, 299
Irish Moss, 86
Irish Soda Bread, 245

Jack Cheese, 8
Jam, Blueberry, 294
Jarlsberg Cheese Soufflé,
Special, 171
Jelly Roll, 281
Juice(s), 24-25, 297
See also Beverages
Juice Extractor, 103

Kale, 37
Kelp, 85
Ketchup, 92
Khaloda (Algerian
Eggplant), 190
Kidney Bean(s), 49
-Chick Pea Sandwich,
122
Four Bean Salad, 218
Tomato Tofu and, 205
Knives, 102
Kofu, 68
Kombu, 85
Kudzu, 89

Lasagna, 194, 198
Leavenings, 89
Leek-Potato Soup, 135-136
Legumes
menu planning and, 109
See also Beans; Lentils;
Peas
Lemon(s), 20
-Egg Soup, Tangy, 128
Rice, 183, 184
Tea Bread, 246

Lentil(s), 50
  Casserole, 206
  Soup, 128, 129, 130, 131
Lettuce, 37-38
Lima Beans, 38
  dried, 50
  Soup, 132
Limes, 20
Liver, Vegetarian
  Chopped, 120
Loganberries, 18

Macaroni
  Salad, 212, 218
  with Vegetables, Greek
    Style, 198
  Walnut Tahini, 198
Mace, 98
Mangoes, 20
Manicotti, Grandma's
  Baked, 194
Maple Sugar, 90
Maple Syrups, 90
Marjoram, 95
Mayonnaise, 93, 225
Meatballs, Vegetarian, 170
Melons, 21
Menus, 107-110
Milk, 3-4, 90
Millet, 64; sprouts, 80
  Soup, 124, 137
  Tofu à la King with, 207
Minestrone, 138
Mint, 95
  Julep, 300
Miso, 56, 57, 88
  Mushroom and Tofu
    Sautéed in, 201
  Soup, with Tofu, 132
Molasses, 91
Mozzarella Cheese, 8
  Eggplant Parmesan
    Sesame, 176
  Pizza, 191
  Soufflé, Triple Cheese,
    172
  Spaghetti Squash with
    Tomato Sauce and,
    177
  Zucchini Parmigiana,
    180
Muenster Cheese, 8
  Cauliflower with
    Almonds and, 175
  in Cheddar Brussels
    Sprouts Casserole,
    174-175
  Soufflé, 171, 172
  in Squash-Onion
    Casserole, 179
  Vegetable Munch,
    Cheesey, 172
  Zucchini Parmigiana,
    180
Muffins
  Apple, 249

Banana Bran, 250
  Bran, 251
  Corn, 252
  Currant Bran, 250
  Gary's Magic, 252
  Three-Grain, 251
  Whole Wheat, 253
Mung Beans, 50
Mung Bean Sprouts, 78
  and Pepper Salad, 215
Mushroom(s), 39
  Lasagna, 194
  Sauce, 231, 233
  Soup, 130, 133, 141
  Stuffed, 153
  Surprise, 152
  and Tofu in miso, 201
Mustard, 92-93
Mustard Greens, 39
Mustard Powder, 96
Mustard Seeds, 80, 96

Navy Beans, 49
  in Minestrone, 138
Nectarines, 21
Noodle(s)
  and Broccoli Casserole,
    195
  Soba Tofu Dinner, 203
  -Vegetable Soup, 139
Nori, 85-86
Nutmeg, 98
Nuts (Nutty), 76
  Candy, 286
  Carrot Cake, 276
  Cheese Spread, 113
  Chews, 285
  menu planning and, 109
  See also individual nuts

Oats (Oatmeal), 64
  Bread, 238
  Cake, 279
  Granola, 254, 255
Oils, 91
Okra, 39
Olive Oil, 91
Omelets, 13-14
Onion(s), 40
  Bread, 239
  Wild, 25
Orange(s), 21-22
  Drinks, 300, 301, 303
  Ordinary, 260-261
Oregano, 96
  Grilled Tomatoes with,
    162

Pancakes
  Baked Apple, 257
  Topping for, 256
  Whole Wheat, 256
Papayas, 22
Paprika, 96-97
Parfait, Pretty, 262

Parmesan Cheese, 8
  Eggplant Parmesan
    Sesame, 176
  Eggplant Parmigiana,
    177
  Tofu-Eggplant
    Parmesan, 204
  Stuffed Tomatoes, 181
Parsley, 96
Parsnips, 40
Pasta, 71, 192-198
  Broccoli, 196
  making your own, 71-72
  pesto sauce for, 94
  Salad, 218
  with Vegetables, Greek
    Style, 198
  Walnut Tahini, 198
  See also Lasagna; Maca-
    roni; Manicotti;
    Noodles; Shells;
    Spaghetti
Peach(es), 22
  -Apricot Custard, 289
  -Banana Compote, 260
  Melba, Low-Calorie, 301
Peanut-Pecan Pie, 268
Peanut Butter
  and Banana, 122
  and Celery, 119
  Cookies, 285
  Soup, 134
Peanut Oil, 91
Pea Pods, Edible or Snow,
  40
Pears, 22
  with Cream, Baked, 261
  with Raisin Stuffing, 261
Peas (Green Peas), 41
  dried, 50-51
  Potatoes and, Herb-
    Buttered, 146
  Salad, 220, 223
Pecan(s), 80
  -Carob Fudge, 282
  -Peanut Pie, 268
Peperonata, 166
Peppers
  cayenne, 96
  chili, 96
  red, 96
  white and black, 98-99
Peppers, Sweet (Green or
  Red), 41
  and Cheese Sandwich,
    Grilled, 123
  in Gazpacho, 143
  Paul's, 186
  Peperonata, 166
  and Sprout Salad, 215
  Stuffed, Grandma's, 154
  with Tofu, 202
  and Yogurt, 154
Pesto, 94
  Paul's Veggie, 232

Pie
  Apple, 264
  Banana Cream, 265
  Carob Cream, 266
  Coconut Custard, 267
  Crusts, 263, 269, 270
  Lemon Coconut, 267
  Peanut Pecan, 268
  Pumpkin, 268, 269, 270
  Strawberry Yogurt, 271
  Tofu, Basic, 272
Pigeon Peas, 51
Piña Colada-Banana Gel, 290
Pineapple(s), 23
  -Orange Fizz, 301
  -Tofu Breakfast Drink, 301
Pine Nuts (Pignolias), 80
Pinto Beans, 51
  Dip, 229
Pistachio Nuts, 80
Pizza, 191
Plums, 23
  Umeboshi, 88-89
Popovers, Whole Wheat, 248
Port Salut, 8
Potato(es), 42-43
  Baked Stuffed, 155
  Kugel, 156
  and Peas, 146
  Soup, 134, 135
  -Yogurt Casserole, 156
Pot cheese, 6
Pots and pans, 100-101
Poundcake, Perfect, 280
Protein, menu planning and, 108-109
Pudding
  Almond, 288-289
  Bananaberry, 289-290
  Blueberry, 290
  Date, 292
  Rice, 292
  Strawberry, 293
Pumpkin Pie, 268, 269, 270
Pumpkin Seeds, 81
Punch, Bubbling Fruit, 296

Raisin(s), 20
  Bread, 235, 237, 238
  -Carrot Salad, 220
  Pears Stuffed with, 261-262
  -Sour Cream Cookies, 287
  -Spice Cake, 280-281
Radishes, 43
Radish Seeds, 81
Raspberries, 18
Ratatouille, 167, 168
Red Peppers, 96
Rice, 64-66
  Lemon, 183, 184

Pudding, 292
  and Vegetables in Red Wine, 187
Rice Vinegar, 92
Ricotta Cheese, 7
  with String Beans, 180
  Tomatoes Stuffed with, 181
Romano Cheese, 8
Rosemary, 97
Rye, 66; sprouts, 80
  Bread, 240

Safflower Oil, 91
Sage, 97
Salads, 209-224
  Basic Tossed, 213
  Chef's, Super, 216
  Four Bean, 218-219
  Garden, 214
  Right from the Garden, 215
  Summer, 220
  Tabbouli, 221, 222
  See also under specific ingredients
Salad Dressings, 225-229
  Cottage Cheese, 7
  Creamy French, 226
  Curry, 226
  for Four Bean Salad, 219
  Garden, 227
  with Garlic, 227
  Sprouts Slaw, 228
  Tofu, 228
  Tomato Juice, 228
  See also Mayonnaise
Salt, 88
Salt-Free Recipes
  Anise-Raisin Bread, 235
  Black-Eyed Peas with Lemon Rice, 183
  Bran Muffins, 251
  Bulghur Casserole, 209
  Cinnamon Bread, 236
  Corn Muffins, 252
  Cream of Sweet Potato Soup, 142
  Green Lima Bean Soup, 132
  Hazelnut-Butter Cookies, 284
  Italian Bulghur and Chick-Peas, 189
  Mushroom Soup with Vegetables, 133
  Nutty Candy, 286
  Onion Bread, 239
  Quick Tomato Sauce, 232
  Sesame Basil Spaghetti, 197
  Sweet Peppers and Yogurt, 154
  Tofu à la King, 207

Tofu-Millet Soup, 137
  Tomato Tofu and Kidney Bean Soup, 205
  Vegetable Soup, 124
  Walnut Tahini Pasta, 198
Sandwiches, 122-123
Sauce
  Almond, 230
  Mushroom, 231, 233
  Pesto, 94, 232
  Tomato, 160, 232
Sautéeing, 105
Scallions, 43-44
Seaweed, 83-87
Seeds, 76, 109
  See also individual types of seeds
Sesame Seed Oil, 91
Sesame Seed Paste. See Tahini
Sesame Seeds, 81
  -Coco-Cooler, 302
  Eggplant Parmesan with, 176
  Spaghetti with Basil and, 197
  Tofu with, 207-208
Shell's, Grandma's Stuffed, 196
Shortenings, 74
Snap Beans. See String Beans
Soba Tofu Dinner, 203
Sorghum Syrup, 91
Soufflé, 171, 172
Soups, 124-145
  See also under specific ingredients
Sour Cream, 10
  -Raisin Cookies, 287
Soybean Curd. See Tofu
Soybean Milk, 53
Soybean Oil, 91
Soybeans, 52-53, 78
Soy Flakes, 55
Soy Flour, 54-55
  in Wheat Berry Bread, 242
Soy Grits, 55
Soy Protein, Textured, 52
Soy Sauce. See Tamari
Spaghetti, Sesame Basil, 197
Spaghetti Squash, 159, 177
Spearmint, Wild, 25
Spices, 93, 97-99
  See also individual spices
Spinach, 44
  Salad, 216
  Soup, Turkish, 136
  Tomatoes Stuffed with Cheese and, 181
Split peas, 51
Spreads, 113-114, 119

Sprouts, 76-77
  See also individual types
    of sprouts
Squash
  Acorn, 157, 158
  Butternut, Ronga's, 158
  Spaghetti, 159, 177
  Summer, 44-45
  Winter, 45
  Yellow, 159, 178, 179
  See also Zucchini
Squash Seeds, 81
Steaming, 103
Stew
  Bean, Thick, 184
  Vegetable, Italian, 166
  Zucchini, 164
Stilton Cheese, 8
Stir frying, 105
Stock, Vegetable, 124
Strawberry(-ies), 17-18
  Pudding, 293
  Soup, Cold, 145
  -Yogurt Gel, 293
  -Yogurt Pie, 271
String Bean(s) (Snap
    Beans), 28
  Casserole, Sal's, 161
  Four Bean Salad, 218
  Italian, 161
  with Ricotta, 180
Sugar, 89-91
Sunflower Seed Oil, 91
Sunflower Seeds, 81-82
  -Banana Cookies, 287
Sweeteners, 89-91
Sweet Potato(es), 45-46
  Soup, Cream of, 142
Swiss Chard, 32
Swiss Cheese, 8
  Casserole, 173
  Soufflé, Triple Cheese,
    172
  and Squash Supreme,
    178
  Vegetable Munch,
    Cheesey, 172
  Yellow Squash with, 178
  Zucchini Parmigiana,
    180
Syrups, 90, 91

Tabbouli, 221, 222
Tahini (Sesame Seed
    Paste), 114
Tamari (Soy Sauce),
    55-56, 88
  Dip, 229
Tangerines, 23
Tarragon, 97
Tempeh, 55
Thickeners, 89
Thyme, 97
Tofu (Soybean Curd),
    58-60
  à la King, 207

-Apple Salad, 210
-Apricot Cheesecake, 277
Breakfast for Two, Hot,
    208
with Butternut Squash,
    199
Casserole, 199, 204, 206
Croquettes, Herby, 200
Dip, 230
-Eggplant Parmesan, 204
and Mushrooms Sautéed
    in Miso, 201
Orleans, 202
Pie, Basic, 272
-Pineapple Breakfast
    Drink, 301
-Pumpkin Pie, 269
Red and Green Peppers
    with, 202
Salad Dressing, 228
Sesame, 207
-Soba Dinner, 203
Soup, 132, 137
Tomato, and Kidney
    Beans, 205
Tomato(es), 46
  Gazpacho, 143
  -Juice Salad Dressing,
    228
  Mangie Momma's, 162
  with Oregano, Grilled,
    162
  Peperonata, 166
  Pizza, 191
  Sauce, 160, 232
  Stuffed, 181, 217
  -Tofu and Kidney Beans,
    205
  Vinaigrette, 217
Topping, Gary's Favorite,
    256
Triticale, 66; loaf, 241
Tropical Delight, 262
Turnips, 47
Turtle Beans, 49

Umeboshi Plums, 88-89
Utensils, 101-102

Vegetable(s), 24-26,
    146-170
  Casserole, Green, 173
  cooking techniques for,
    103-106
  cutting, 106
  frozen, 105-106
  juices, 24-25
  menu planning and,
    109-110
  Munch, Cheesey, 172
  Pasta with, Greek Style,
    198
  Rice and, in Red Wine,
    187
  Sautéed, 168-169
  Soup, 133, 138, 139

Stew, Italian, 166
Stock, 124
-Yogurt Surprise, 169
  See also individual
    vegetables
Vinegars, 92

Wakame, 85
Walnut, 82
  Date Nut Bread with,
    244
  Pasta with Tahini and,
    198
Watermelon, 21
Wheat Berry Bread, 242
Wheat Bran, 67
Wheat Germ, 67, 68
Wheat Gluten, 67, 68
Wheat Meal, 67-68
Wheat Sprouts, 79
Whole Wheat, 66-68
  Bread, 234, 242, 246.
    See also Bread
  Jelly Roll, 281
  Muffins, 251, 253
  Pancakes, 256
  Pasta. *See* Pasta
  Pastry Pie Crust,
    Crunchy, 263
  Pizza with Fresh
    Tomatoes, 191
  See also Bulghur
Wine, Rice and
  Vegetables in, 187
Wine Vinegar, 92
Wok, 100-101

Yams, 45-46
Yeast
  for bread making, 73
  nutritional, 89
Yogurt, 4, 9-10
  -Banana Cheese Pie, 266
  Fruit Juice Drink, 303
  -Potato Casserole, 156
  -Strawberry Gel, 293
  -Strawberry Pie, 271
  Sweet Peppers and, 154
  -Tofu Casserole, 204
  -Vegetable Surprise, 169

Zucchini, 44-55
  Bread, Sweet, 247
  -Cheese Supreme, 178
  and Chick-Pea Curry,
    182
  Frittata, 164-165
  Fritters, 117
  -Onion Casserole, 179
  Parmigiana, 180
  Ratatouille, 167, 168
    Grandma's, 167
    Supreme, 168
  Stew, 164
  Stuffed, 163, 165